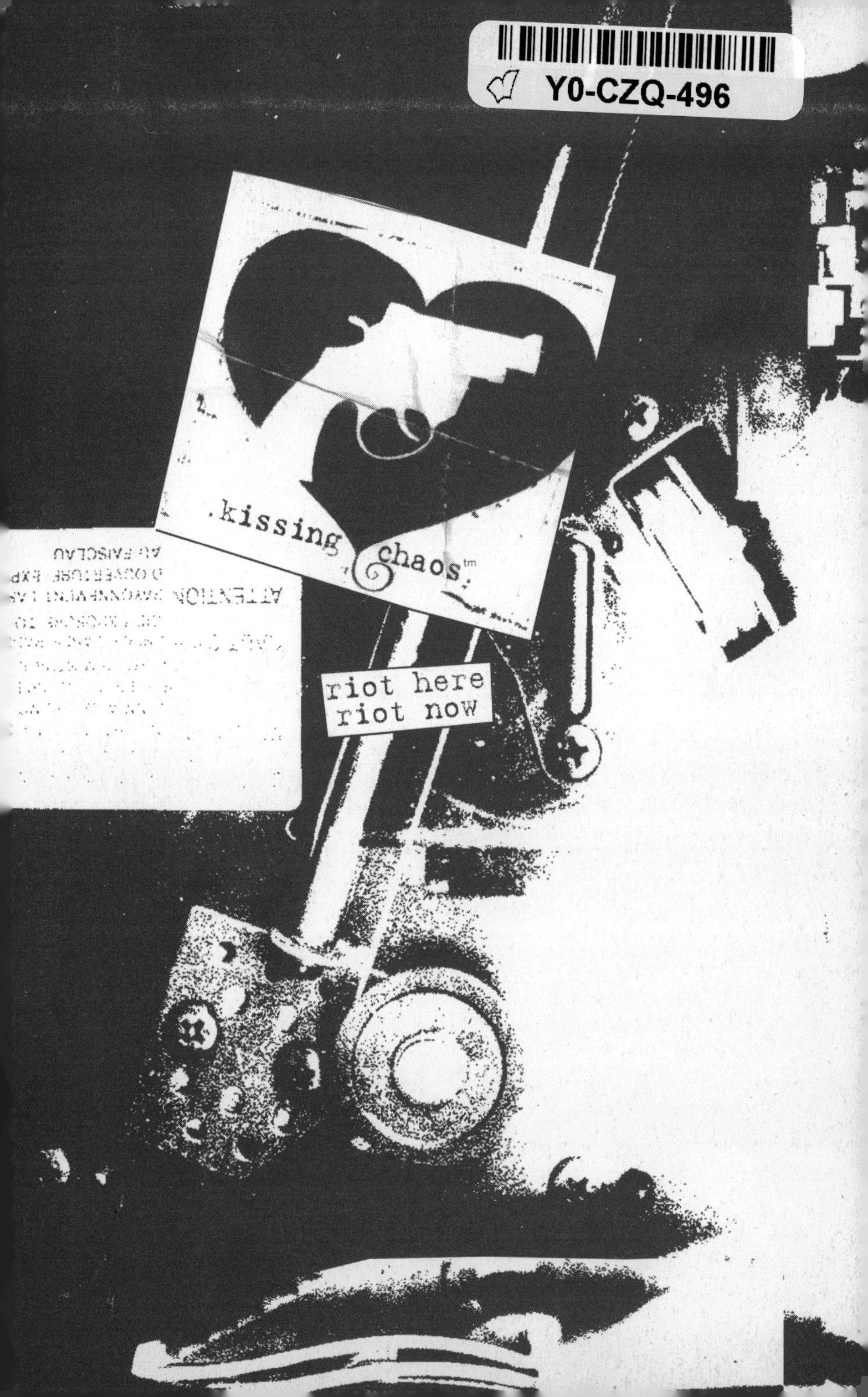
.kissing chaos™
riot here
riot now

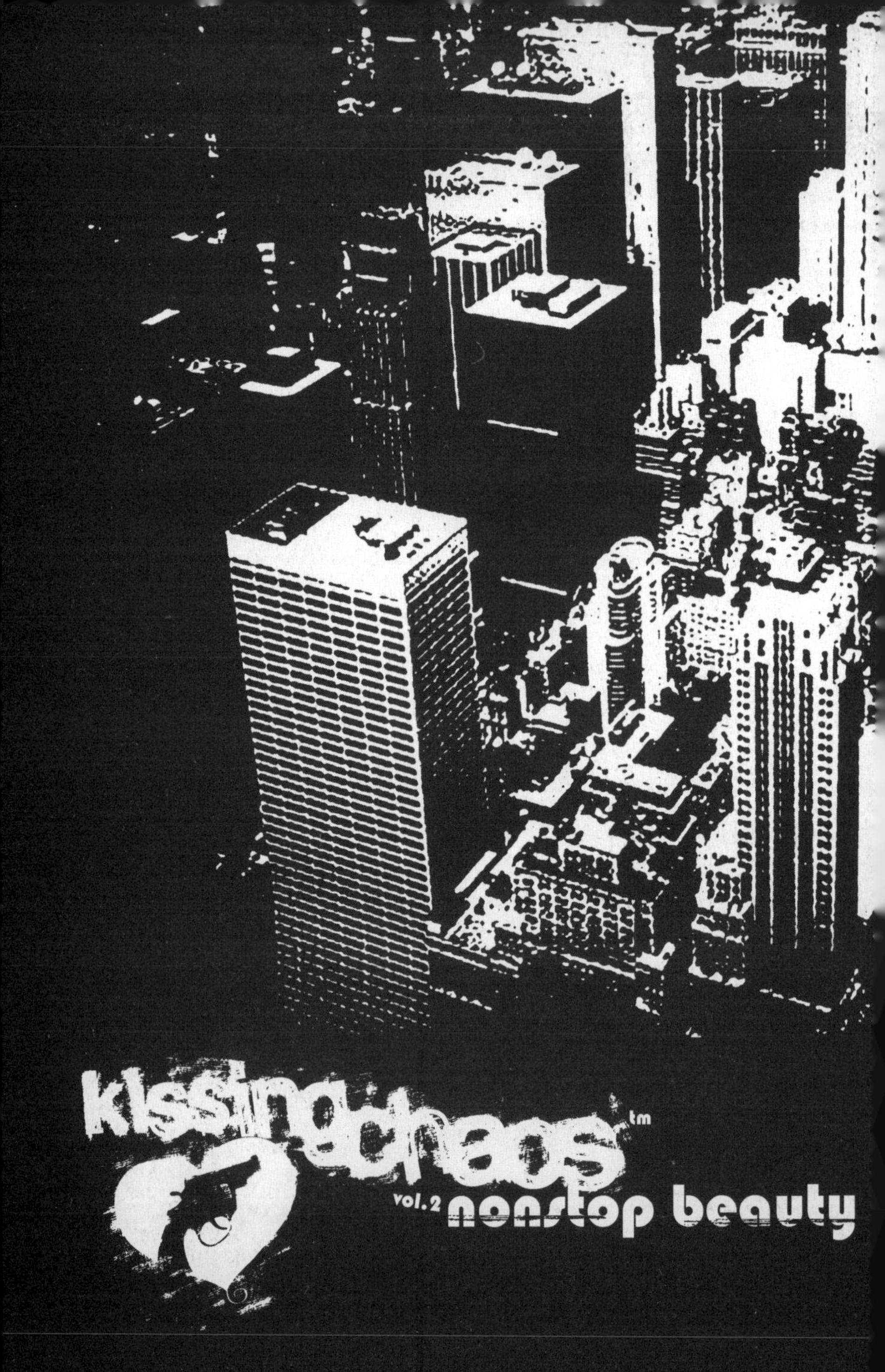
kissing chaos tm
vol. 2 nonstop beauty

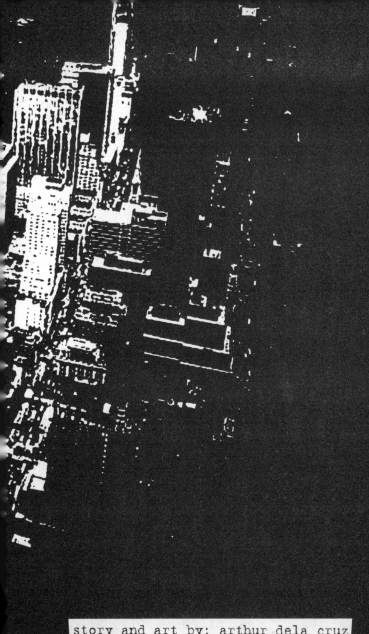

story and art by: arthur dela cruz

book design: arthur dela cruz

edited by: jamie s. rich

cover layout:kalah allen

Published by Oni Press, Inc.
Joe Nozemack, publisher
Jamie S. Rich, editor in chief
James Lucas Jones, associate editor

This collects issues 1-4 of the Oni Press comics series
Kissing Chaos: Nonstop Beauty.™

ONI PRESS, INC.
6336 SE Milwaukie Avenue, PMB30
Portland, OR 97202
USA

www.kissingchaos.com
www.onipress.com

First edition: September 2003
ISBN 1-929998-64-3

1 3 5 7 9 10 8 6 4 2
PRINTED IN CANADA

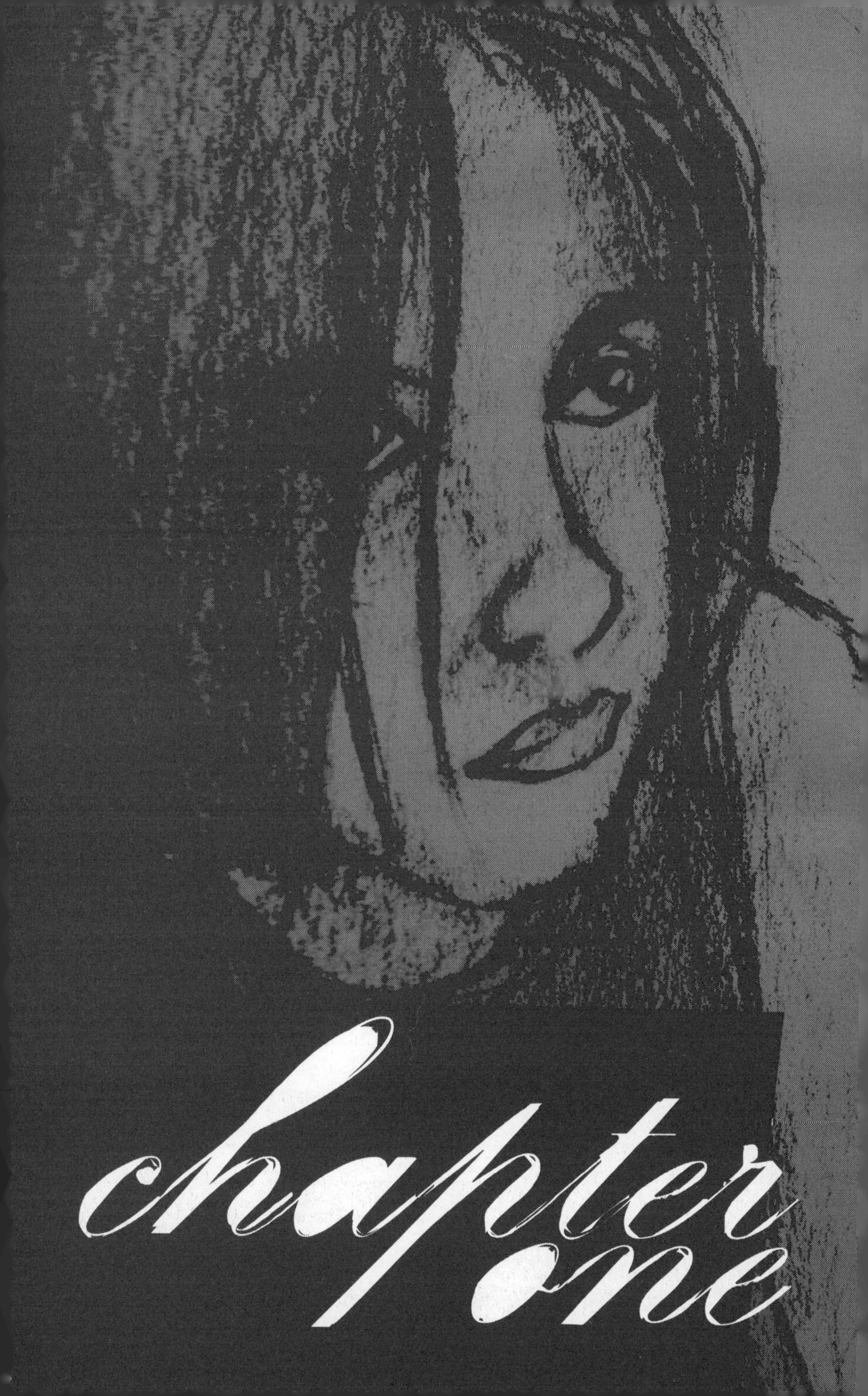
chapter
one

for a kiss can never be absolutely defined.

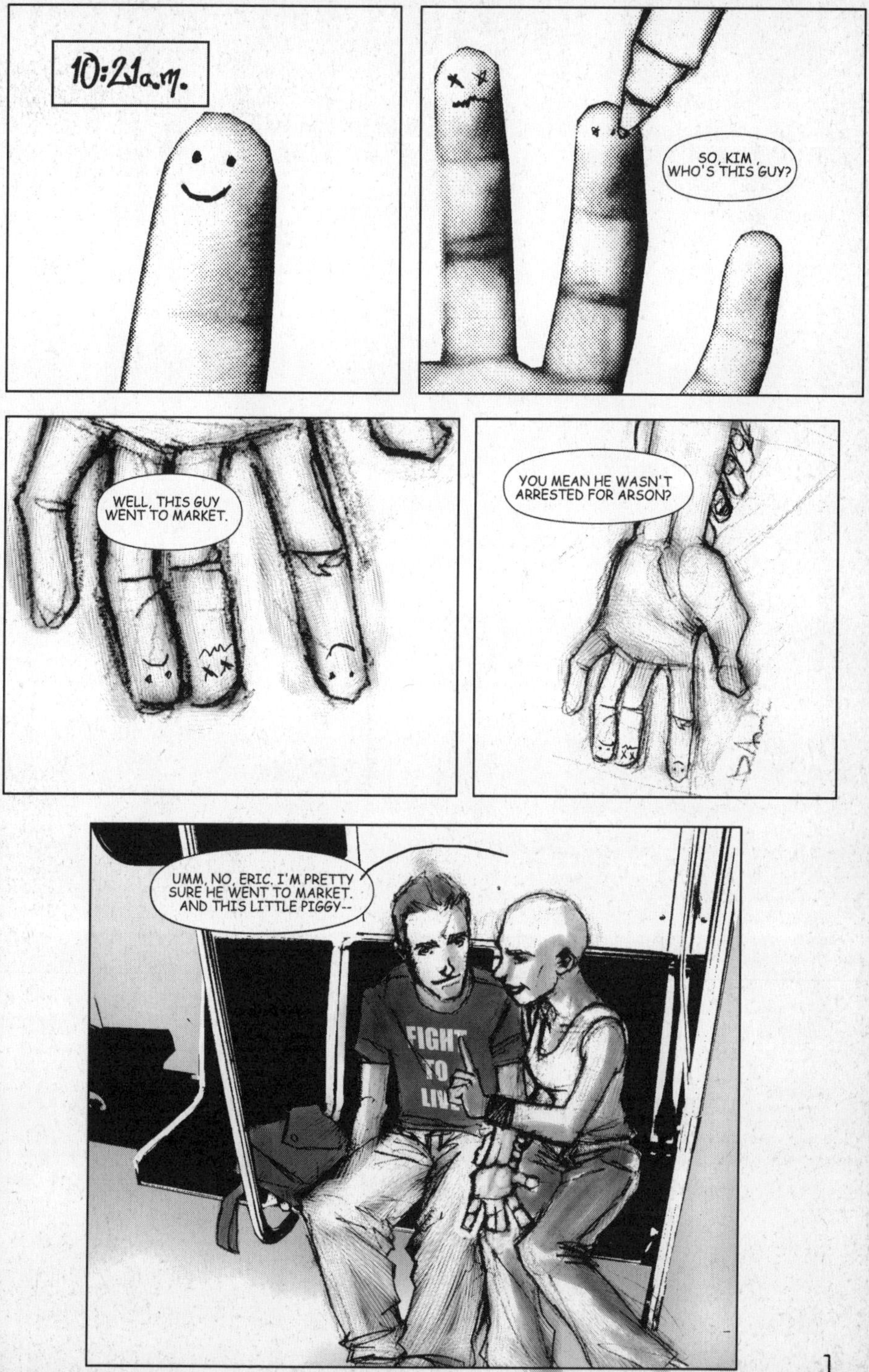
10:21 a.m.
SO, KIM, WHO'S THIS GUY?
WELL, THIS GUY WENT TO MARKET.
YOU MEAN HE WASN'T ARRESTED FOR ARSON?
UMM, NO, ERIC. I'M PRETTY SURE HE WENT TO MARKET. AND THIS LITTLE PIGGY--
FIGHT TO LIVE

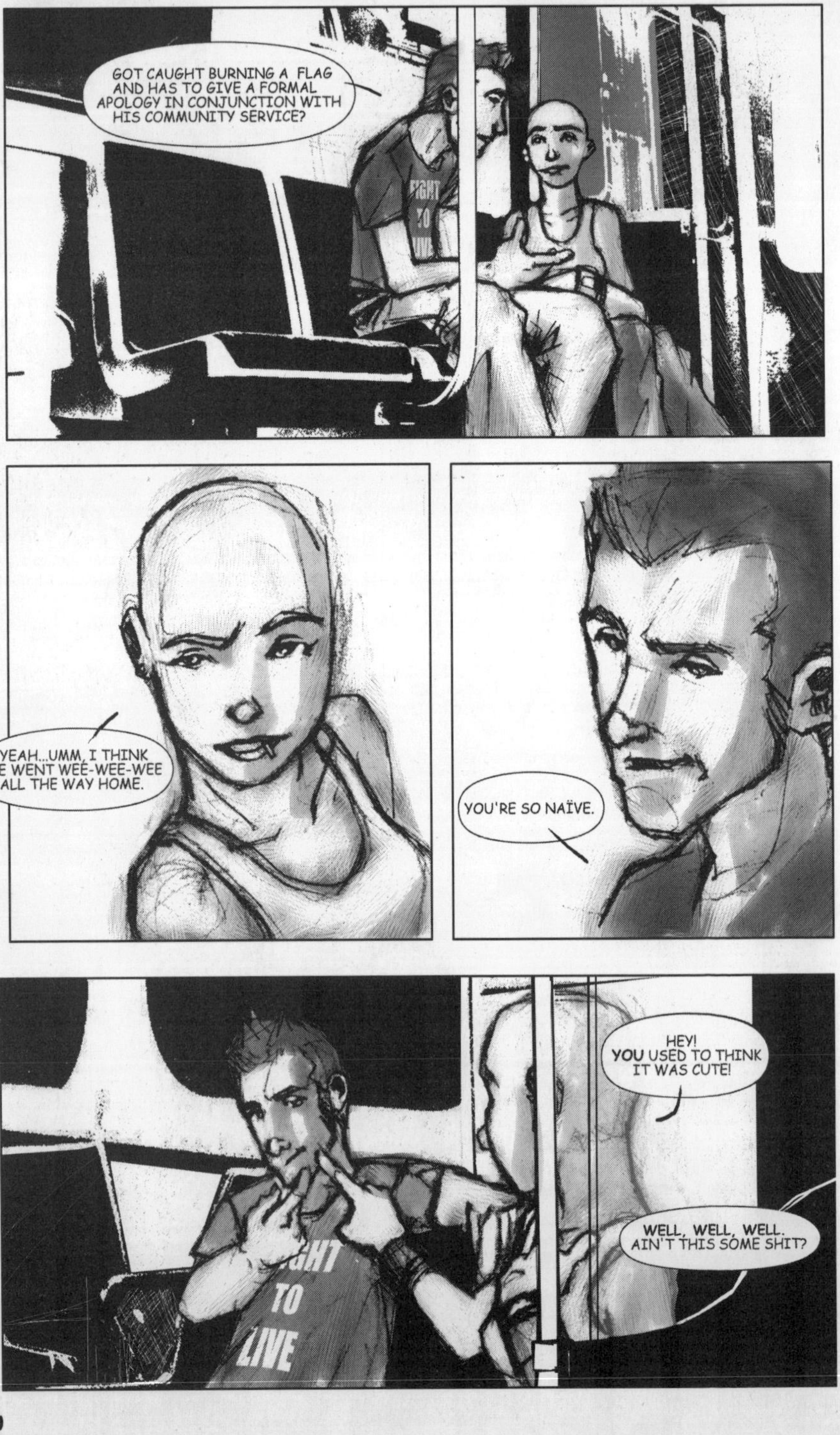
GOT CAUGHT BURNING A FLAG AND HAS TO GIVE A FORMAL APOLOGY IN CONJUNCTION WITH HIS COMMUNITY SERVICE?
FIGHT TO LIVE
YEAH...UMM, I THINK HE WENT WEE-WEE-WEE ALL THE WAY HOME.
YOU'RE SO NAÏVE.
HEY! **YOU** USED TO THINK IT WAS CUTE!
WELL, WELL, WELL. AIN'T THIS SOME SHIT?
TO LIVE

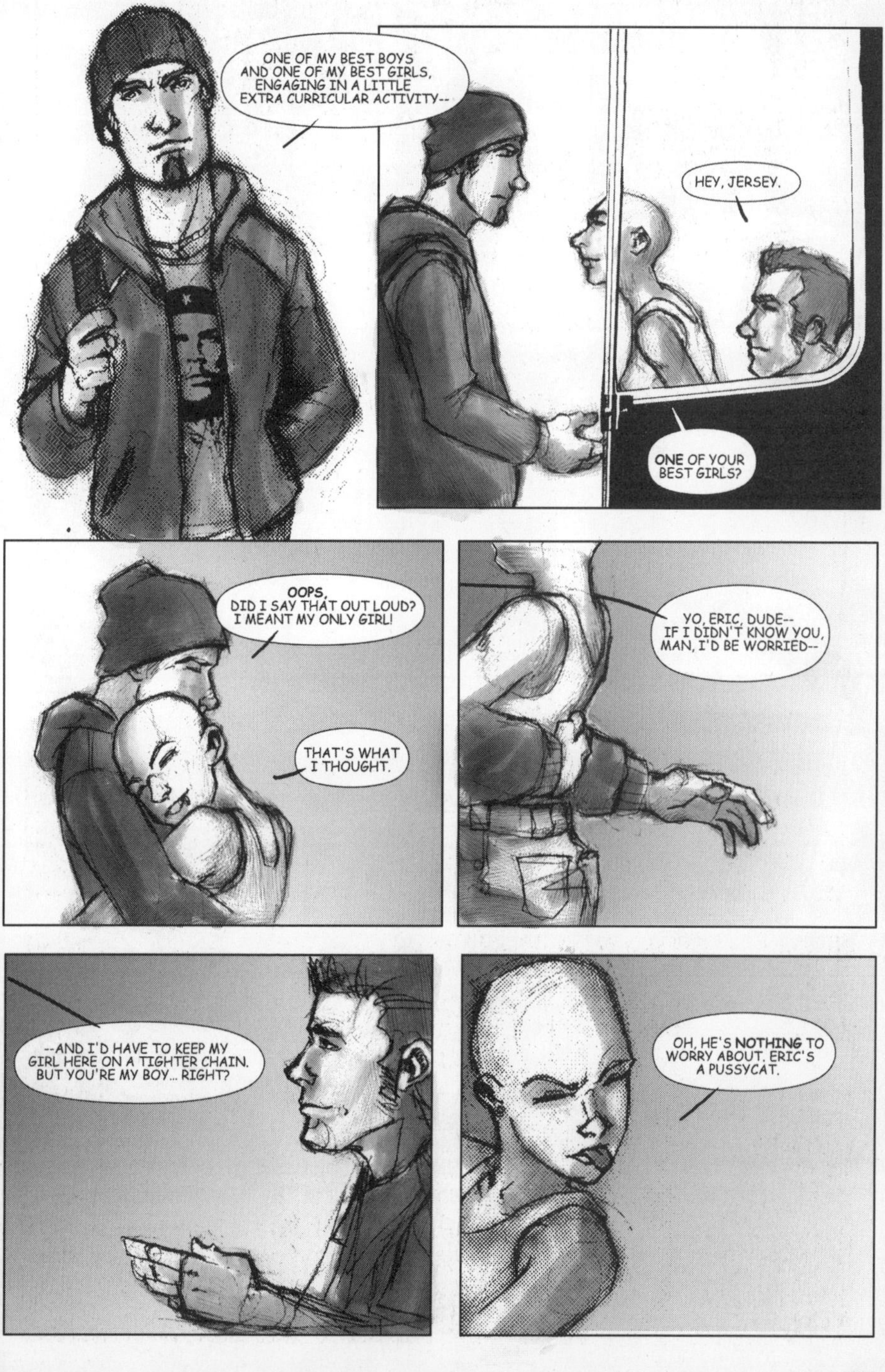
ONE OF MY BEST BOYS AND ONE OF MY BEST GIRLS, ENGAGING IN A LITTLE EXTRA CURRICULAR ACTIVITY--
HEY, JERSEY.
ONE OF YOUR BEST GIRLS?
OOPS, DID I SAY THAT OUT LOUD? I MEANT MY ONLY GIRL!
THAT'S WHAT I THOUGHT.
YO, ERIC, DUDE-- IF I DIDN'T KNOW YOU, MAN, I'D BE WORRIED--
--AND I'D HAVE TO KEEP MY GIRL HERE ON A TIGHTER CHAIN. BUT YOU'RE MY BOY... RIGHT?
OH, HE'S NOTHING TO WORRY ABOUT. ERIC'S A PUSSYCAT.

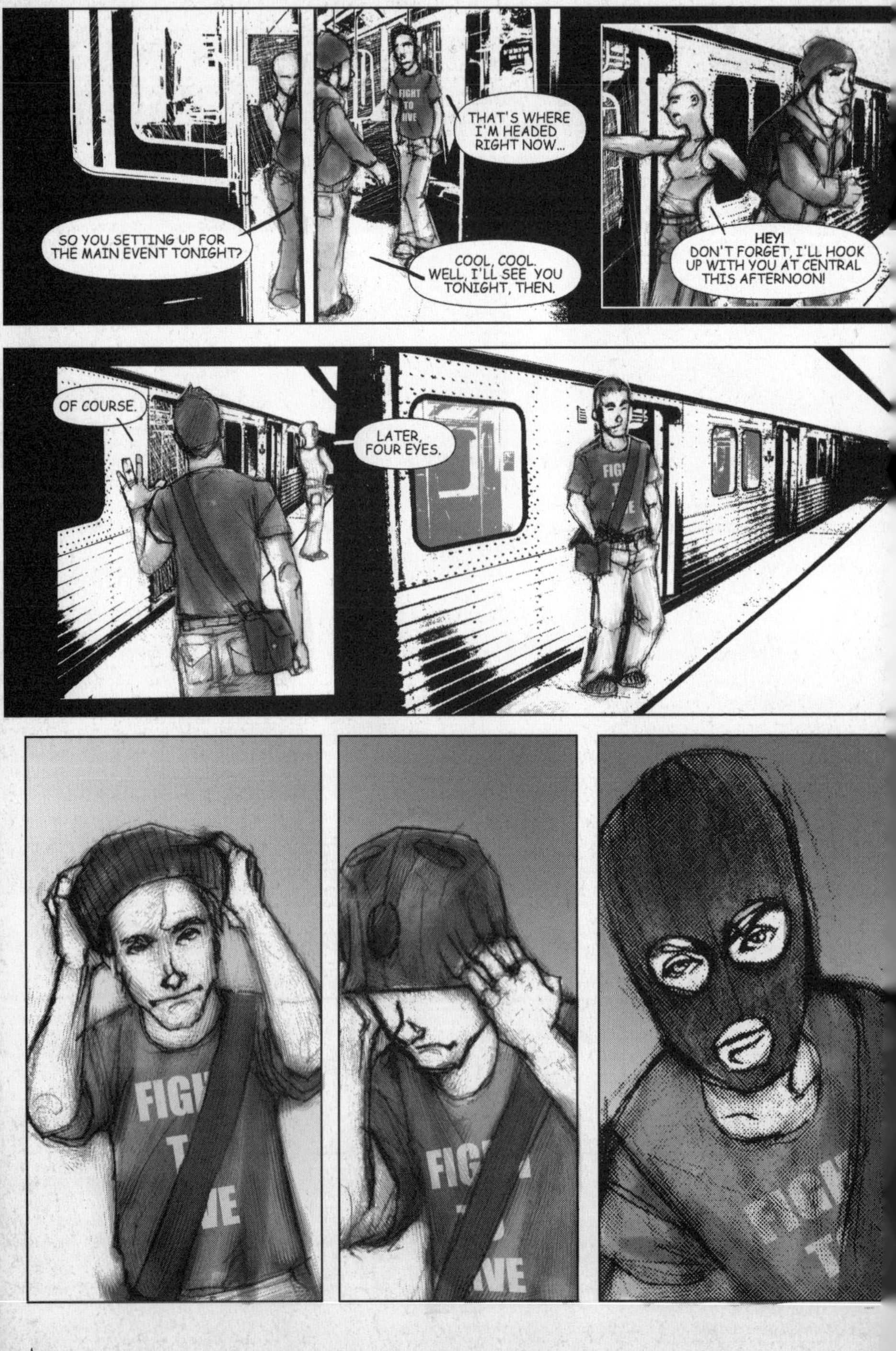

SO YOU SETTING UP FOR THE MAIN EVENT TONIGHT?
THAT'S WHERE I'M HEADED RIGHT NOW...
COOL, COOL. WELL, I'LL SEE YOU TONIGHT, THEN.
HEY! DON'T FORGET, I'LL HOOK UP WITH YOU AT CENTRAL THIS AFTERNOON!
OF COURSE.
LATER, FOUR EYES.

I HAVE NO STORIES.

I HAVE NOTHING TO SAY.

N OTHING OF ANY IMPORTANCE, ANYWAY.

CALL ME WHAT YOU WANT--SHY, A WALLFLOWER, AN INTROVERT.

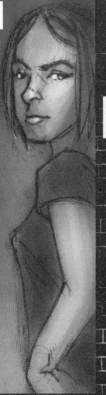

ANY WAY YOU CUT IT, WHILE PEOPLE ARE OUT THERE EXPERIENCING LIFE, I'M MORE LIKE AN INNOCENT BYSTANDER.

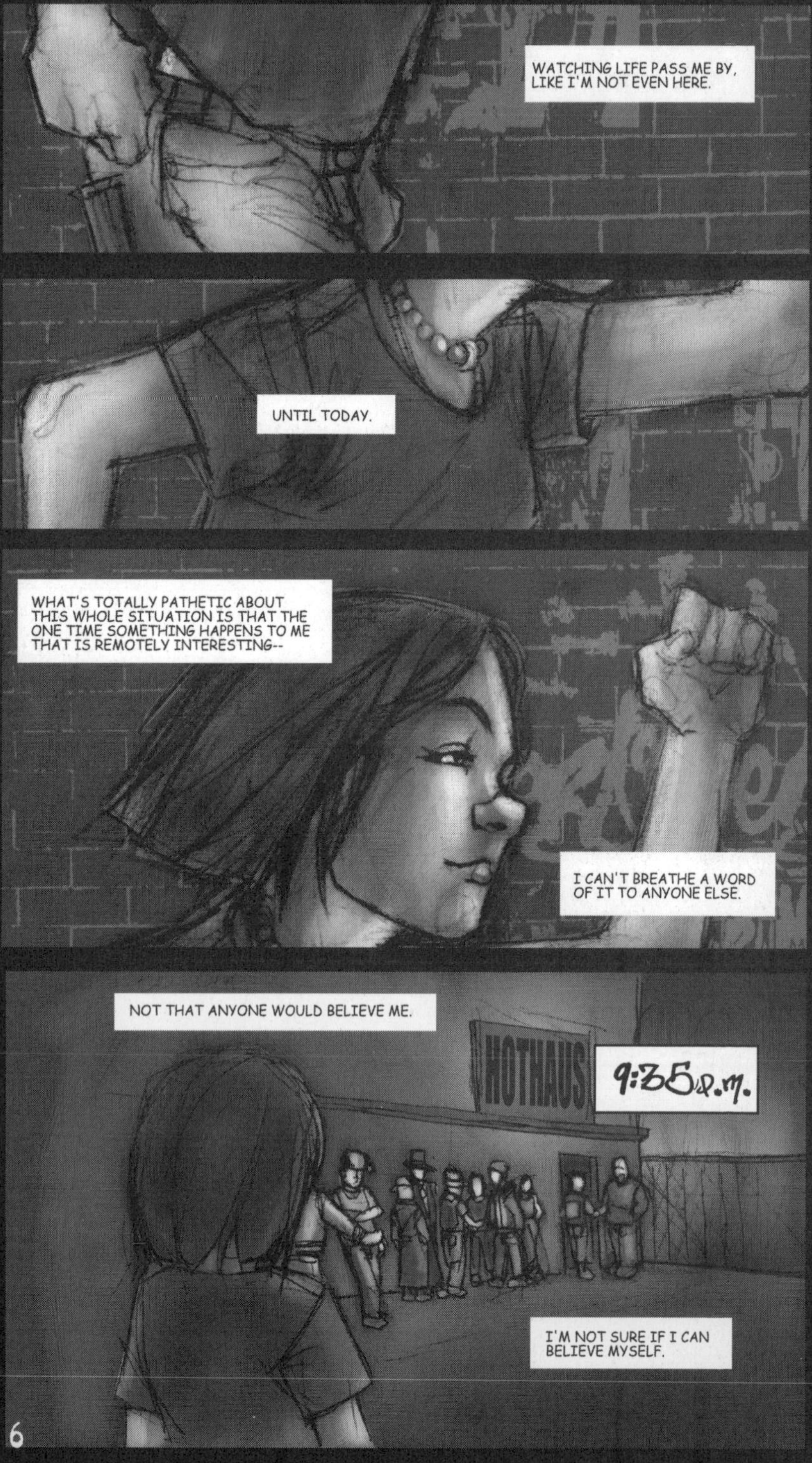
WATCHING LIFE PASS ME BY, LIKE I'M NOT EVEN HERE.
UNTIL TODAY.
WHAT'S TOTALLY PATHETIC ABOUT THIS WHOLE SITUATION IS THAT THE ONE TIME SOMETHING HAPPENS TO ME THAT IS REMOTELY INTERESTING--
I CAN'T BREATHE A WORD OF IT TO ANYONE ELSE.
NOT THAT ANYONE WOULD BELIEVE ME.
HOTHAUS
9:35 p.m.
I'M NOT SURE IF I CAN BELIEVE MYSELF.

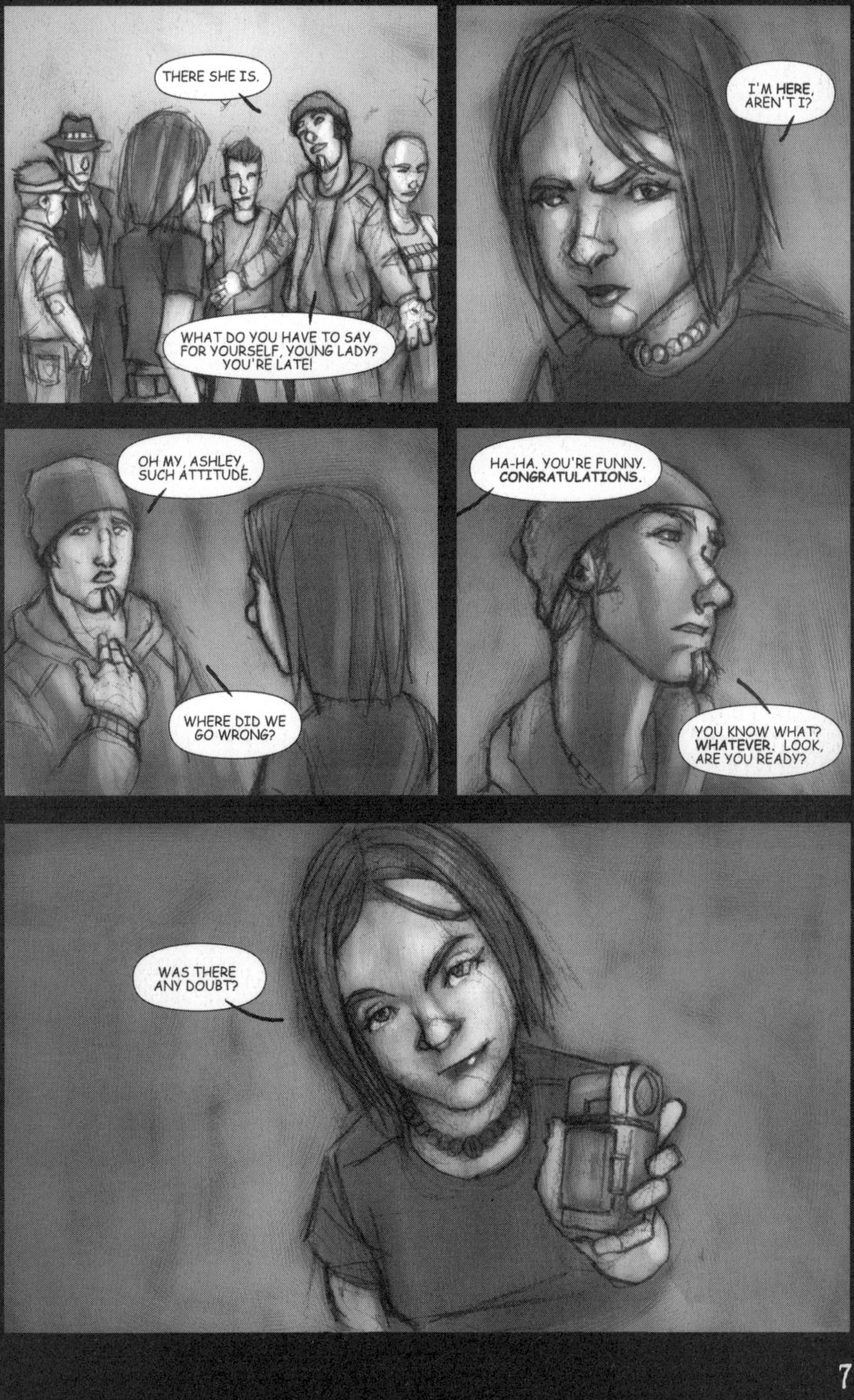

THERE SHE IS.
WHAT DO YOU HAVE TO SAY FOR YOURSELF, YOUNG LADY? YOU'RE LATE!
I'M HERE, AREN'T I?
OH MY, ASHLEY, SUCH ATTITUDE.
WHERE DID WE GO WRONG?
HA-HA. YOU'RE FUNNY. CONGRATULATIONS.
YOU KNOW WHAT? WHATEVER. LOOK, ARE YOU READY?
WAS THERE ANY DOUBT?

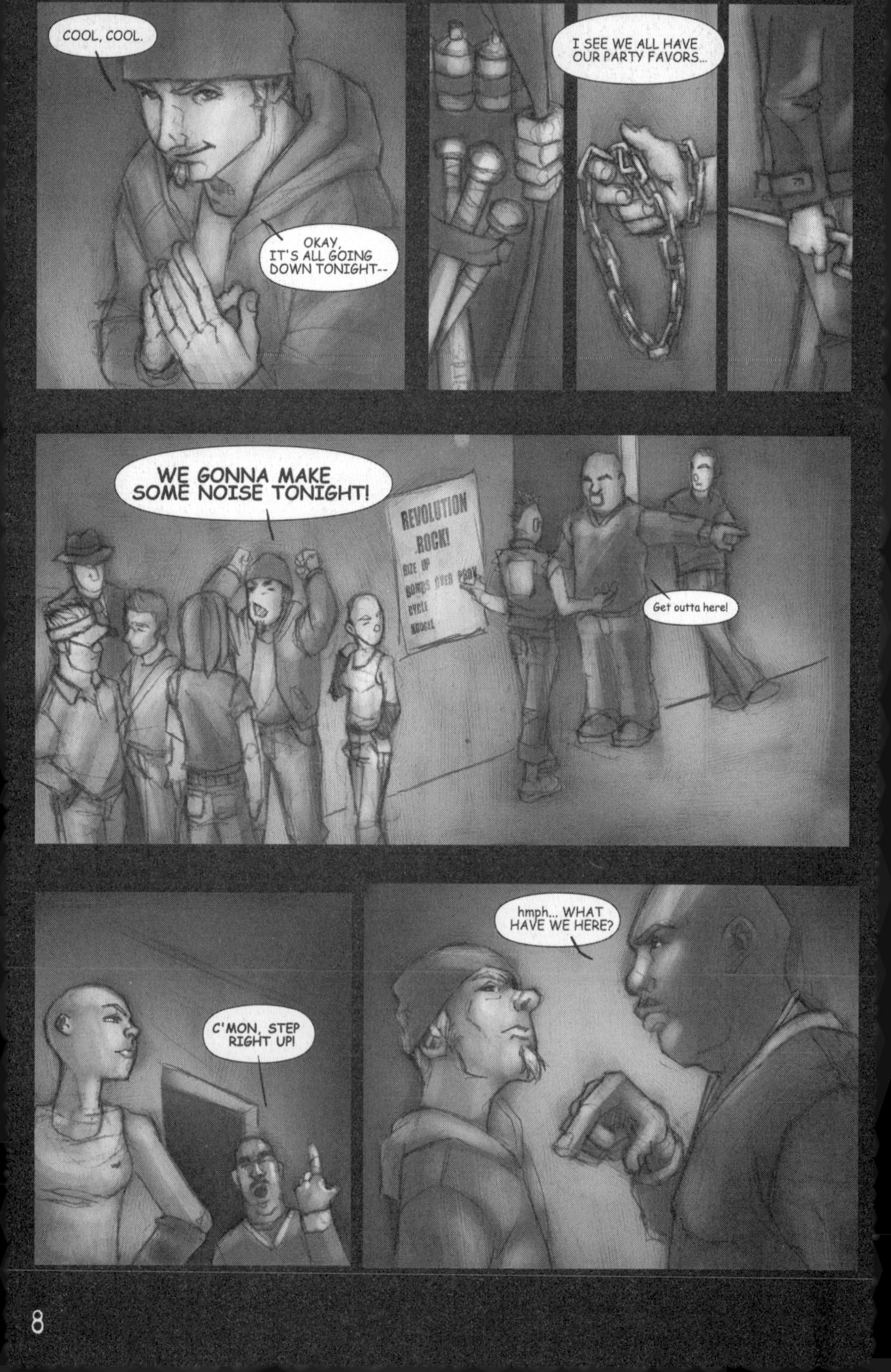

COOL, COOL.
OKAY, IT'S ALL GOING DOWN TONIGHT--
I SEE WE ALL HAVE OUR PARTY FAVORS...
WE GONNA MAKE SOME NOISE TONIGHT!
REVOLUTION ROCK!
Get outta here!
C'MON, STEP RIGHT UP!
hmph... WHAT HAVE WE HERE?

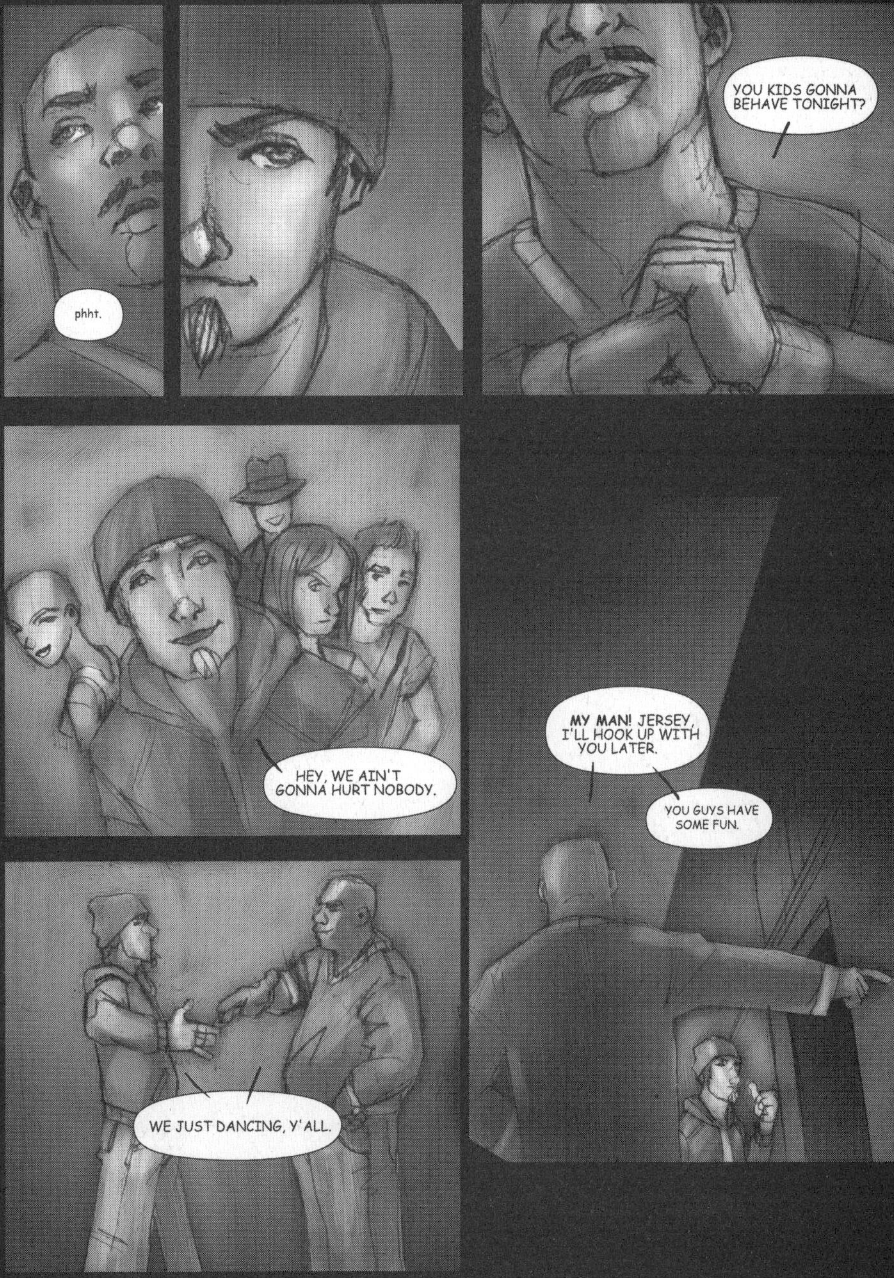
phht.
YOU KIDS GONNA BEHAVE TONIGHT?
HEY, WE AIN'T GONNA HURT NOBODY.
WE JUST DANCING, Y'ALL.
MY MAN! JERSEY, I'LL HOOK UP WITH YOU LATER.
YOU GUYS HAVE SOME FUN.

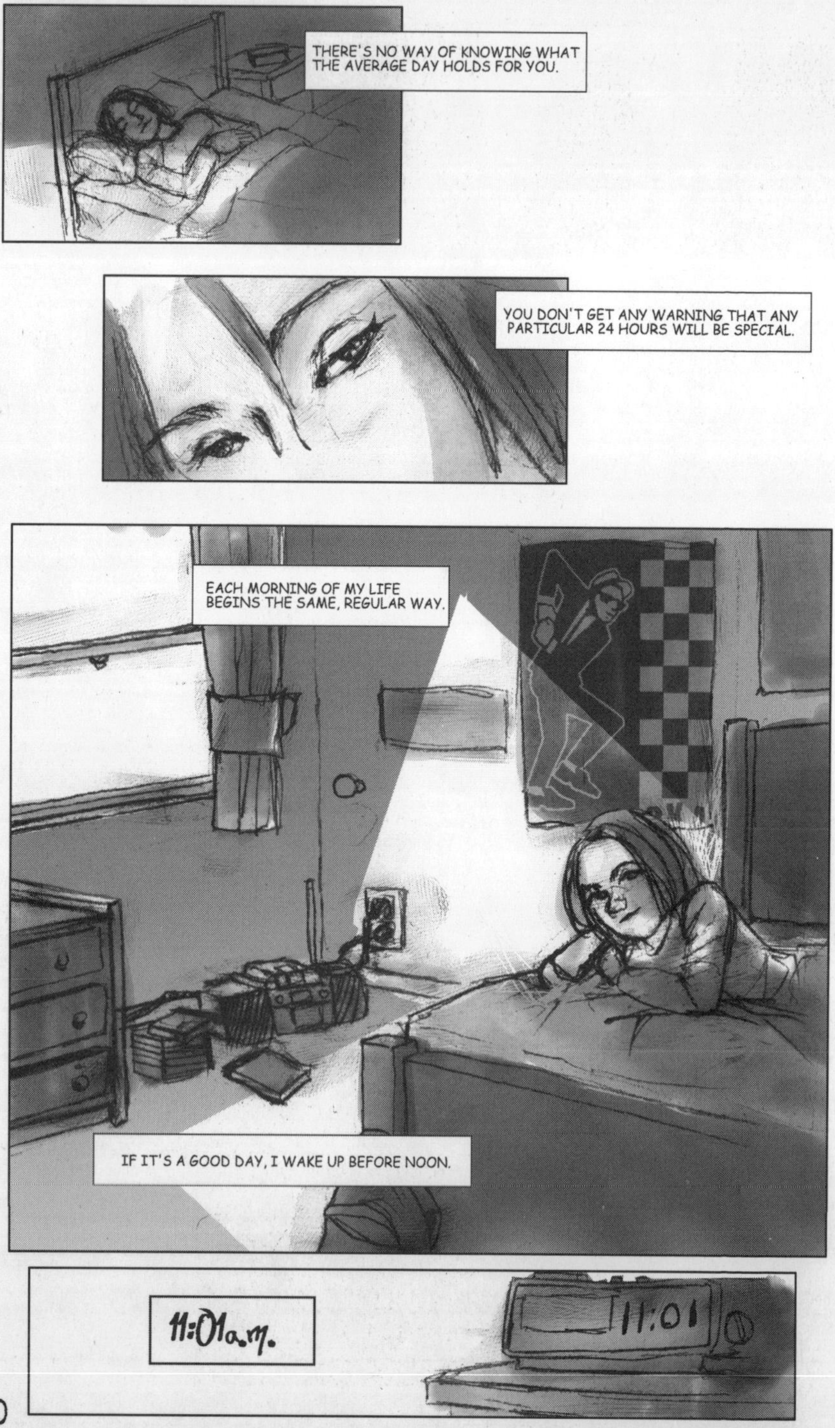
THERE'S NO WAY OF KNOWING WHAT THE AVERAGE DAY HOLDS FOR YOU.
YOU DON'T GET ANY WARNING THAT ANY PARTICULAR 24 HOURS WILL BE SPECIAL.
EACH MORNING OF MY LIFE BEGINS THE SAME, REGULAR WAY.
IF IT'S A GOOD DAY, I WAKE UP BEFORE NOON.
11:01 a.m.
11:01

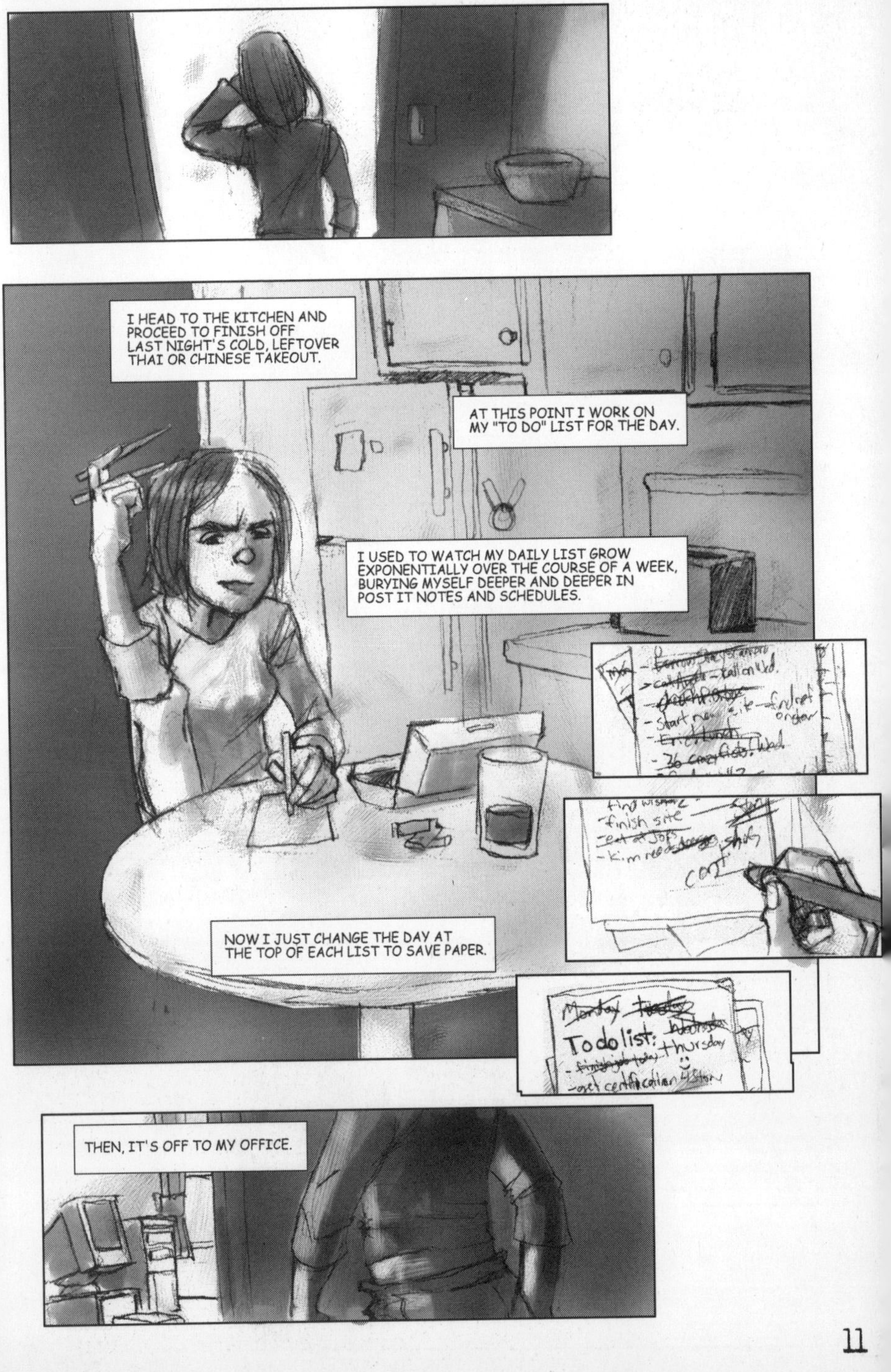
I HEAD TO THE KITCHEN AND PROCEED TO FINISH OFF LAST NIGHT'S COLD, LEFTOVER THAI OR CHINESE TAKEOUT.
AT THIS POINT I WORK ON MY "TO DO" LIST FOR THE DAY.
I USED TO WATCH MY DAILY LIST GROW EXPONENTIALLY OVER THE COURSE OF A WEEK, BURYING MYSELF DEEPER AND DEEPER IN POST IT NOTES AND SCHEDULES.
NOW I JUST CHANGE THE DAY AT THE TOP OF EACH LIST TO SAVE PAPER.
Todo list:
thursday
THEN, IT'S OFF TO MY OFFICE.

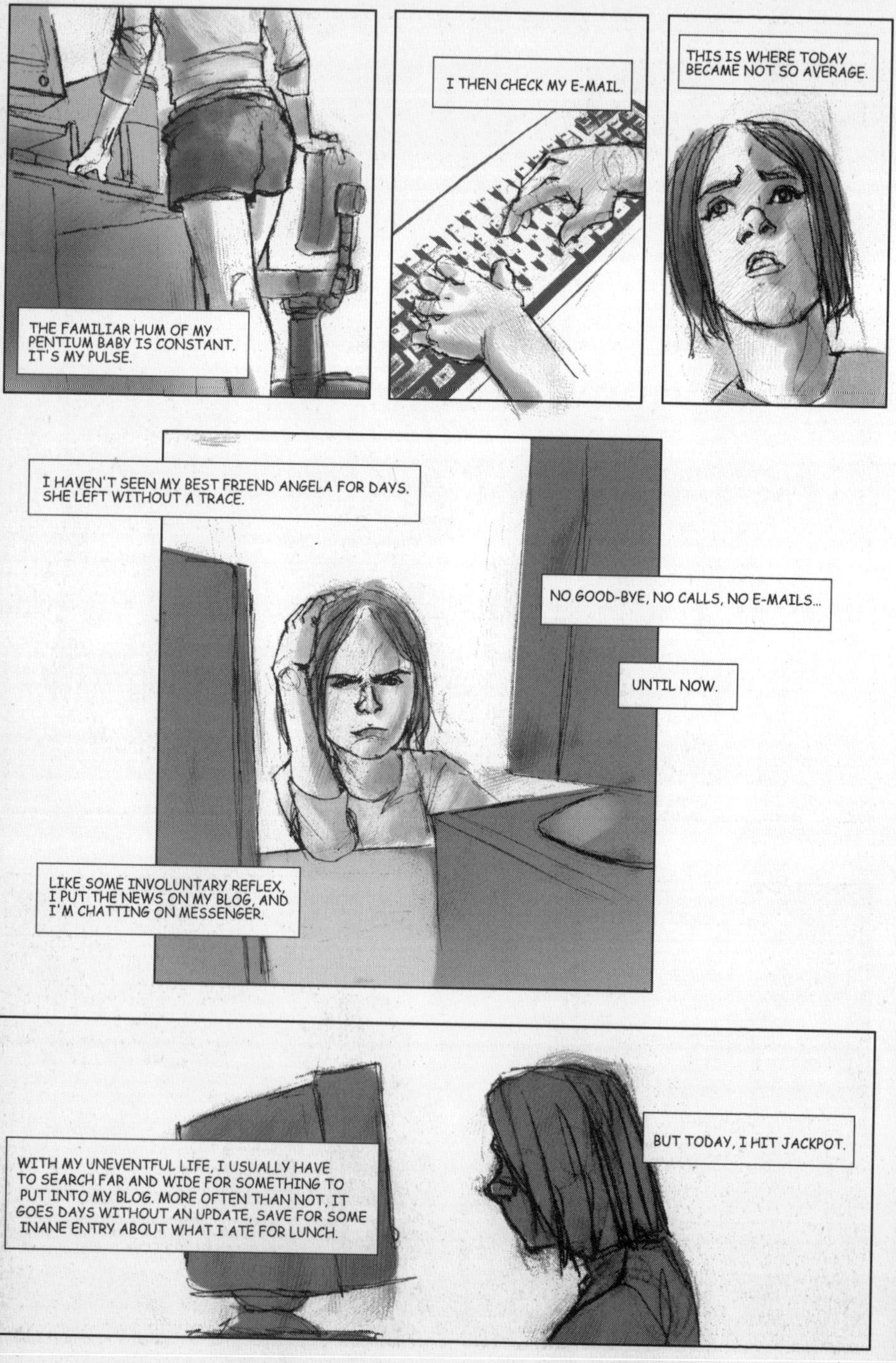
THE FAMILIAR HUM OF MY PENTIUM BABY IS CONSTANT. IT'S MY PULSE.
I THEN CHECK MY E-MAIL.
THIS IS WHERE TODAY BECAME NOT SO AVERAGE.
I HAVEN'T SEEN MY BEST FRIEND ANGELA FOR DAYS. SHE LEFT WITHOUT A TRACE.
NO GOOD-BYE, NO CALLS, NO E-MAILS...
UNTIL NOW.
LIKE SOME INVOLUNTARY REFLEX, I PUT THE NEWS ON MY BLOG, AND I'M CHATTING ON MESSENGER.
WITH MY UNEVENTFUL LIFE, I USUALLY HAVE TO SEARCH FAR AND WIDE FOR SOMETHING TO PUT INTO MY BLOG. MORE OFTEN THAN NOT, IT GOES DAYS WITHOUT AN UPDATE, SAVE FOR SOME INANE ENTRY ABOUT WHAT I ATE FOR LUNCH.
BUT TODAY, I HIT JACKPOT.

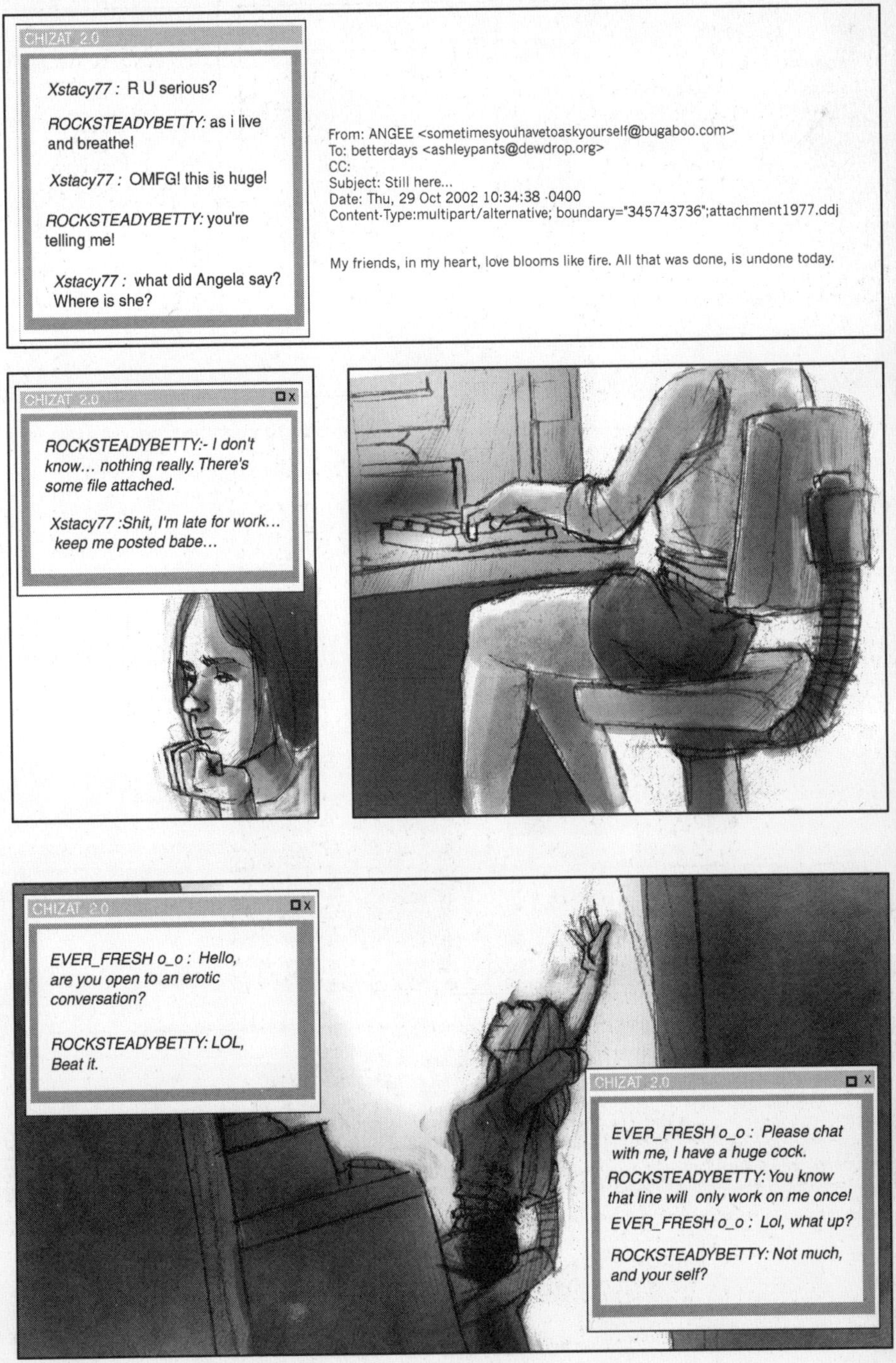
CHIZAT 2.0
Xstacy77 : R U serious?
ROCKSTEADYBETTY: as i live and breathe!
Xstacy77 : OMFG! this is huge!
ROCKSTEADYBETTY: you're telling me!
Xstacy77 : what did Angela say? Where is she?
From: ANGEE <sometimesyouhavetoaskyourself@bugaboo.com>
To: betterdays <ashleypants@dewdrop.org>
CC:
Subject: Still here...
Date: Thu, 29 Oct 2002 10:34:38 -0400
Content-Type:multipart/alternative; boundary="345743736";attachment1977.ddj
My friends, in my heart, love blooms like fire. All that was done, is undone today.
CHIZAT 2.0
ROCKSTEADYBETTY:- I don't know... nothing really. There's some file attached.
Xstacy77 :Shit, I'm late for work... keep me posted babe...
CHIZAT 2.0
EVER_FRESH o_o : Hello, are you open to an erotic conversation?
ROCKSTEADYBETTY: LOL, Beat it.
CHIZAT 2.0
EVER_FRESH o_o : Please chat with me, I have a huge cock.
ROCKSTEADYBETTY: You know that line will only work on me once!
EVER_FRESH o_o : Lol, what up?
ROCKSTEADYBETTY: Not much, and your self?

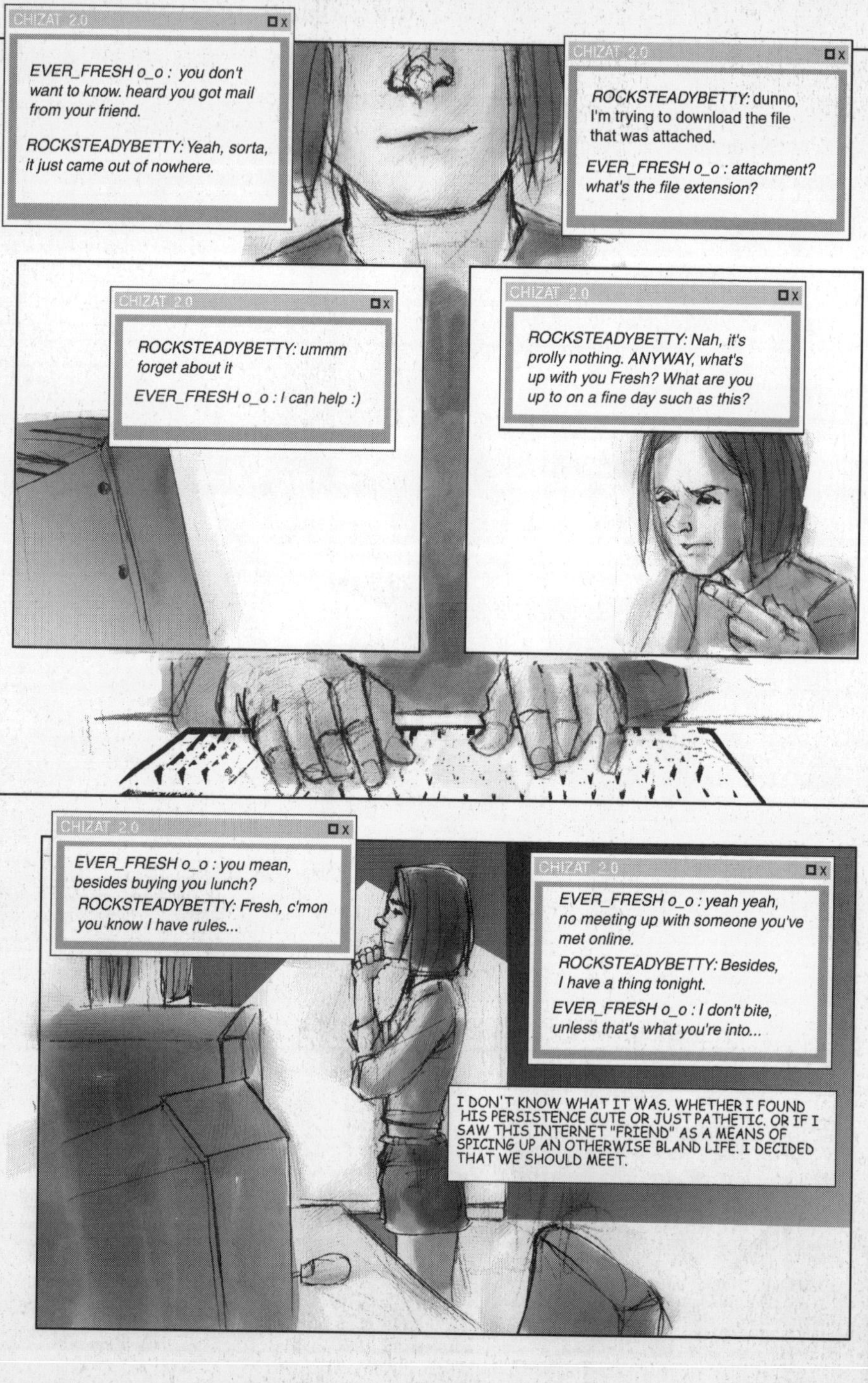
CHIZAT 2.0
EVER_FRESH o_o : you don't want to know. heard you got mail from your friend.
ROCKSTEADYBETTY: Yeah, sorta, it just came out of nowhere.
CHIZAT 2.0
ROCKSTEADYBETTY: dunno, I'm trying to download the file that was attached.
EVER_FRESH o_o : attachment? what's the file extension?
CHIZAT 2.0
ROCKSTEADYBETTY: ummm forget about it
EVER_FRESH o_o : I can help :)
CHIZAT 2.0
ROCKSTEADYBETTY: Nah, it's prolly nothing. ANYWAY, what's up with you Fresh? What are you up to on a fine day such as this?
CHIZAT 2.0
EVER_FRESH o_o : you mean, besides buying you lunch?
ROCKSTEADYBETTY: Fresh, c'mon you know I have rules...
CHIZAT 2.0
EVER_FRESH o_o : yeah yeah, no meeting up with someone you've met online.
ROCKSTEADYBETTY: Besides, I have a thing tonight.
EVER_FRESH o_o : I don't bite, unless that's what you're into...
I DON'T KNOW WHAT IT WAS. WHETHER I FOUND HIS PERSISTENCE CUTE OR JUST PATHETIC. OR IF I SAW THIS INTERNET "FRIEND" AS A MEANS OF SPICING UP AN OTHERWISE BLAND LIFE. I DECIDED THAT WE SHOULD MEET.

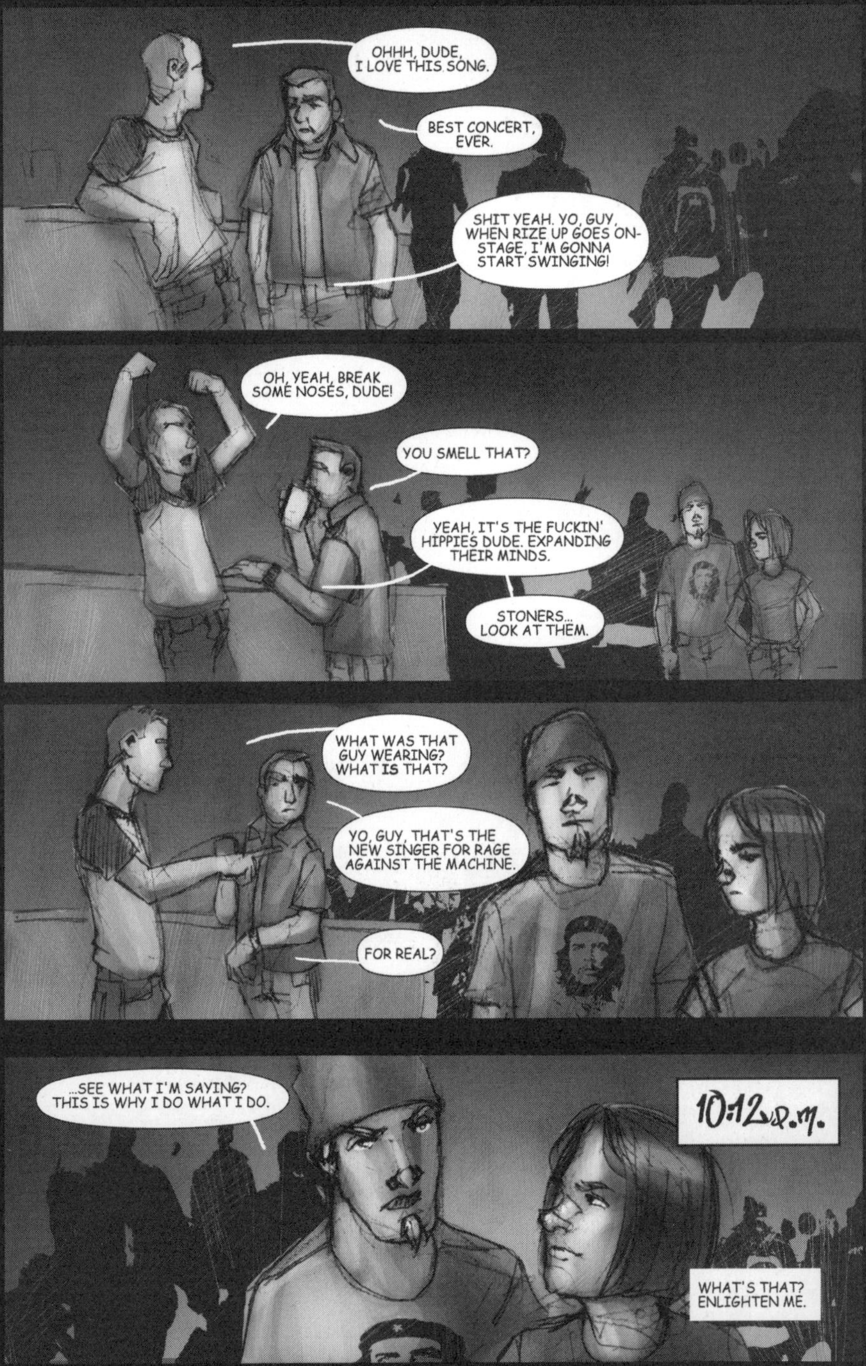
OHHH, DUDE, I LOVE THIS SONG.
BEST CONCERT, EVER.
SHIT YEAH. YO, GUY, WHEN RIZE UP GOES ON-STAGE, I'M GONNA START SWINGING!
OH, YEAH, BREAK SOME NOSES, DUDE!
YOU SMELL THAT?
YEAH, IT'S THE FUCKIN' HIPPIES DUDE. EXPANDING THEIR MINDS.
STONERS... LOOK AT THEM.
WHAT WAS THAT GUY WEARING? WHAT **IS** THAT?
YO, GUY, THAT'S THE NEW SINGER FOR RAGE AGAINST THE MACHINE.
FOR REAL?
...SEE WHAT I'M SAYING? THIS IS WHY I DO WHAT I DO.
10:12 p.m.
WHAT'S THAT? ENLIGHTEN ME.

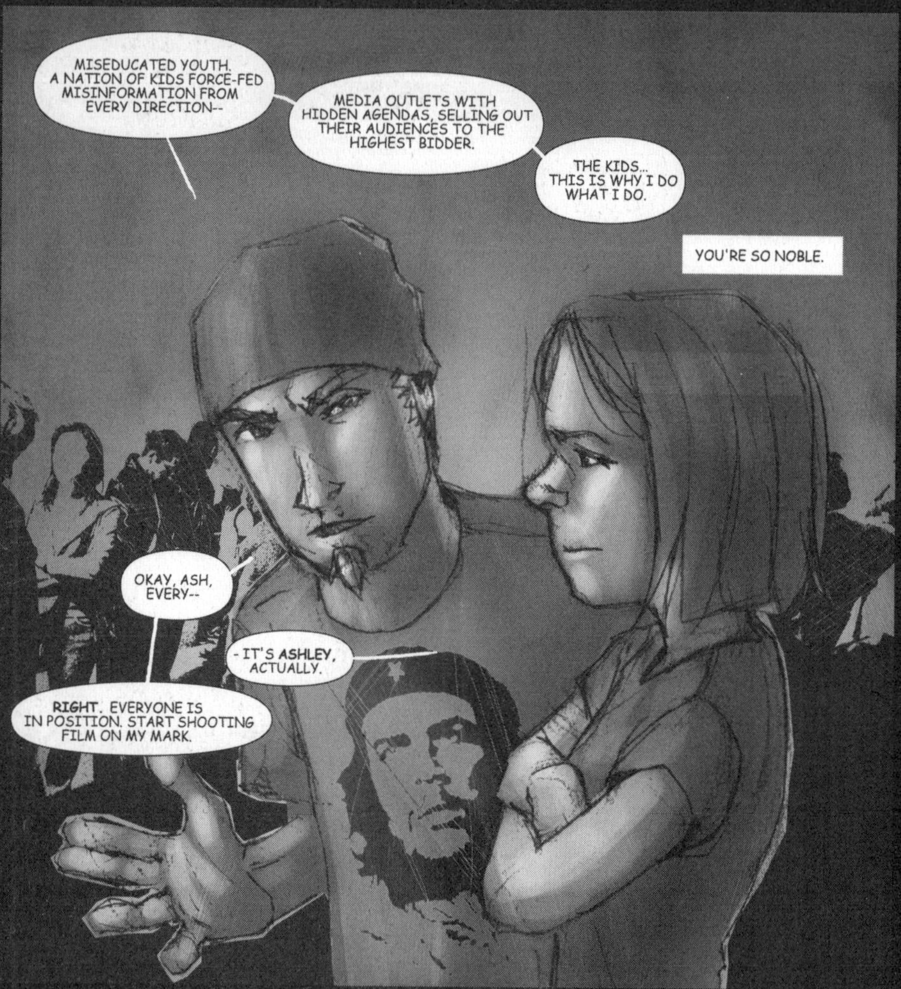
MISEDUCATED YOUTH. A NATION OF KIDS FORCE-FED MISINFORMATION FROM EVERY DIRECTION--
MEDIA OUTLETS WITH HIDDEN AGENDAS, SELLING OUT THEIR AUDIENCES TO THE HIGHEST BIDDER.
THE KIDS... THIS IS WHY I DO WHAT I DO.
YOU'RE SO NOBLE.
OKAY, ASH, EVERY--
- IT'S **ASHLEY**, ACTUALLY.
RIGHT. EVERYONE IS IN POSITION. START SHOOTING FILM ON MY MARK.

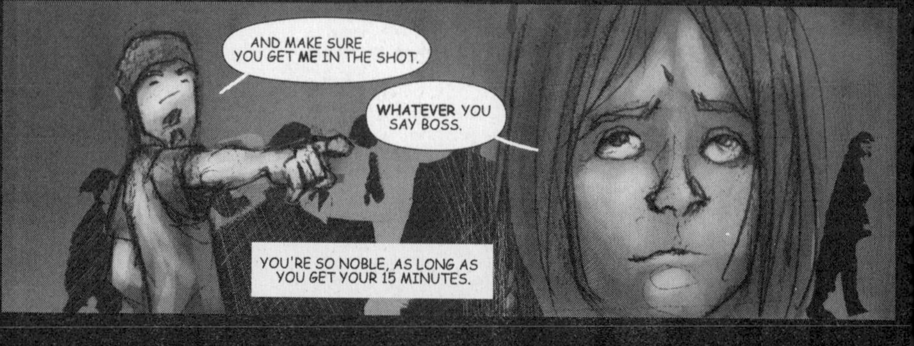
AND MAKE SURE YOU GET **ME** IN THE SHOT.
WHATEVER YOU SAY BOSS.
YOU'RE SO NOBLE, AS LONG AS YOU GET YOUR 15 MINUTES.

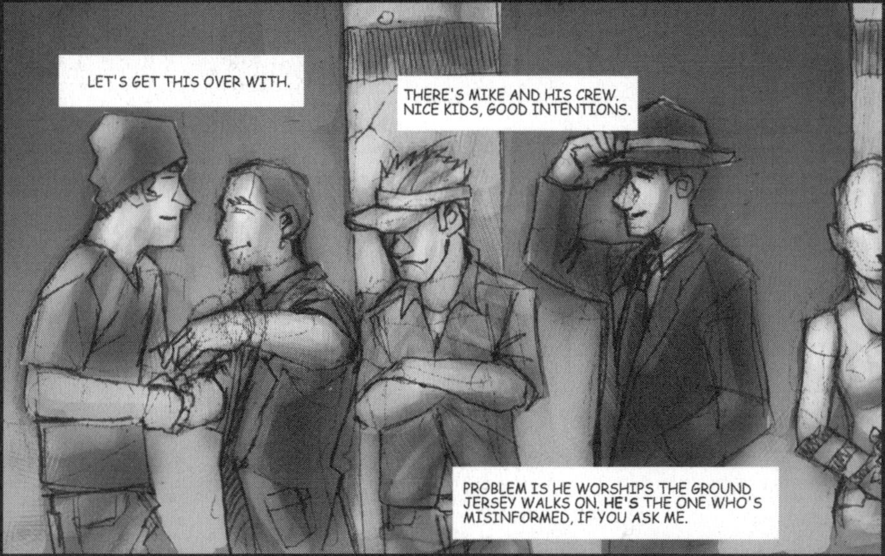
LET'S GET THIS OVER WITH.
THERE'S MIKE AND HIS CREW. NICE KIDS, GOOD INTENTIONS.
PROBLEM IS HE WORSHIPS THE GROUND JERSEY WALKS ON. HE'S THE ONE WHO'S MISINFORMED, IF YOU ASK ME.

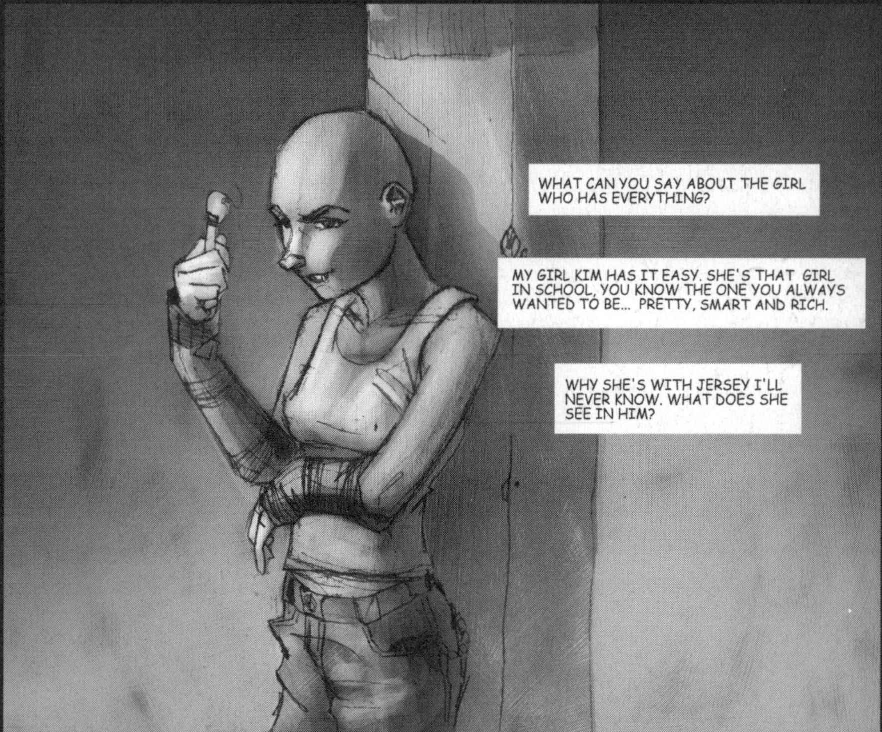
WHAT CAN YOU SAY ABOUT THE GIRL WHO HAS EVERYTHING?
MY GIRL KIM HAS IT EASY. SHE'S THAT GIRL IN SCHOOL, YOU KNOW THE ONE YOU ALWAYS WANTED TO BE... PRETTY, SMART AND RICH.
WHY SHE'S WITH JERSEY I'LL NEVER KNOW. WHAT DOES SHE SEE IN HIM?

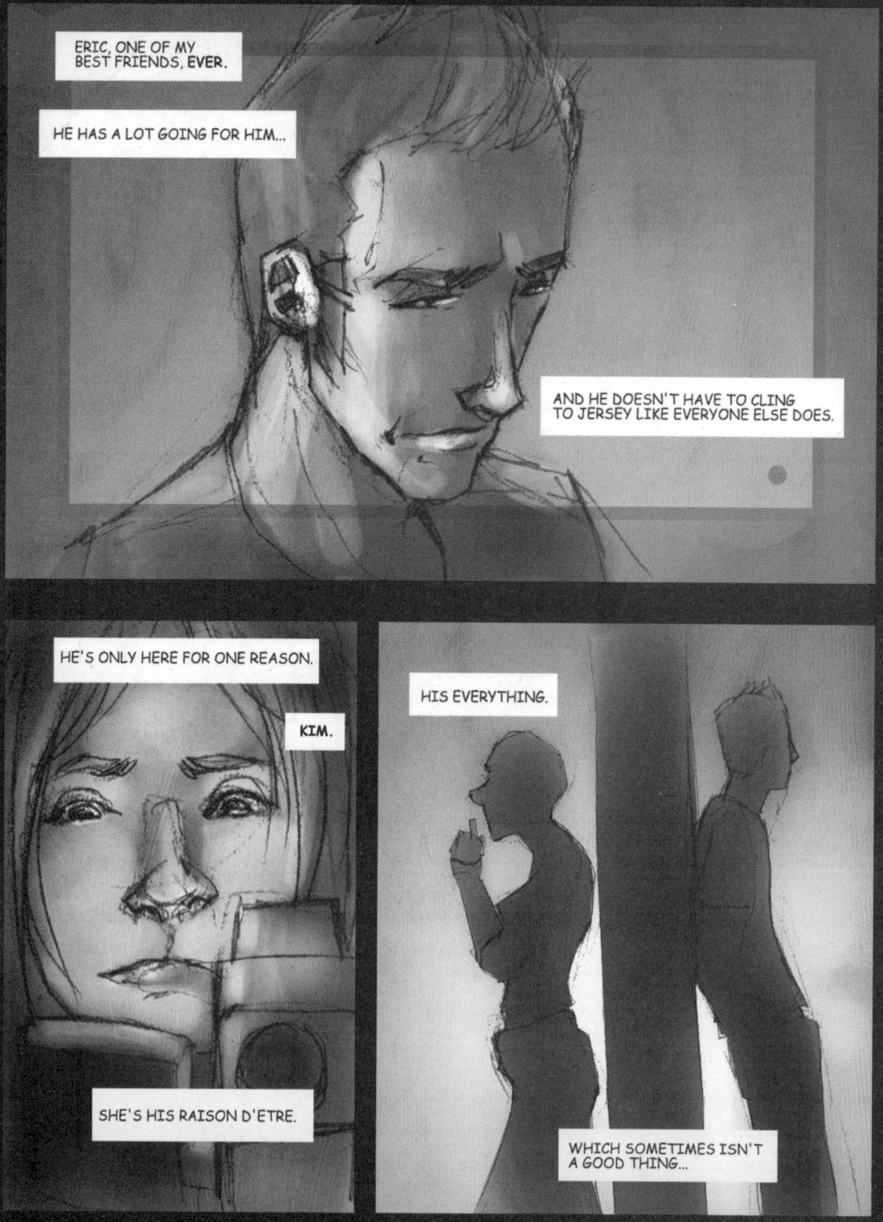
ERIC, ONE OF MY BEST FRIENDS, **EVER.**
HE HAS A LOT GOING FOR HIM...
AND HE DOESN'T HAVE TO CLING TO JERSEY LIKE EVERYONE ELSE DOES.
HE'S ONLY HERE FOR ONE REASON.
KIM.
SHE'S HIS RAISON D'ETRE.
HIS EVERYTHING.
WHICH SOMETIMES ISN'T A GOOD THING...

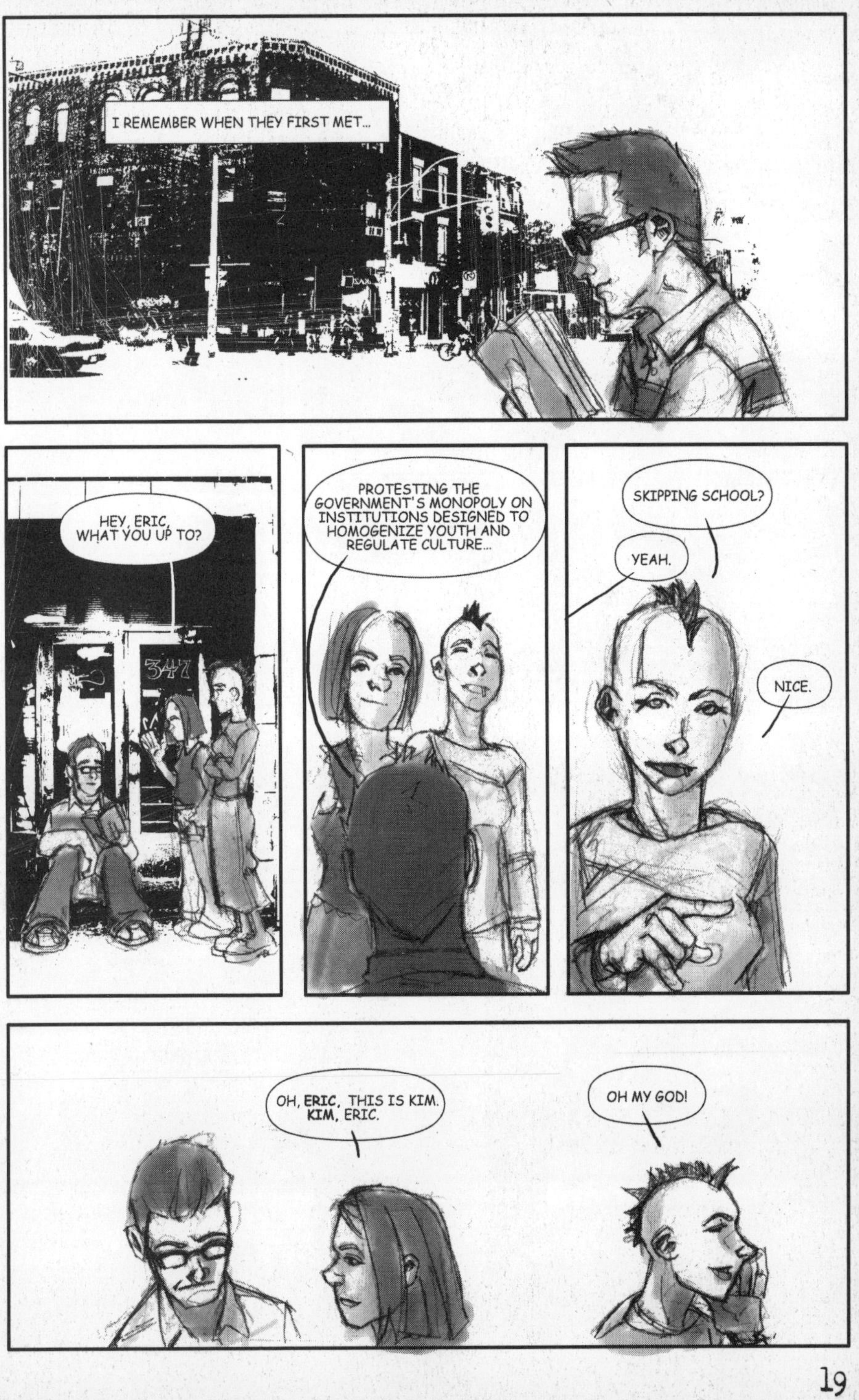
I REMEMBER WHEN THEY FIRST MET...
HEY, ERIC, WHAT YOU UP TO?
PROTESTING THE GOVERNMENT'S MONOPOLY ON INSTITUTIONS DESIGNED TO HOMOGENIZE YOUTH AND REGULATE CULTURE...
SKIPPING SCHOOL?
YEAH.
NICE.
OH, ERIC, THIS IS KIM. KIM, ERIC.
OH MY GOD!

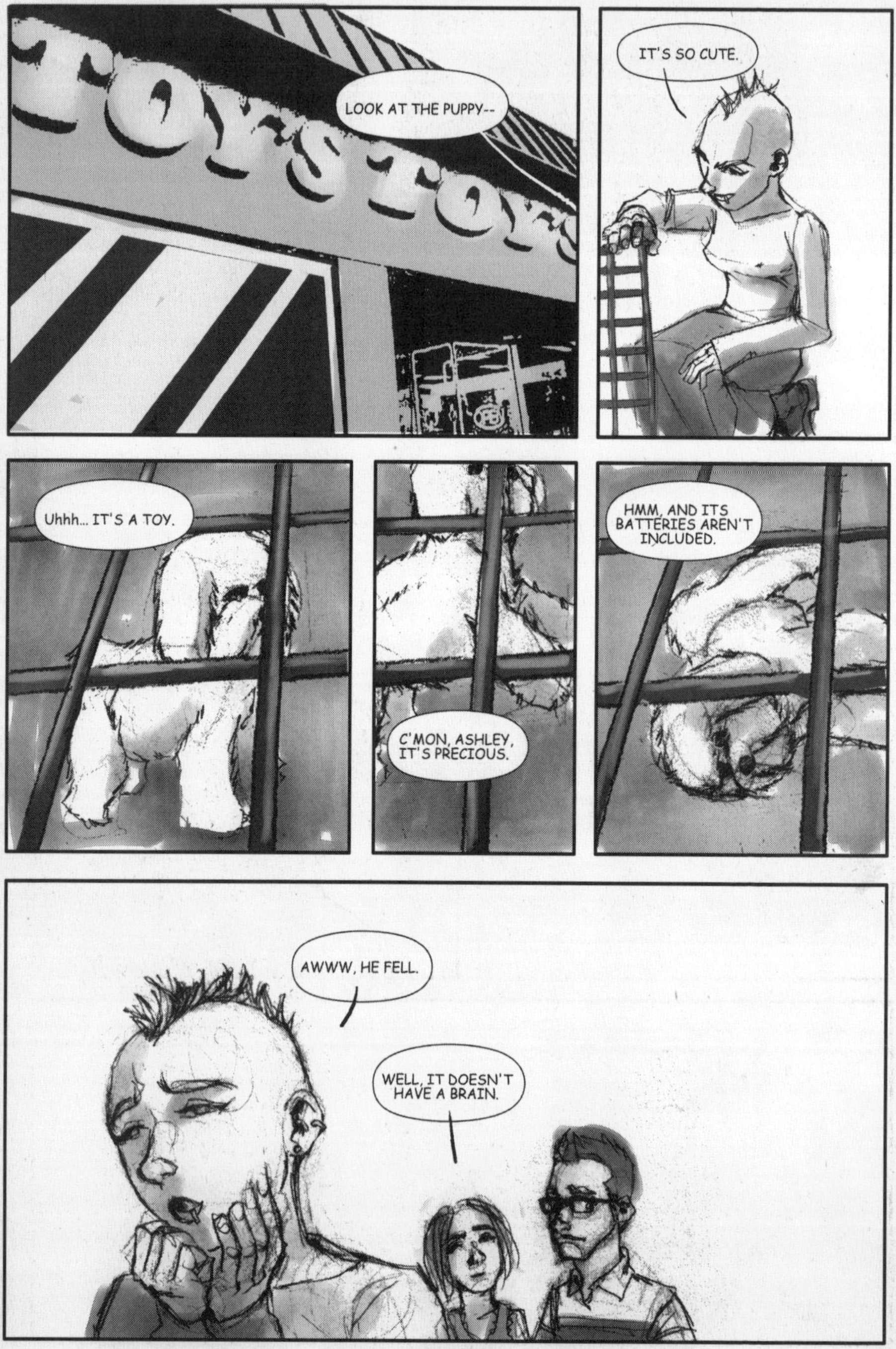
LOOK AT THE PUPPY--
IT'S SO CUTE.
Uhhh... IT'S A TOY.
C'MON, ASHLEY, IT'S PRECIOUS.
HMM, AND ITS BATTERIES AREN'T INCLUDED.
AWWW, HE FELL.
WELL, IT DOESN'T HAVE A BRAIN.

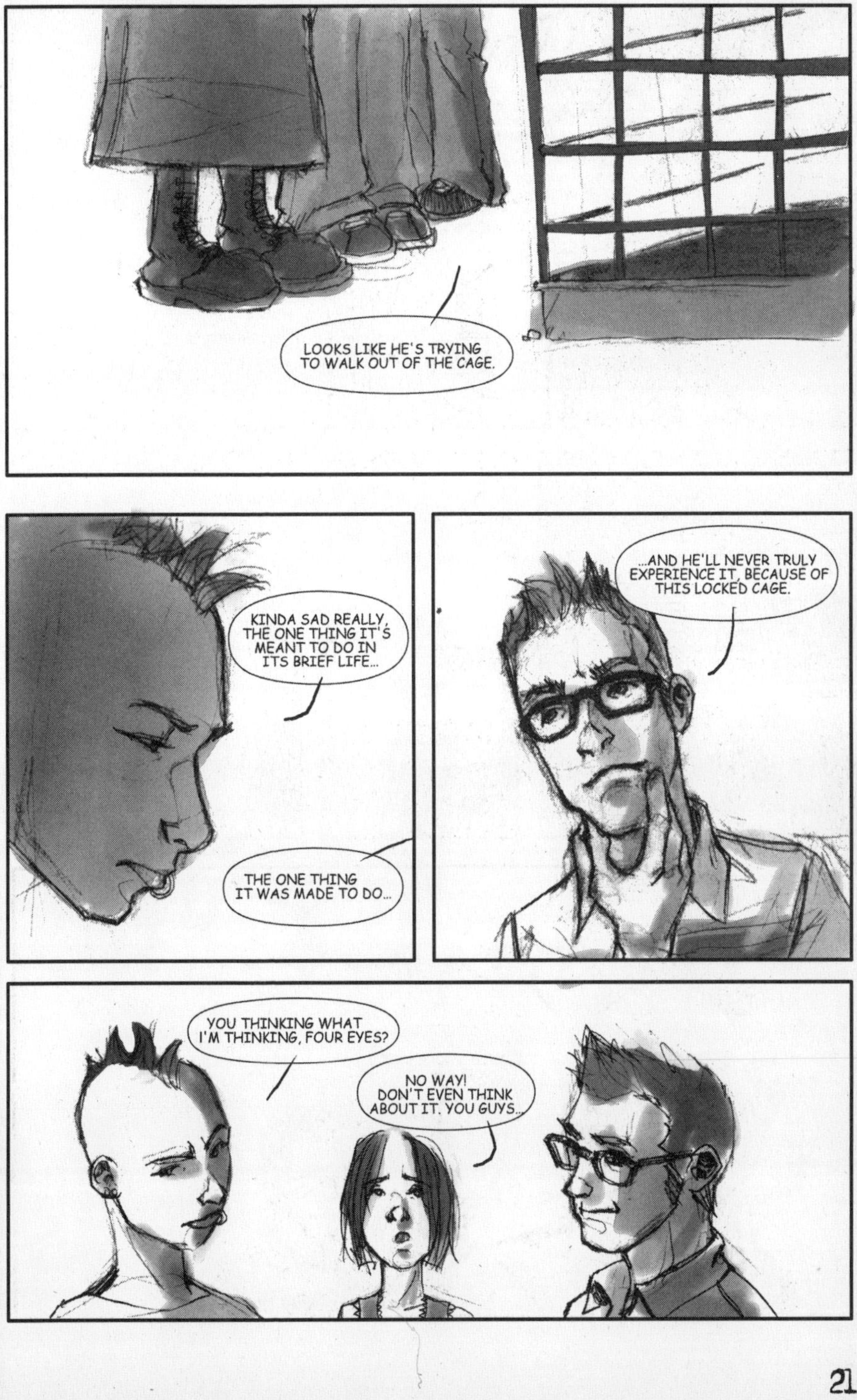

LOOKS LIKE HE'S TRYING TO WALK OUT OF THE CAGE.
KINDA SAD REALLY, THE ONE THING IT'S MEANT TO DO IN ITS BRIEF LIFE...
THE ONE THING IT WAS MADE TO DO...
...AND HE'LL NEVER TRULY EXPERIENCE IT, BECAUSE OF THIS LOCKED CAGE.
YOU THINKING WHAT I'M THINKING, FOUR EYES?
NO WAY! DON'T EVEN THINK ABOUT IT. YOU GUYS...

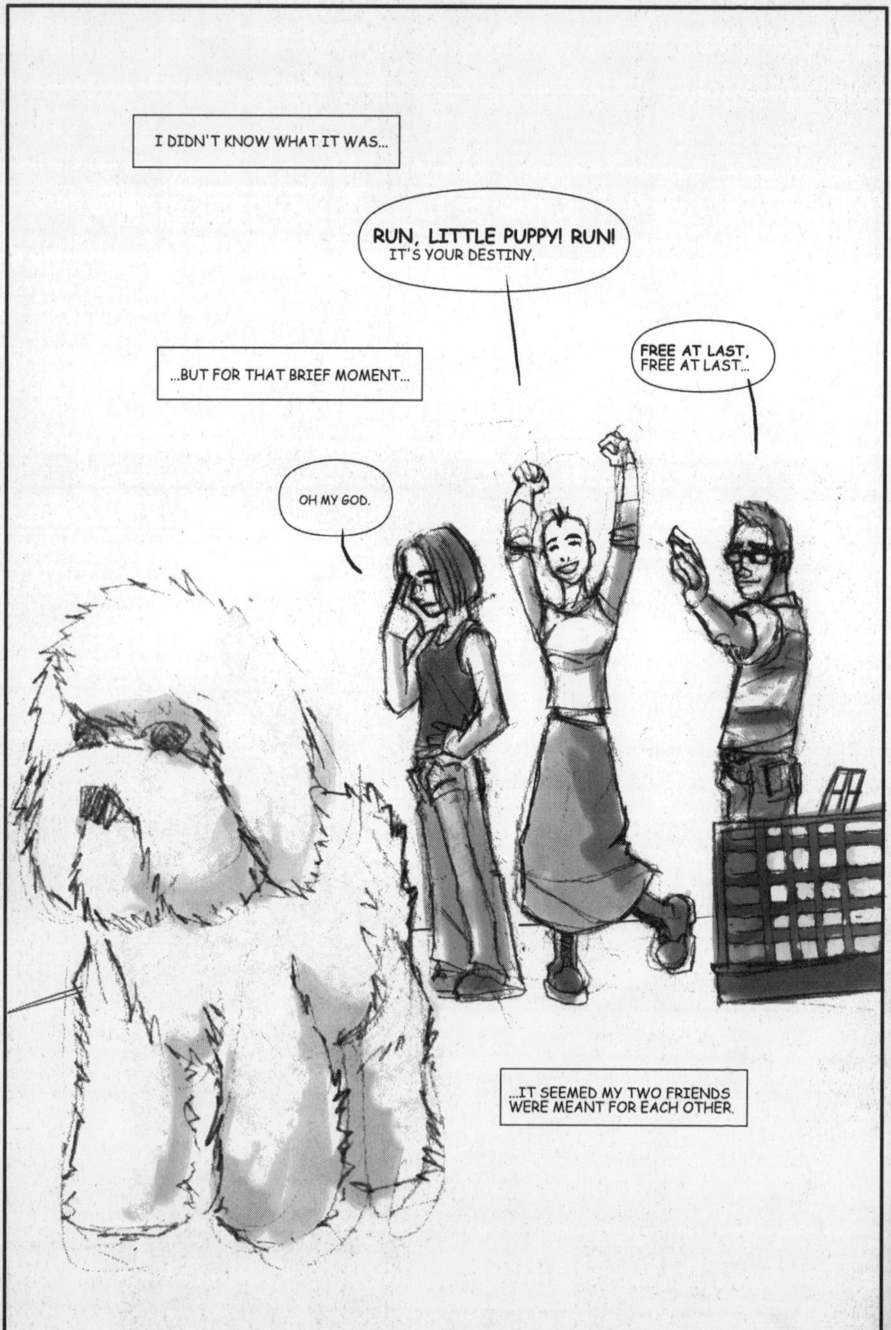
I DIDN'T KNOW WHAT IT WAS...
RUN, LITTLE PUPPY! RUN! IT'S YOUR DESTINY.
...BUT FOR THAT BRIEF MOMENT...
FREE AT LAST, FREE AT LAST...
OH MY GOD.
...IT SEEMED MY TWO FRIENDS WERE MEANT FOR EACH OTHER.

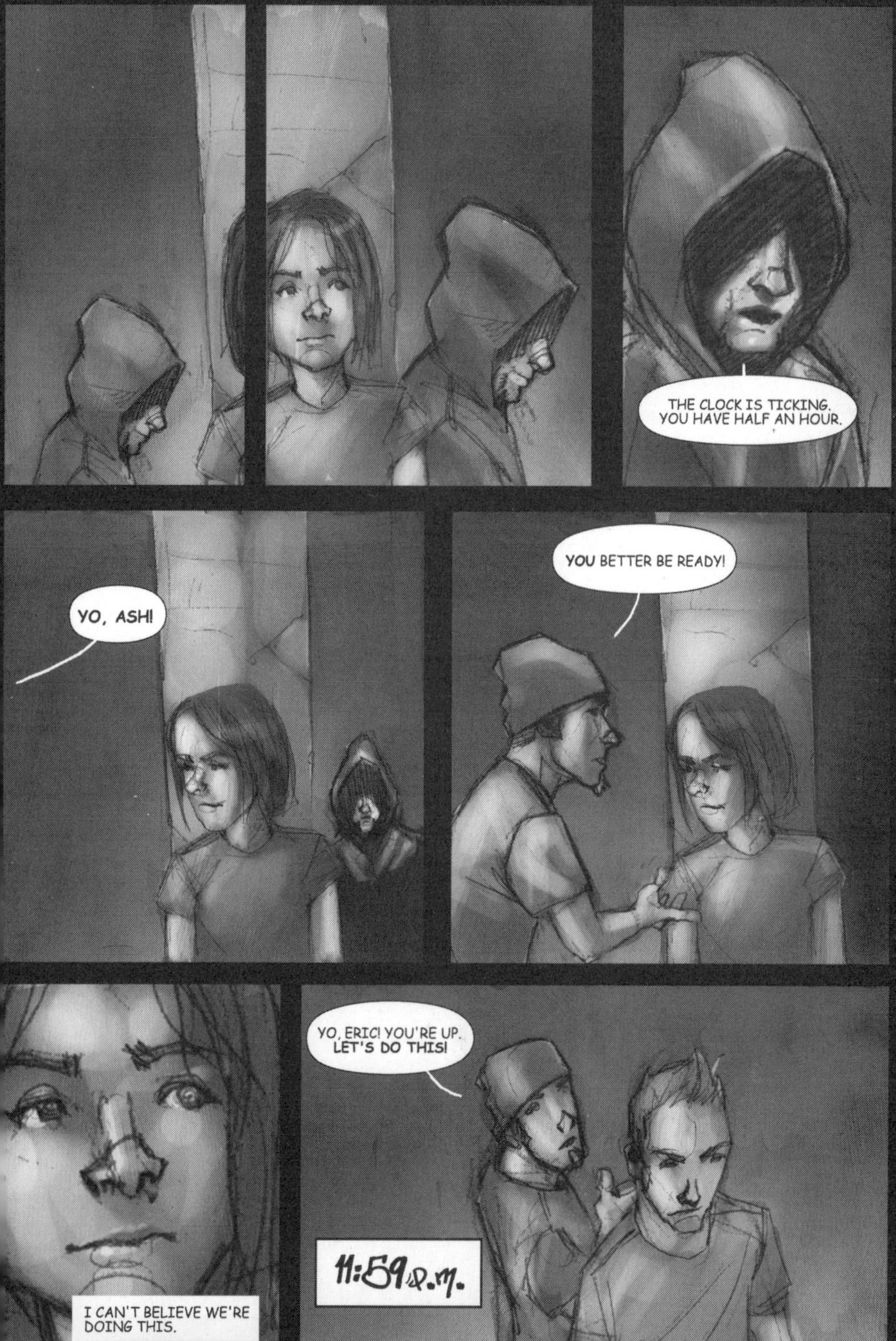
THE CLOCK IS TICKING. YOU HAVE HALF AN HOUR.
YO, ASH!
YOU BETTER BE READY!
I CAN'T BELIEVE WE'RE DOING THIS.
YO, ERIC! YOU'RE UP. LET'S DO THIS!
11:59 p.m.

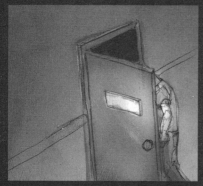

SHOWTIME...

12:00 a.m.

24

chapter two

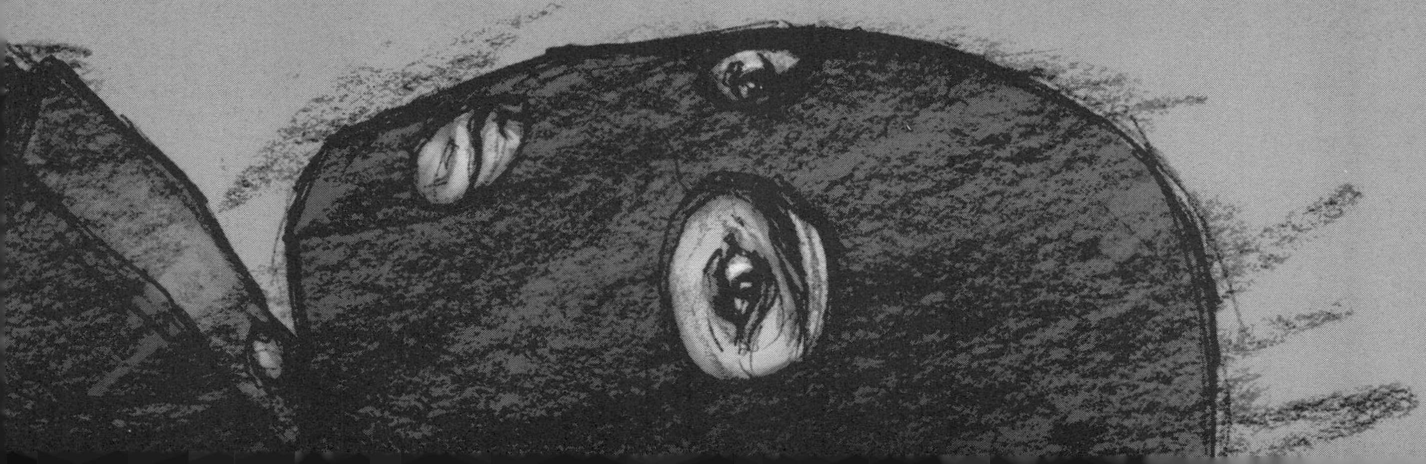

because each kiss is different from the one
before and the one after.

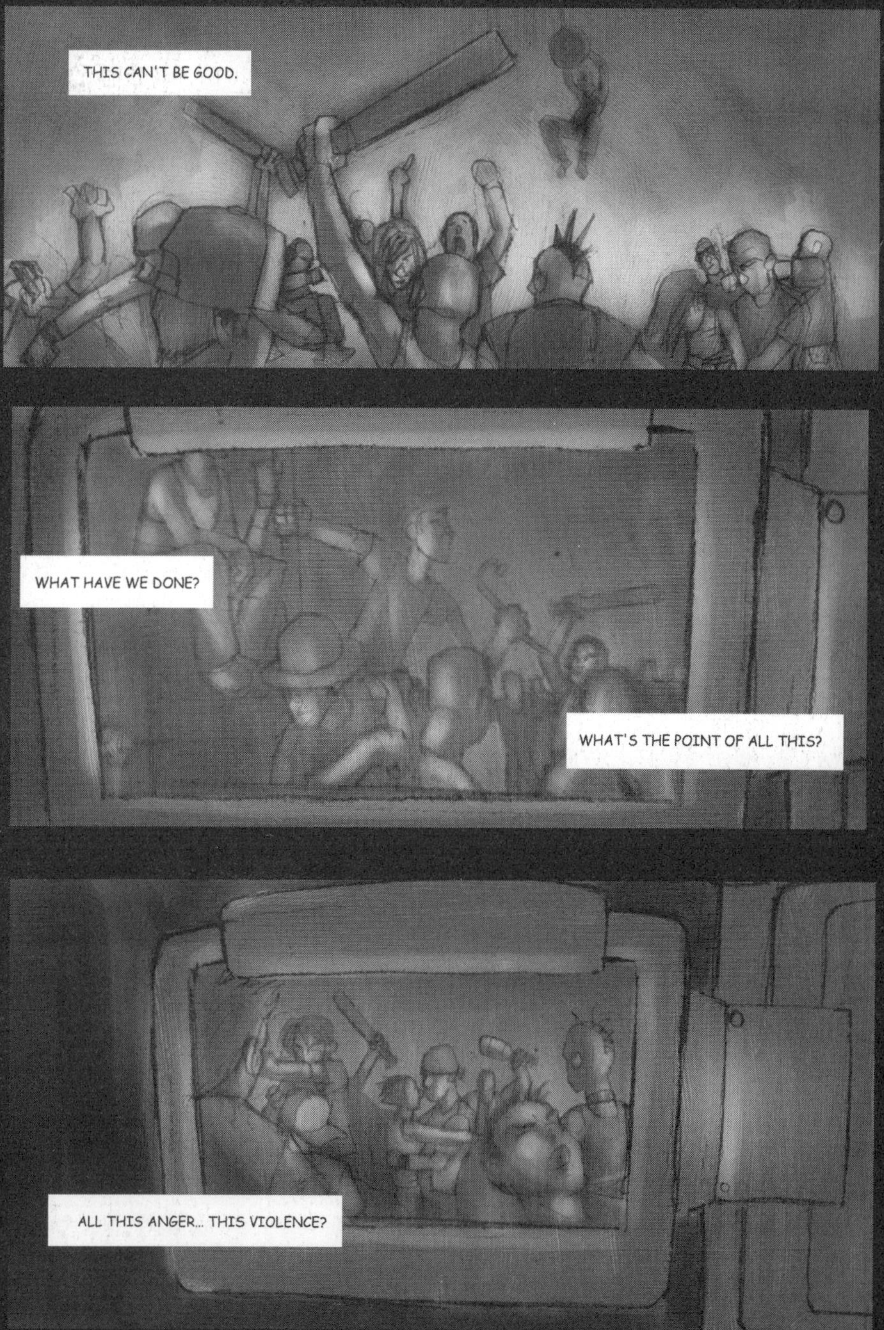
THIS CAN'T BE GOOD.
WHAT HAVE WE DONE?
WHAT'S THE POINT OF ALL THIS?
ALL THIS ANGER... THIS VIOLENCE?

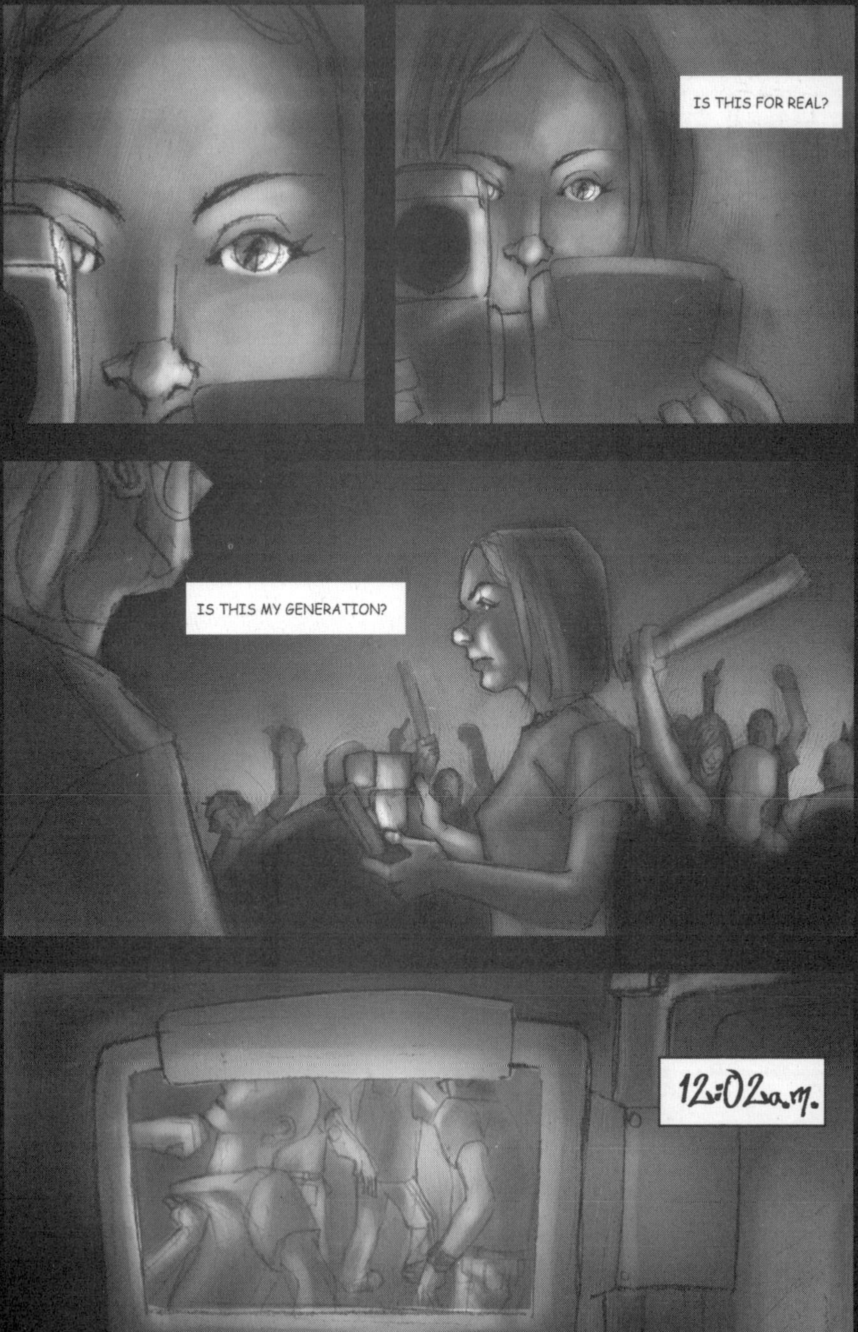
IS THIS FOR REAL?
IS THIS MY GENERATION?
12:02a.m.

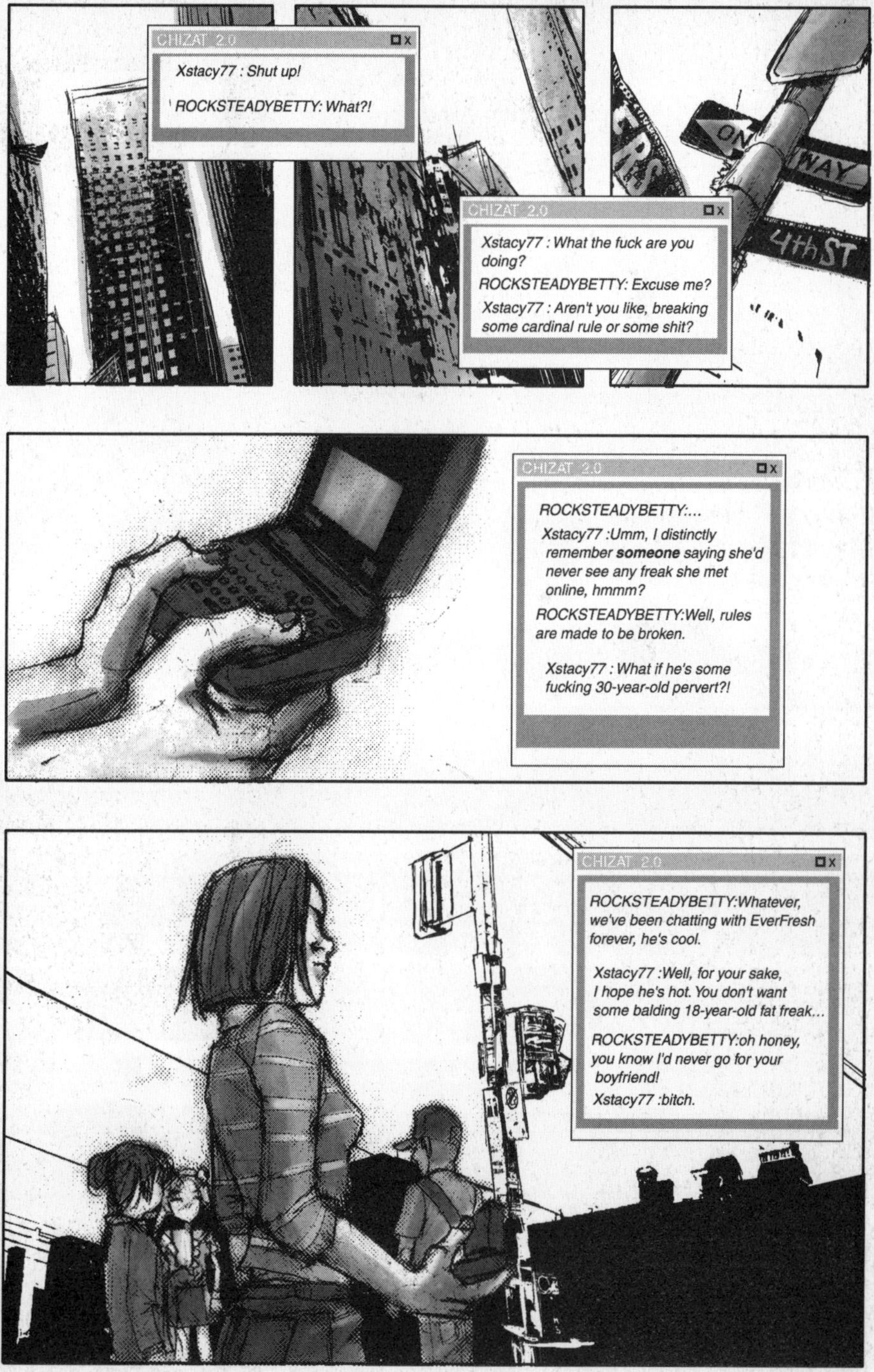
CHIZAT 2.0
Xstacy77 : Shut up!
ROCKSTEADYBETTY: What?!
CHIZAT 2.0
Xstacy77 : What the fuck are you doing?
ROCKSTEADYBETTY: Excuse me?
Xstacy77 : Aren't you like, breaking some cardinal rule or some shit?
4th ST
CHIZAT 2.0
ROCKSTEADYBETTY:...
Xstacy77 :Umm, I distinctly remember **someone** saying she'd never see any freak she met online, hmmm?
ROCKSTEADYBETTY:Well, rules are made to be broken.
Xstacy77 : What if he's some fucking 30-year-old pervert?!
CHIZAT 2.0
ROCKSTEADYBETTY:Whatever, we've been chatting with EverFresh forever, he's cool.
Xstacy77 :Well, for your sake, I hope he's hot. You don't want some balding 18-year-old fat freak...
ROCKSTEADYBETTY:oh honey, you know I'd never go for your boyfriend!
Xstacy77 :bitch.

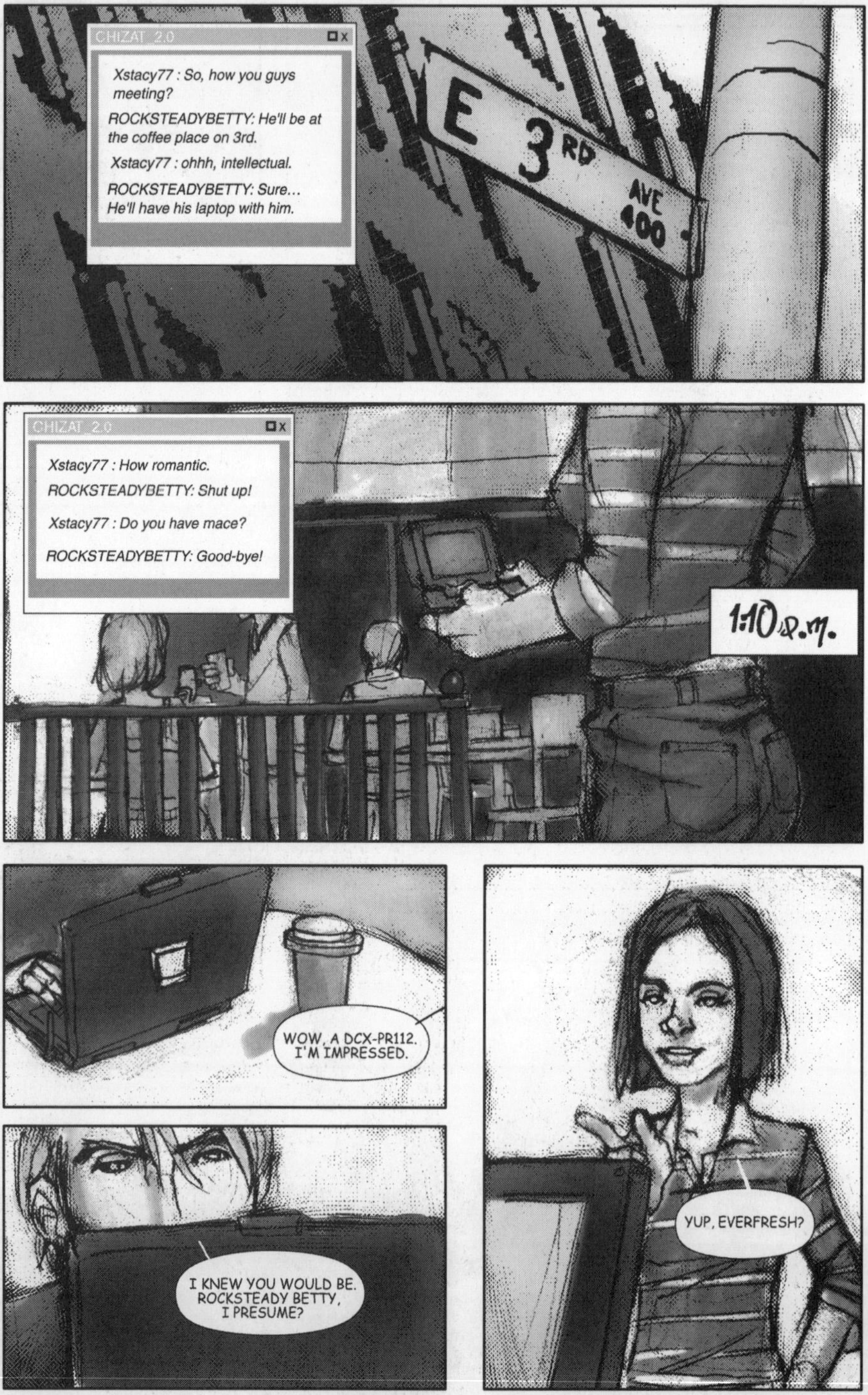
CHIZAT_2.0
Xstacy77 : So, how you guys meeting?
ROCKSTEADYBETTY: He'll be at the coffee place on 3rd.
Xstacy77 : ohhh, intellectual.
ROCKSTEADYBETTY: Sure… He'll have his laptop with him.
E 3RD AVE 400
CHIZAT_2.0
Xstacy77 : How romantic.
ROCKSTEADYBETTY: Shut up!
Xstacy77 : Do you have mace?
ROCKSTEADYBETTY: Good-bye!
1:10 p.m.
WOW, A DCX-PR112. I'M IMPRESSED.
I KNEW YOU WOULD BE. ROCKSTEADY BETTY, I PRESUME?
YUP, EVERFRESH?

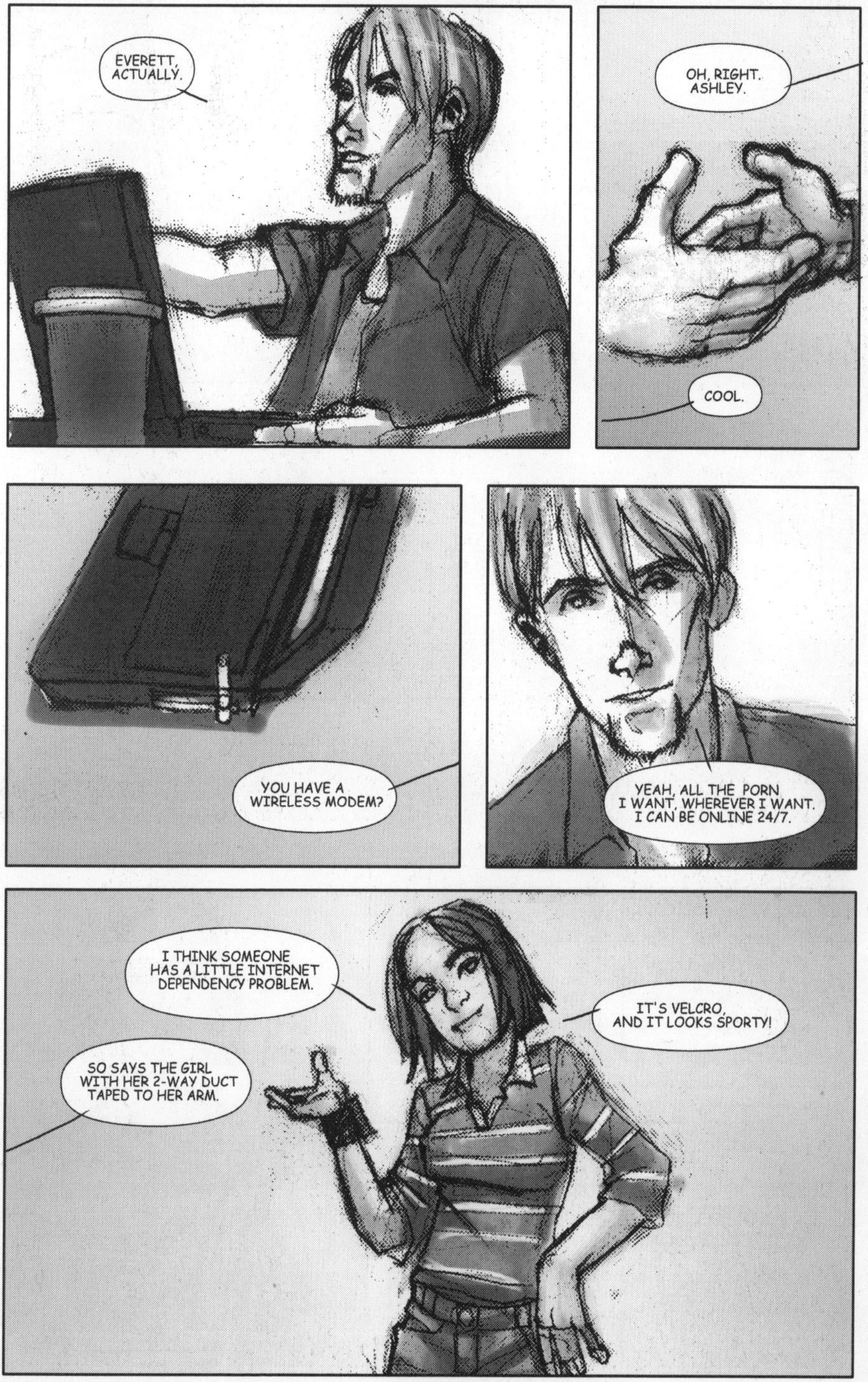
EVERETT, ACTUALLY.
OH, RIGHT. ASHLEY.
COOL.
YOU HAVE A WIRELESS MODEM?
YEAH, ALL THE PORN I WANT, WHEREVER I WANT. I CAN BE ONLINE 24/7.
I THINK SOMEONE HAS A LITTLE INTERNET DEPENDENCY PROBLEM.
SO SAYS THE GIRL WITH HER 2-WAY DUCT TAPED TO HER ARM.
IT'S VELCRO, AND IT LOOKS SPORTY!

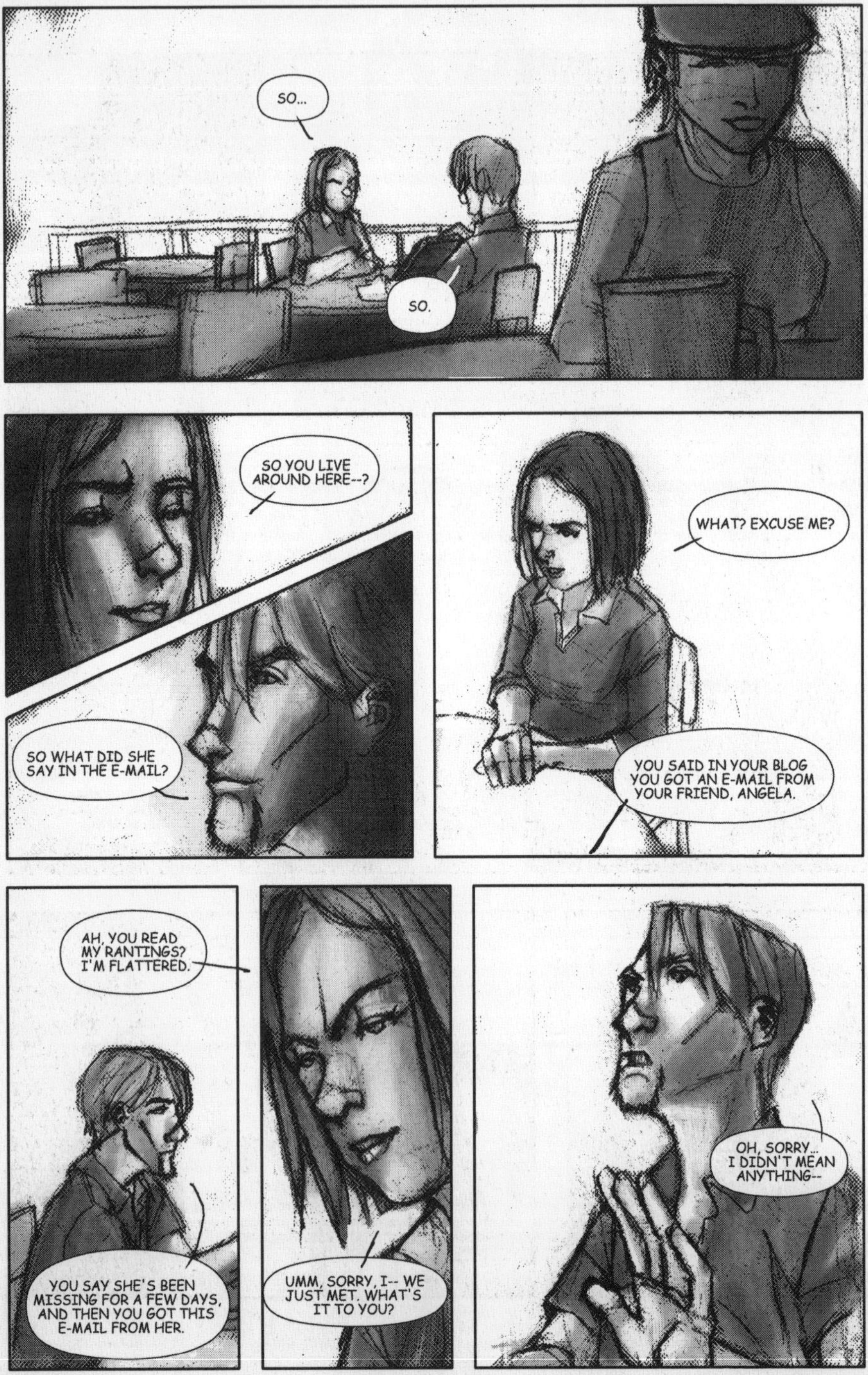
SO...
SO.
SO YOU LIVE AROUND HERE--?
SO WHAT DID SHE SAY IN THE E-MAIL?
WHAT? EXCUSE ME?
YOU SAID IN YOUR BLOG YOU GOT AN E-MAIL FROM YOUR FRIEND, ANGELA.
AH, YOU READ MY RANTINGS? I'M FLATTERED.
YOU SAY SHE'S BEEN MISSING FOR A FEW DAYS, AND THEN YOU GOT THIS E-MAIL FROM HER.
UMM, SORRY, I-- WE JUST MET. WHAT'S IT TO YOU?
OH, SORRY... I DIDN'T MEAN ANYTHING--

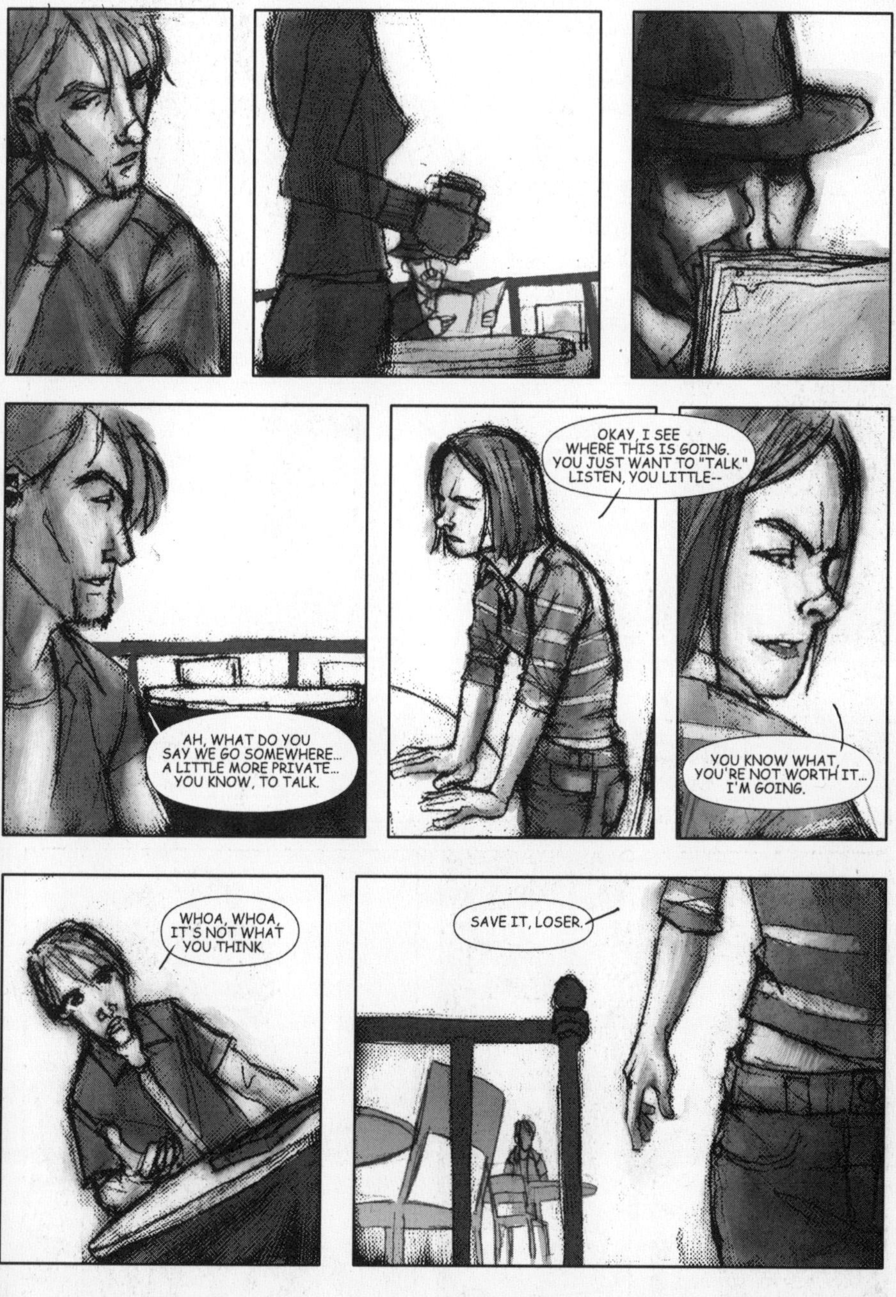
AH, WHAT DO YOU SAY WE GO SOMEWHERE... A LITTLE MORE PRIVATE... YOU KNOW, TO TALK.
OKAY, I SEE WHERE THIS IS GOING. YOU JUST WANT TO "TALK." LISTEN, YOU LITTLE--
YOU KNOW WHAT, YOU'RE NOT WORTH IT... I'M GOING.
WHOA, WHOA, IT'S NOT WHAT YOU THINK.
SAVE IT, LOSER.

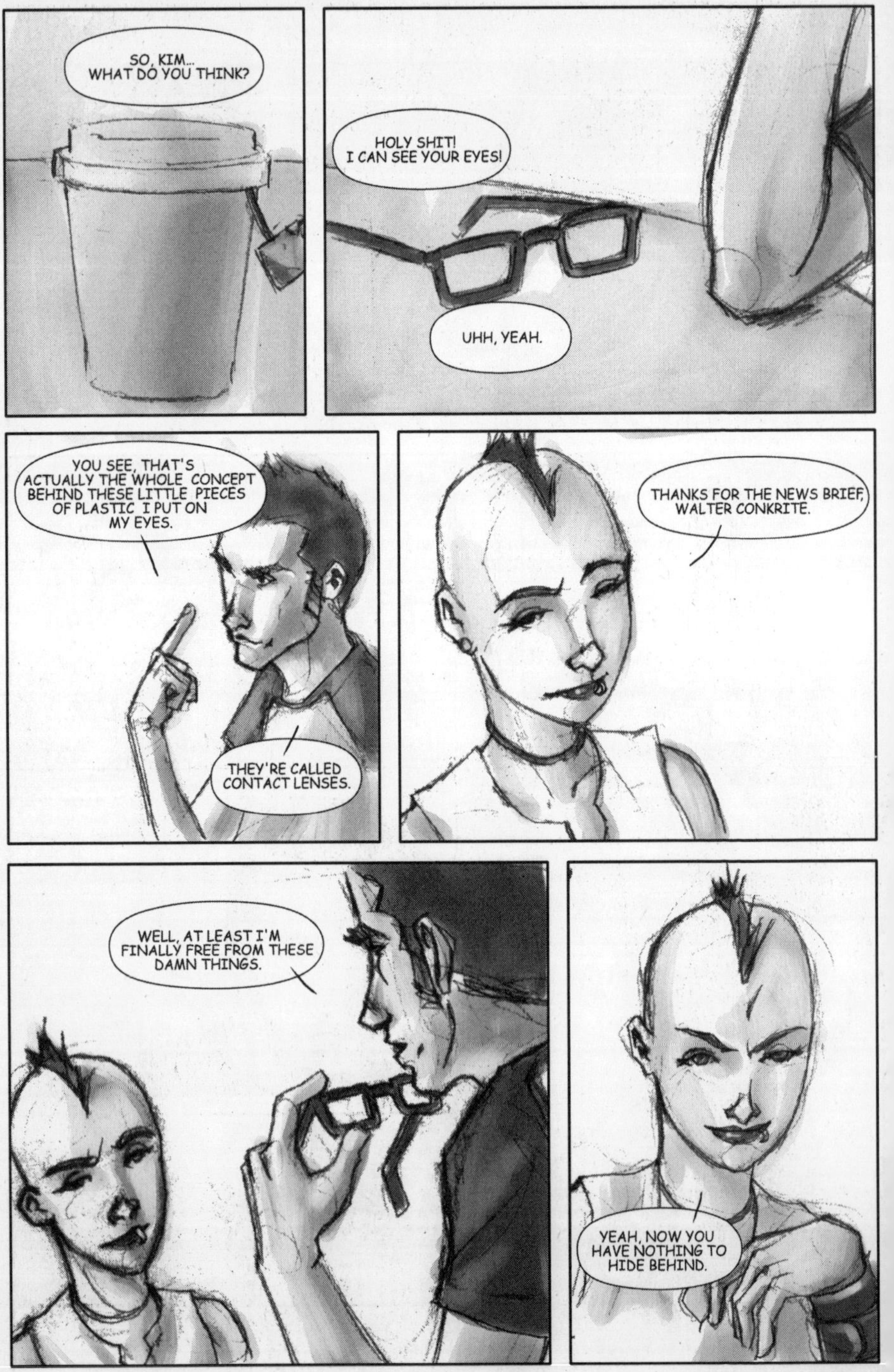
SO, KIM... WHAT DO YOU THINK?
HOLY SHIT! I CAN SEE YOUR EYES!
UHH, YEAH.
YOU SEE, THAT'S ACTUALLY THE WHOLE CONCEPT BEHIND THESE LITTLE PIECES OF PLASTIC I PUT ON MY EYES.
THEY'RE CALLED CONTACT LENSES.
THANKS FOR THE NEWS BRIEF, WALTER CONKRITE.
WELL, AT LEAST I'M FINALLY FREE FROM THESE DAMN THINGS.
YEAH, NOW YOU HAVE NOTHING TO HIDE BEHIND.

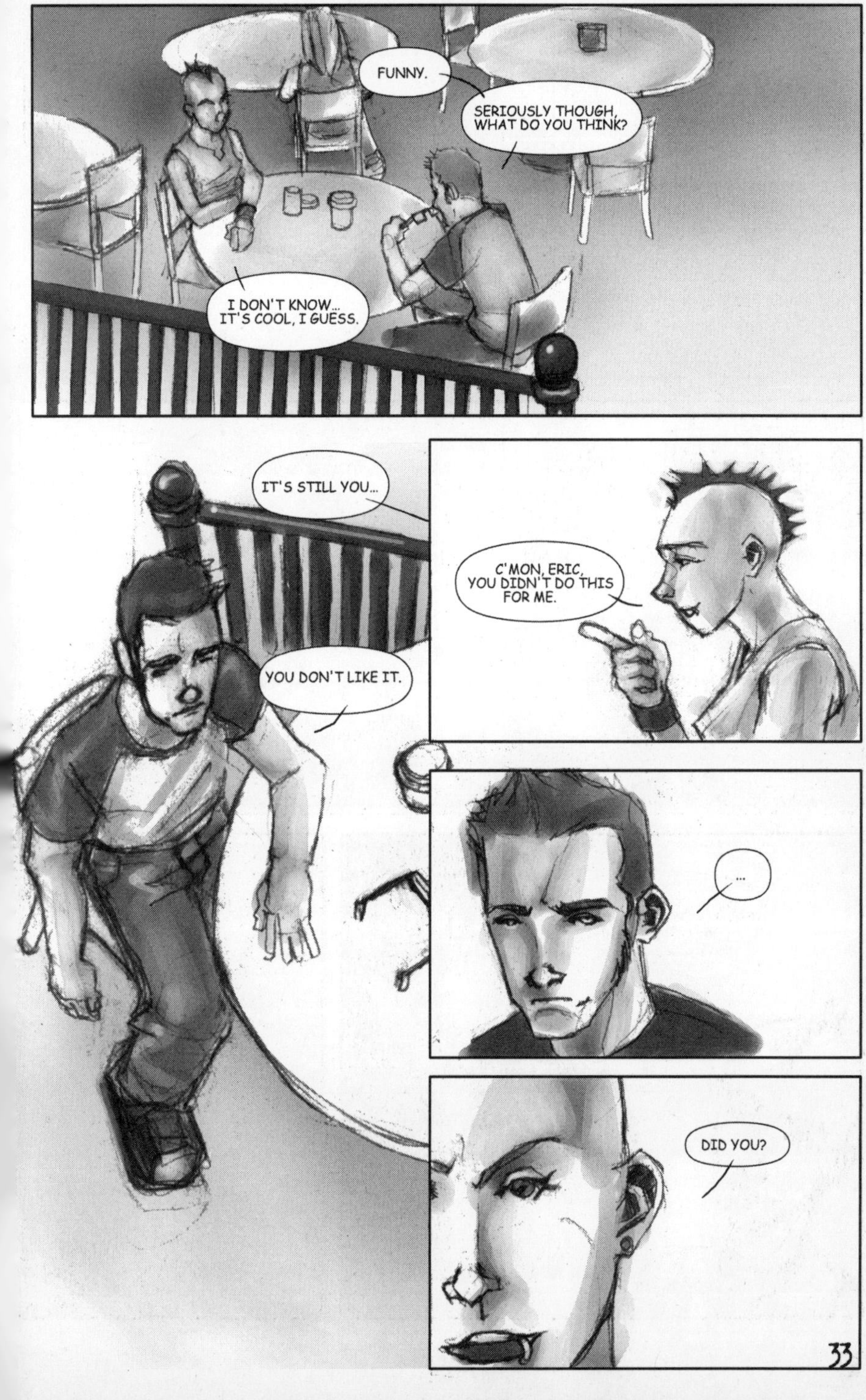
FUNNY.
SERIOUSLY THOUGH, WHAT DO YOU THINK?
I DON'T KNOW... IT'S COOL, I GUESS.
IT'S STILL YOU...
C'MON, ERIC, YOU DIDN'T DO THIS FOR ME.
YOU DON'T LIKE IT.
...
DID YOU?

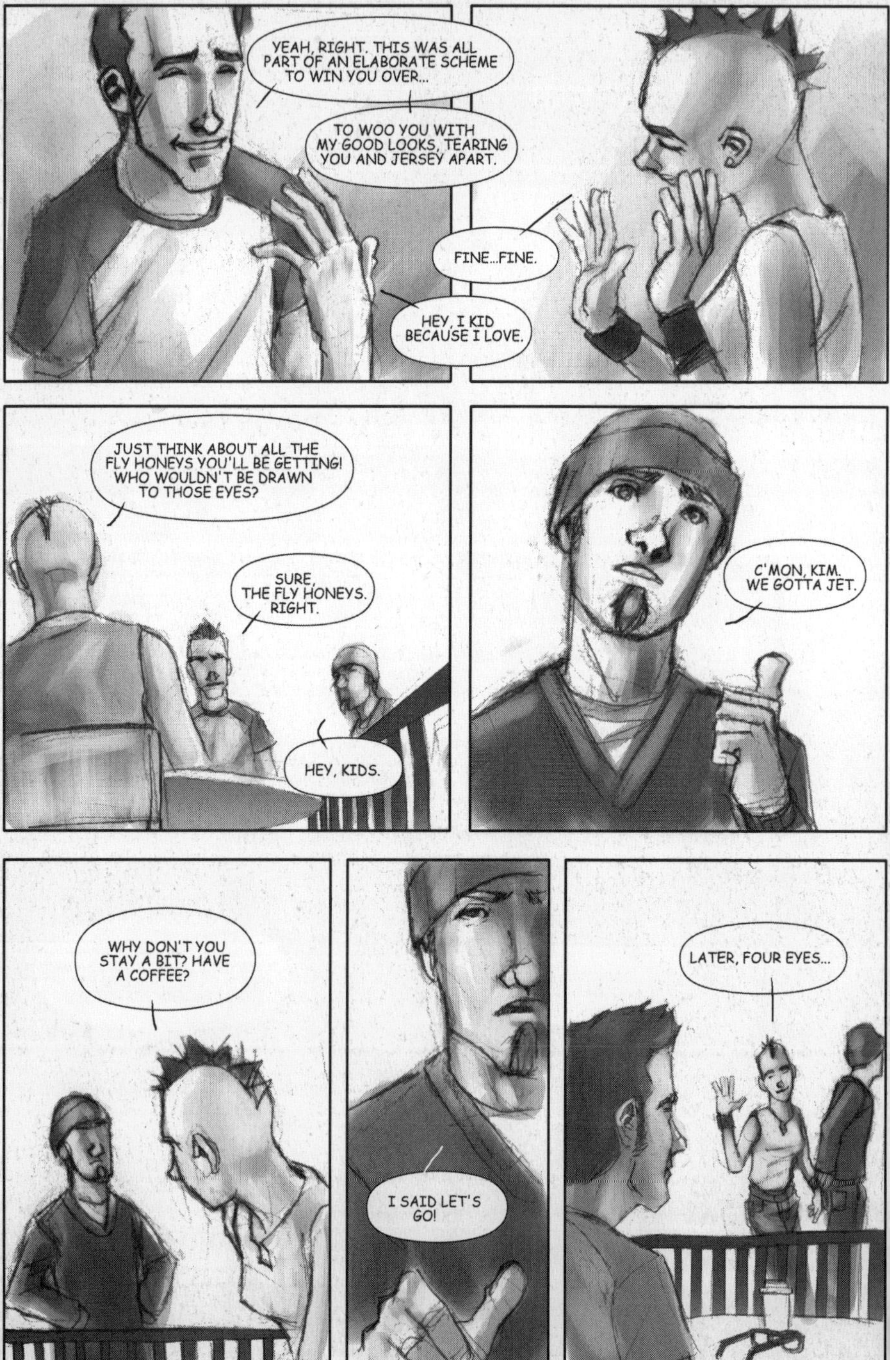
YEAH, RIGHT. THIS WAS ALL PART OF AN ELABORATE SCHEME TO WIN YOU OVER...
TO WOO YOU WITH MY GOOD LOOKS, TEARING YOU AND JERSEY APART.
HEY, I KID BECAUSE I LOVE.
FINE...FINE.
JUST THINK ABOUT ALL THE FLY HONEYS YOU'LL BE GETTING! WHO WOULDN'T BE DRAWN TO THOSE EYES?
SURE, THE FLY HONEYS. RIGHT.
HEY, KIDS.
C'MON, KIM. WE GOTTA JET.
WHY DON'T YOU STAY A BIT? HAVE A COFFEE?
I SAID LET'S GO!
LATER, FOUR EYES...

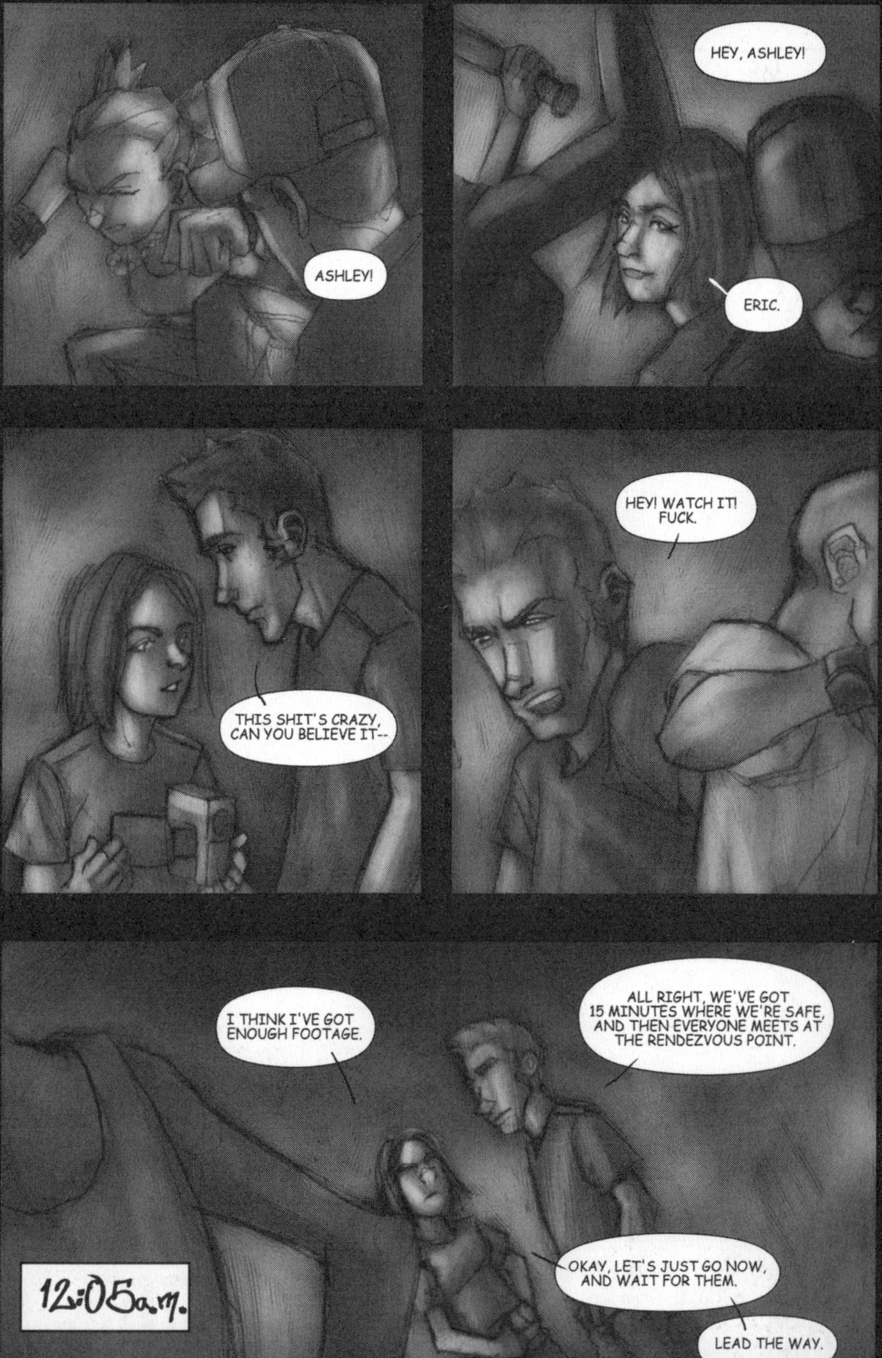
ASHLEY!
HEY, ASHLEY!
ERIC.
THIS SHIT'S CRAZY, CAN YOU BELIEVE IT--
HEY! WATCH IT! FUCK.
I THINK I'VE GOT ENOUGH FOOTAGE.
ALL RIGHT, WE'VE GOT 15 MINUTES WHERE WE'RE SAFE, AND THEN EVERYONE MEETS AT THE RENDEZVOUS POINT.
12:05a.m.
OKAY, LET'S JUST GO NOW, AND WAIT FOR THEM.
LEAD THE WAY.

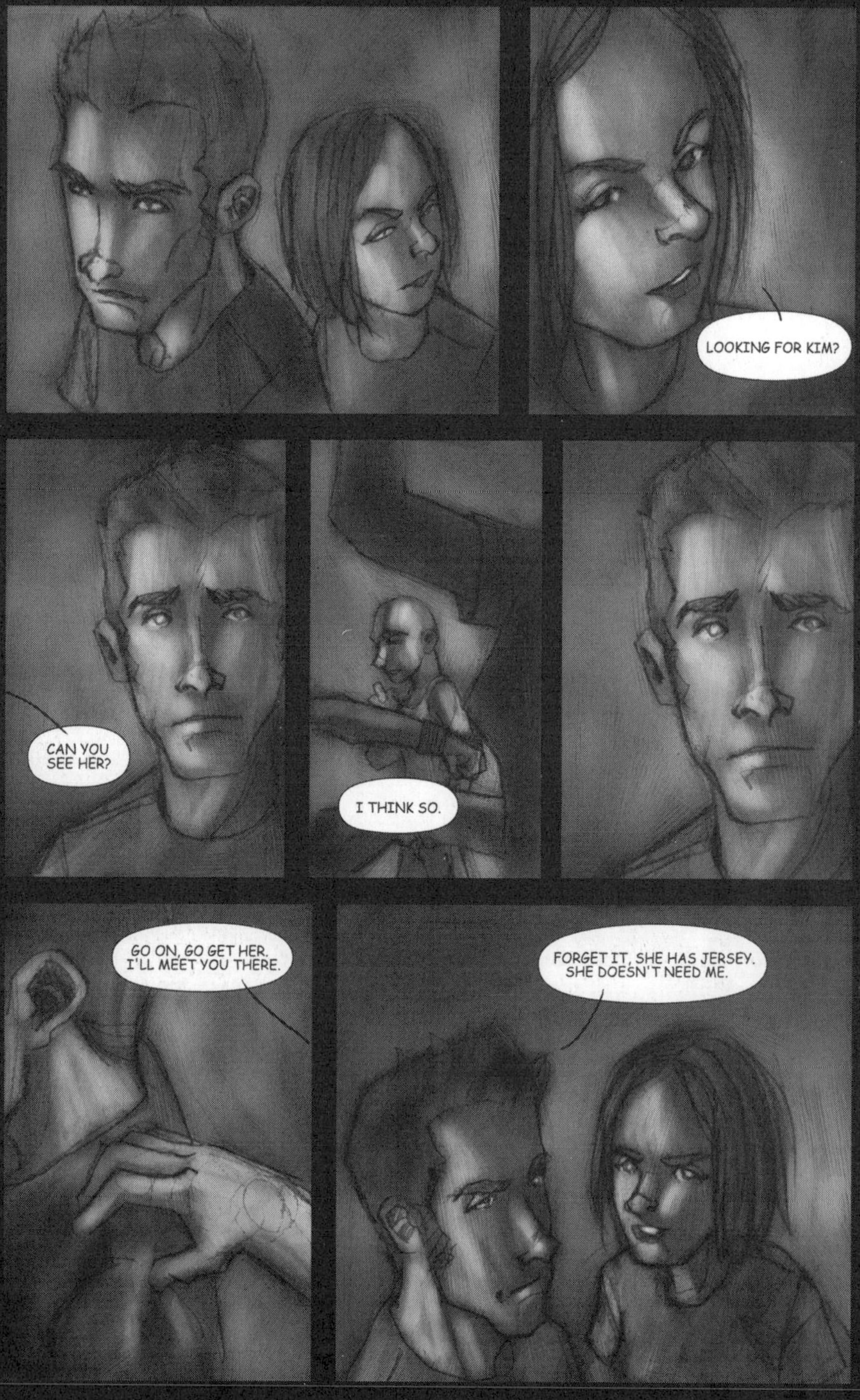
LOOKING FOR KIM?
CAN YOU SEE HER?
I THINK SO.
GO ON, GO GET HER. I'LL MEET YOU THERE.
FORGET IT, SHE HAS JERSEY. SHE DOESN'T NEED ME.

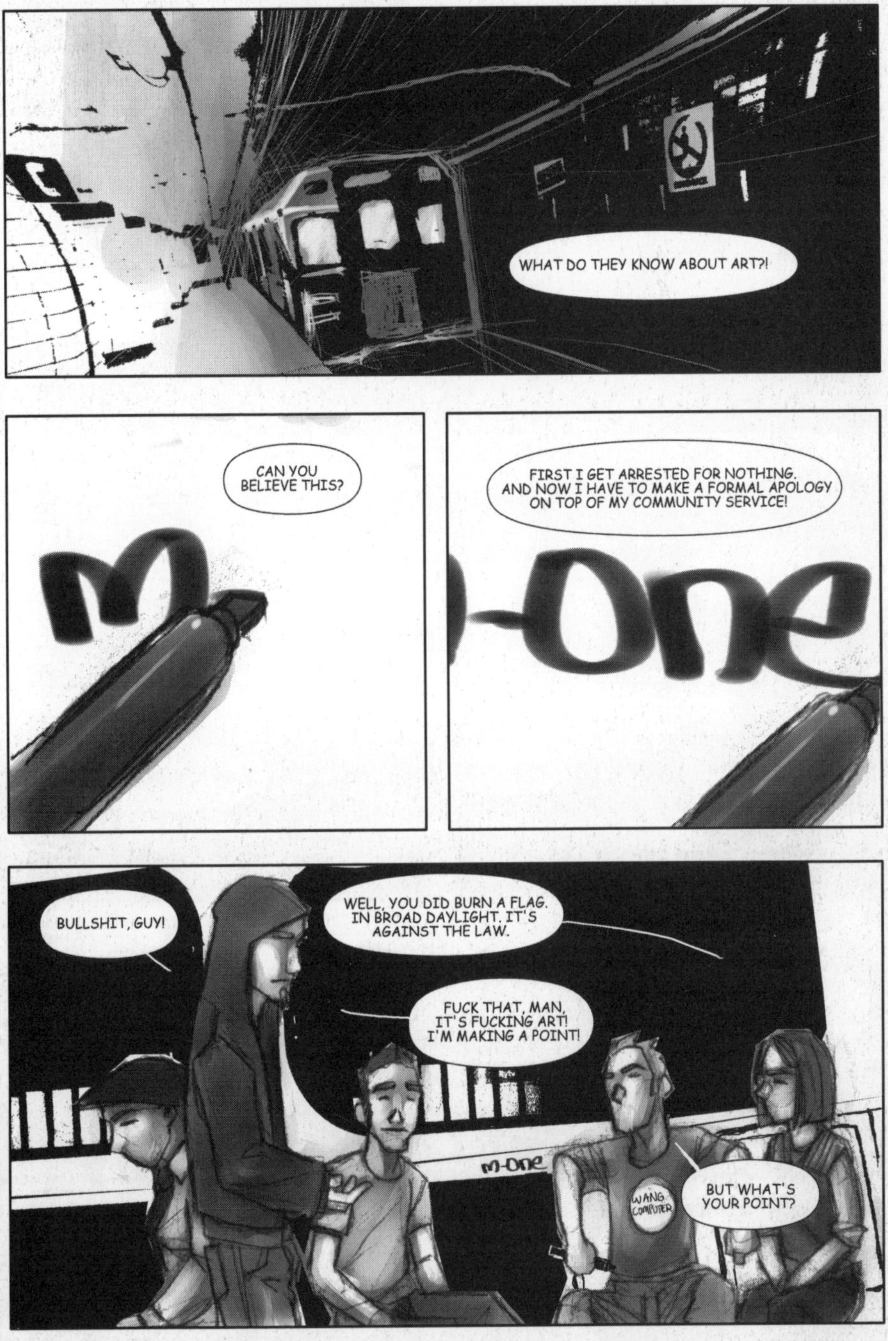
WHAT DO THEY KNOW ABOUT ART?!
CAN YOU BELIEVE THIS?
FIRST I GET ARRESTED FOR NOTHING. AND NOW I HAVE TO MAKE A FORMAL APOLOGY ON TOP OF MY COMMUNITY SERVICE!
BULLSHIT, GUY!
WELL, YOU DID BURN A FLAG. IN BROAD DAYLIGHT. IT'S AGAINST THE LAW.
FUCK THAT, MAN, IT'S FUCKING ART! I'M MAKING A POINT!
M-ONE
WANG COMPUTER
BUT WHAT'S YOUR POINT?

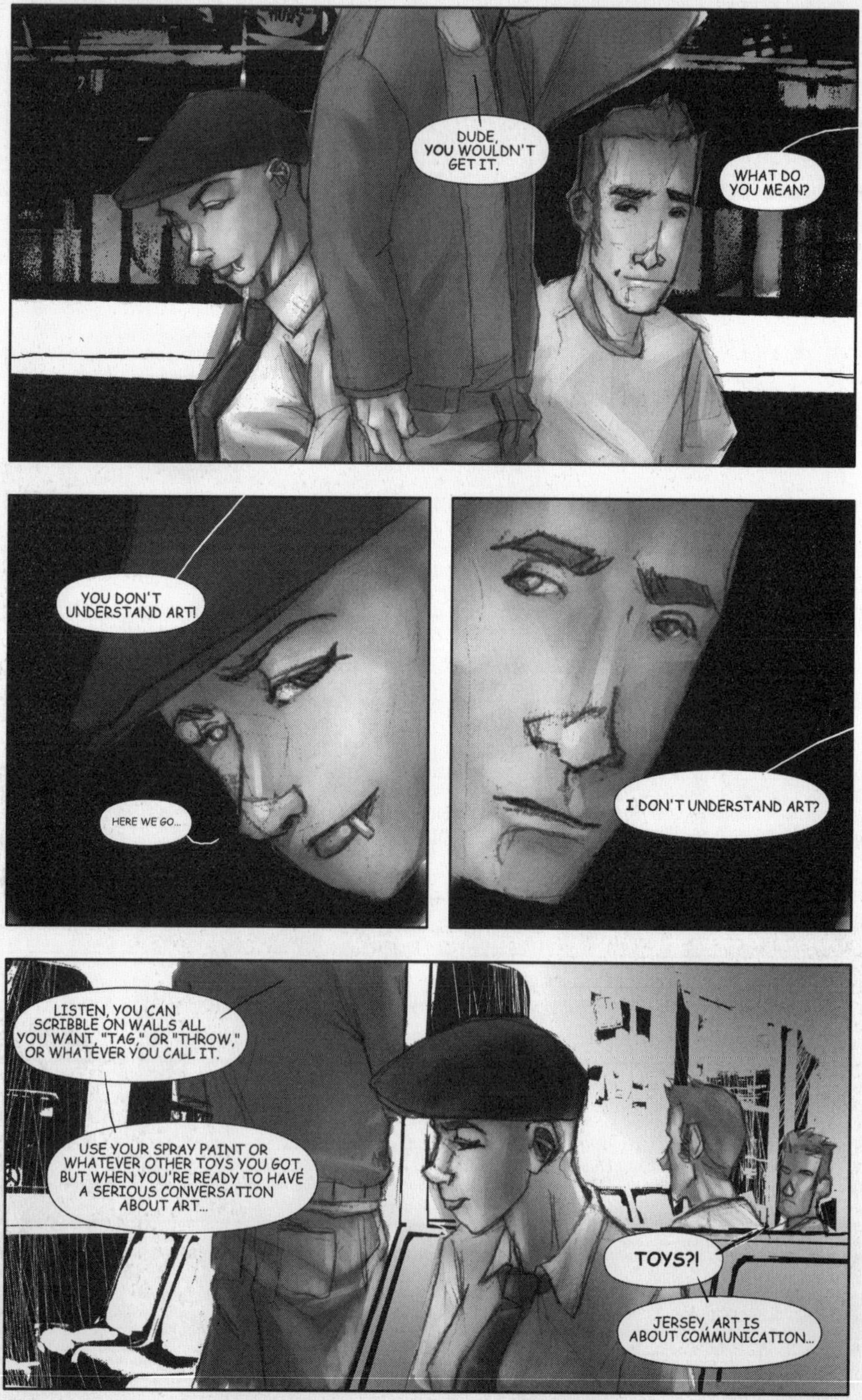
DUDE, YOU WOULDN'T GET IT.
WHAT DO YOU MEAN?
YOU DON'T UNDERSTAND ART!
HERE WE GO...
I DON'T UNDERSTAND ART?
LISTEN, YOU CAN SCRIBBLE ON WALLS ALL YOU WANT, "TAG," OR "THROW," OR WHATEVER YOU CALL IT.
USE YOUR SPRAY PAINT OR WHATEVER OTHER TOYS YOU GOT, BUT WHEN YOU'RE READY TO HAVE A SERIOUS CONVERSATION ABOUT ART...
TOYS?!
JERSEY, ART IS ABOUT COMMUNICATION...

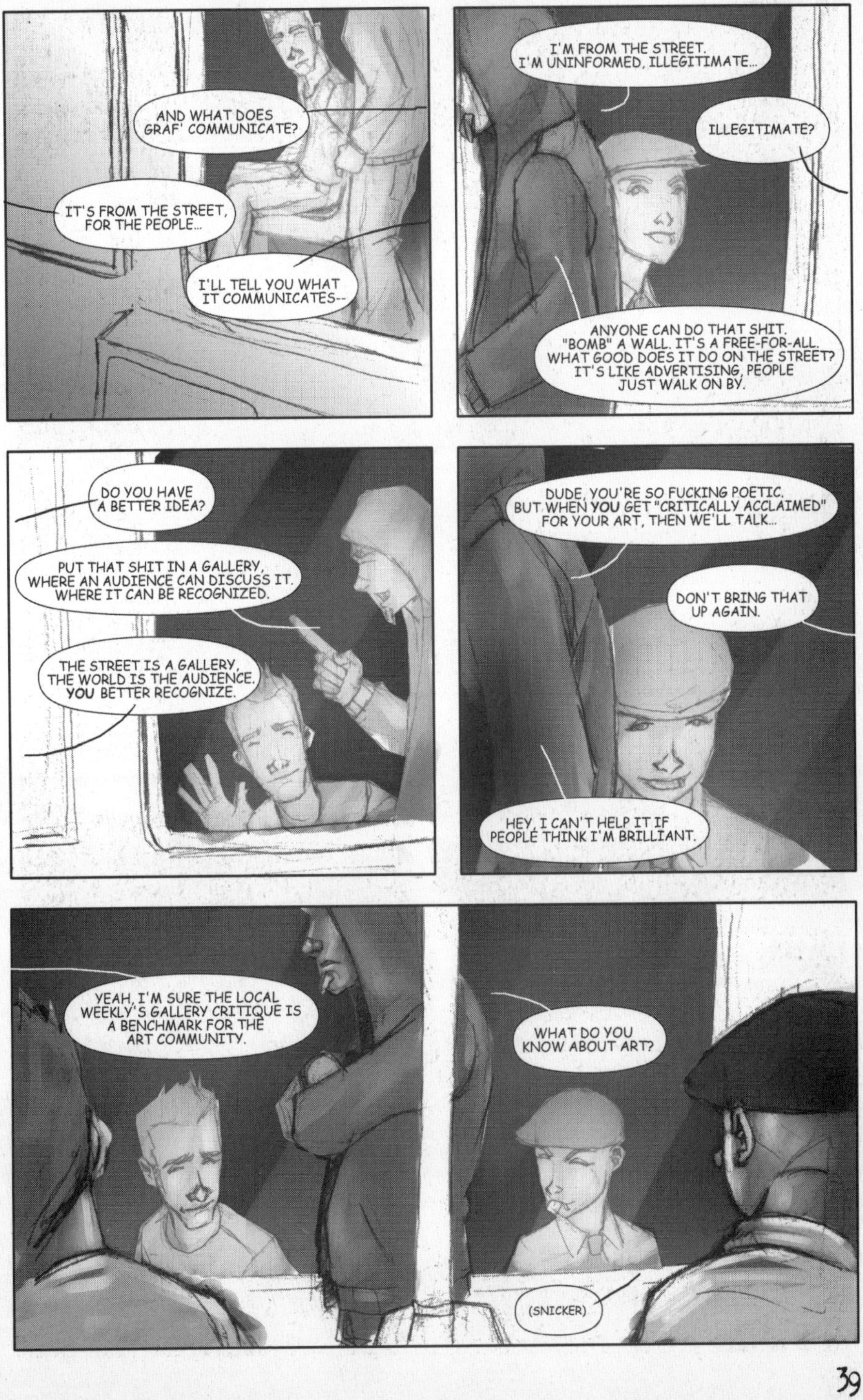
AND WHAT DOES GRAF' COMMUNICATE?
IT'S FROM THE STREET, FOR THE PEOPLE...
I'LL TELL YOU WHAT IT COMMUNICATES--
I'M FROM THE STREET. I'M UNINFORMED, ILLEGITIMATE...
ILLEGITIMATE?
ANYONE CAN DO THAT SHIT. "BOMB" A WALL. IT'S A FREE-FOR-ALL. WHAT GOOD DOES IT DO ON THE STREET? IT'S LIKE ADVERTISING, PEOPLE JUST WALK ON BY.
DO YOU HAVE A BETTER IDEA?
PUT THAT SHIT IN A GALLERY, WHERE AN AUDIENCE CAN DISCUSS IT. WHERE IT CAN BE RECOGNIZED.
THE STREET IS A GALLERY, THE WORLD IS THE AUDIENCE. YOU BETTER RECOGNIZE.
DUDE, YOU'RE SO FUCKING POETIC. BUT WHEN YOU GET "CRITICALLY ACCLAIMED" FOR YOUR ART, THEN WE'LL TALK...
DON'T BRING THAT UP AGAIN.
HEY, I CAN'T HELP IT IF PEOPLE THINK I'M BRILLIANT.
YEAH, I'M SURE THE LOCAL WEEKLY'S GALLERY CRITIQUE IS A BENCHMARK FOR THE ART COMMUNITY.
WHAT DO YOU KNOW ABOUT ART?
(SNICKER)

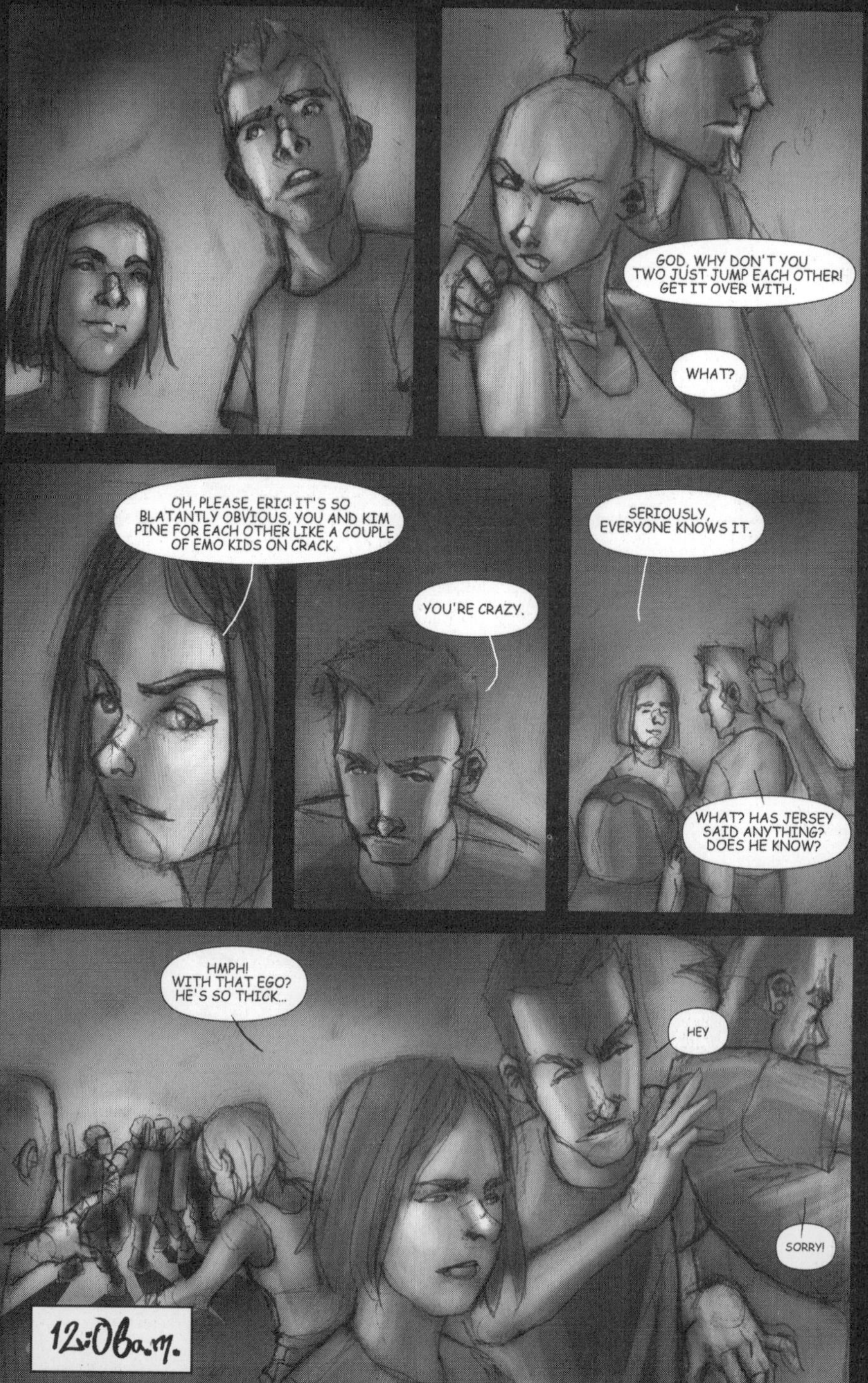
GOD, WHY DON'T YOU TWO JUST JUMP EACH OTHER! GET IT OVER WITH.
WHAT?
OH, PLEASE, ERIC! IT'S SO BLATANTLY OBVIOUS, YOU AND KIM PINE FOR EACH OTHER LIKE A COUPLE OF EMO KIDS ON CRACK.
YOU'RE CRAZY.
SERIOUSLY, EVERYONE KNOWS IT.
WHAT? HAS JERSEY SAID ANYTHING? DOES HE KNOW?
HMPH! WITH THAT EGO? HE'S SO THICK...
HEY
SORRY!
12:06a.m.

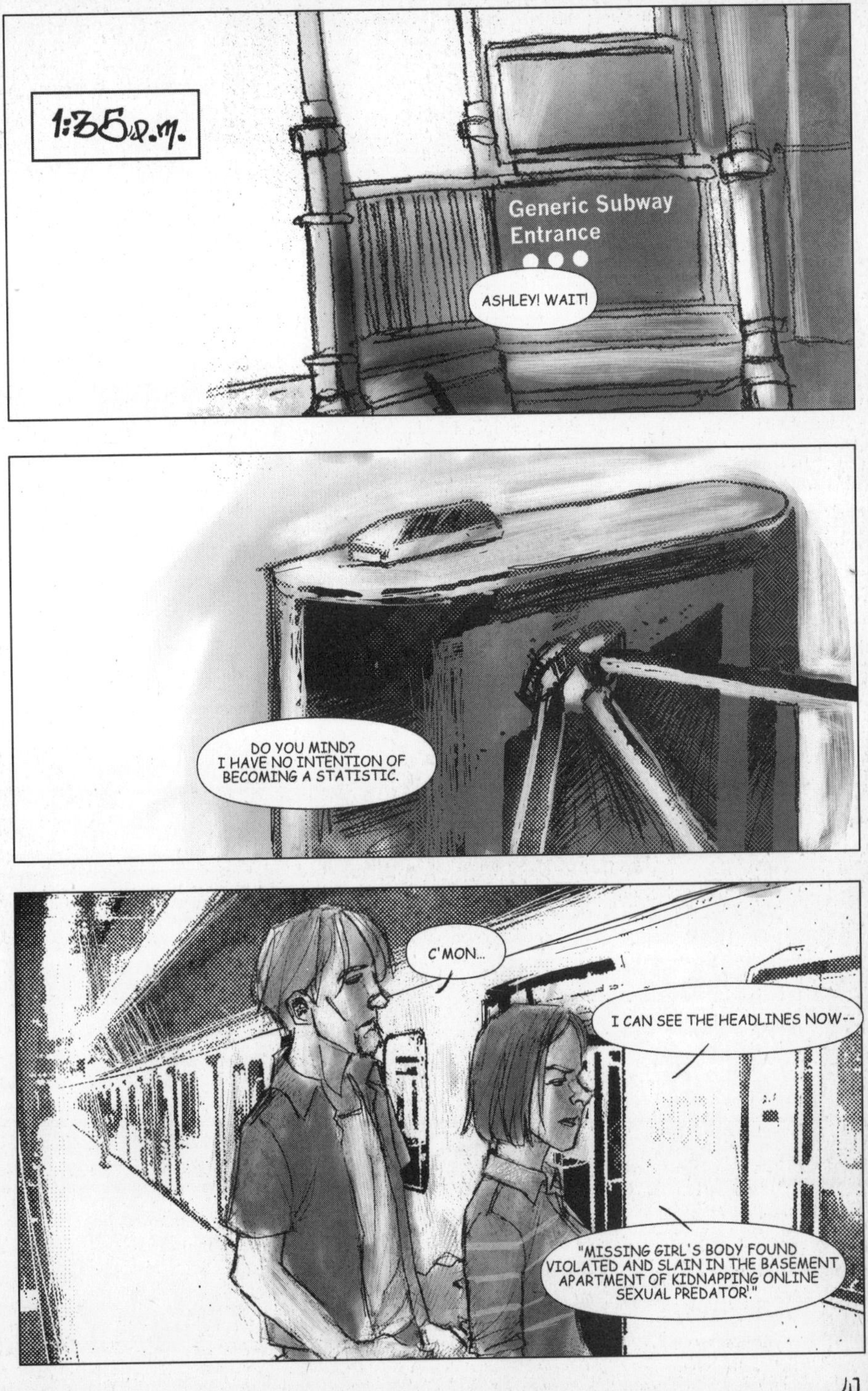
1:35 p.m.
Generic Subway Entrance
ASHLEY! WAIT!
DO YOU MIND? I HAVE NO INTENTION OF BECOMING A STATISTIC.
C'MON...
I CAN SEE THE HEADLINES NOW--
"MISSING GIRL'S BODY FOUND VIOLATED AND SLAIN IN THE BASEMENT APARTMENT OF KIDNAPPING ONLINE SEXUAL PREDATOR."

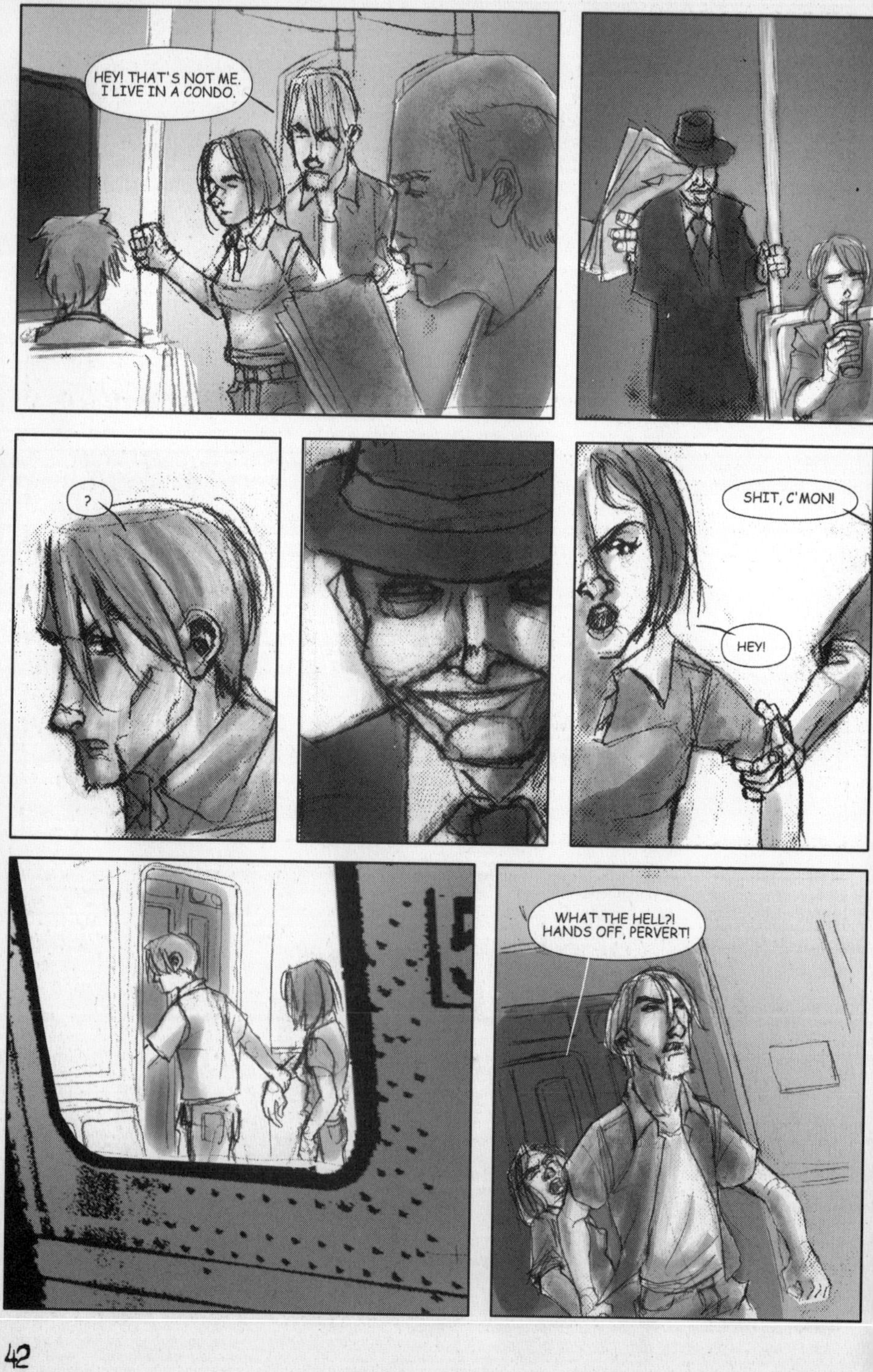
HEY! THAT'S NOT ME. I LIVE IN A CONDO.
?
SHIT, C'MON!
HEY!
WHAT THE HELL?! HANDS OFF, PERVERT!

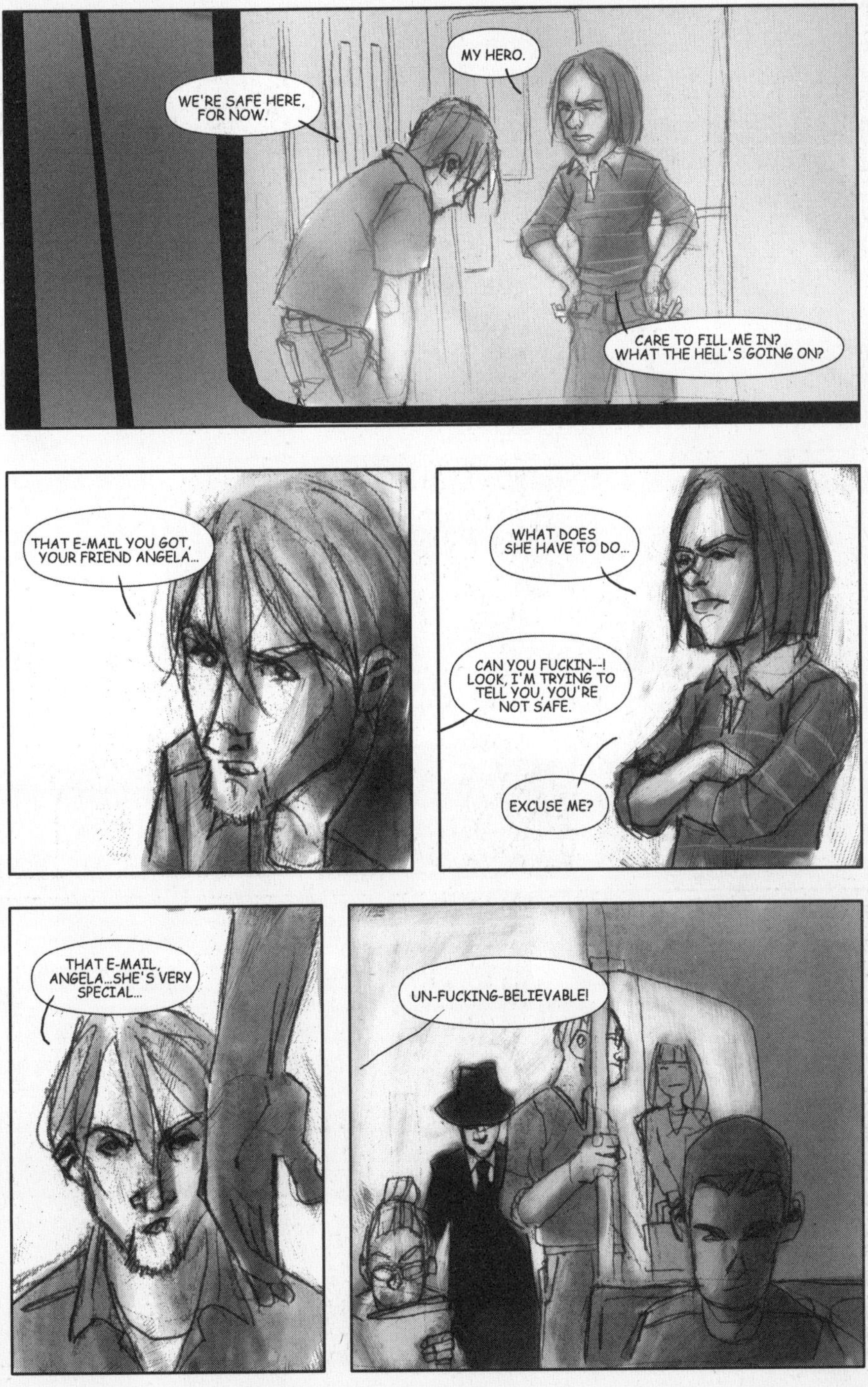
WE'RE SAFE HERE, FOR NOW.
MY HERO.
CARE TO FILL ME IN? WHAT THE HELL'S GOING ON?
THAT E-MAIL YOU GOT, YOUR FRIEND ANGELA...
WHAT DOES SHE HAVE TO DO...
CAN YOU FUCKIN--! LOOK, I'M TRYING TO TELL YOU, YOU'RE NOT SAFE.
EXCUSE ME?
THAT E-MAIL, ANGELA...SHE'S VERY SPECIAL...
UN-FUCKING-BELIEVABLE!

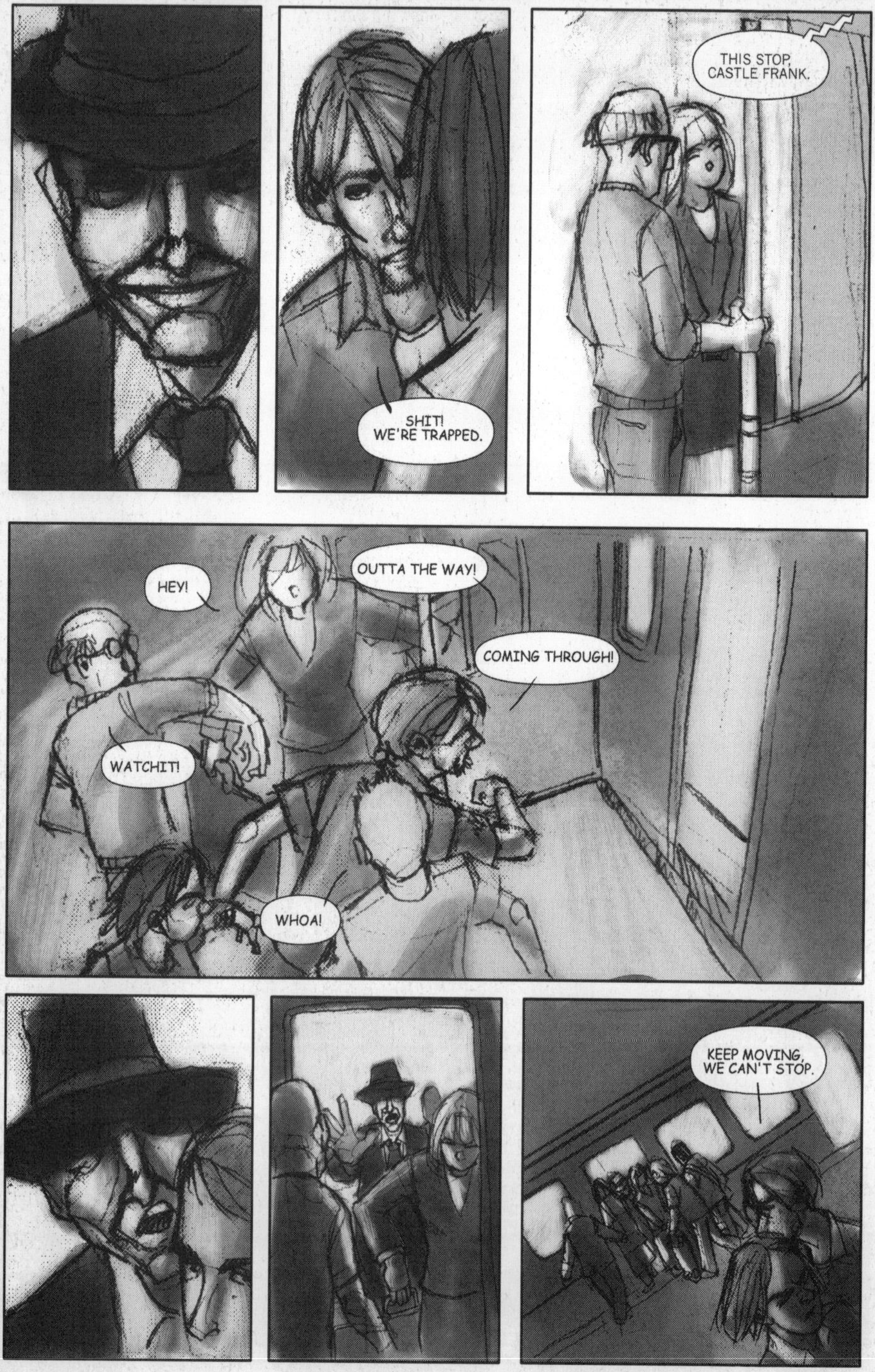
SHIT!
WE'RE TRAPPED.
THIS STOP,
CASTLE FRANK.
HEY!
OUTTA THE WAY!
COMING THROUGH!
WATCHIT!
WHOA!
KEEP MOVING,
WE CAN'T STOP.

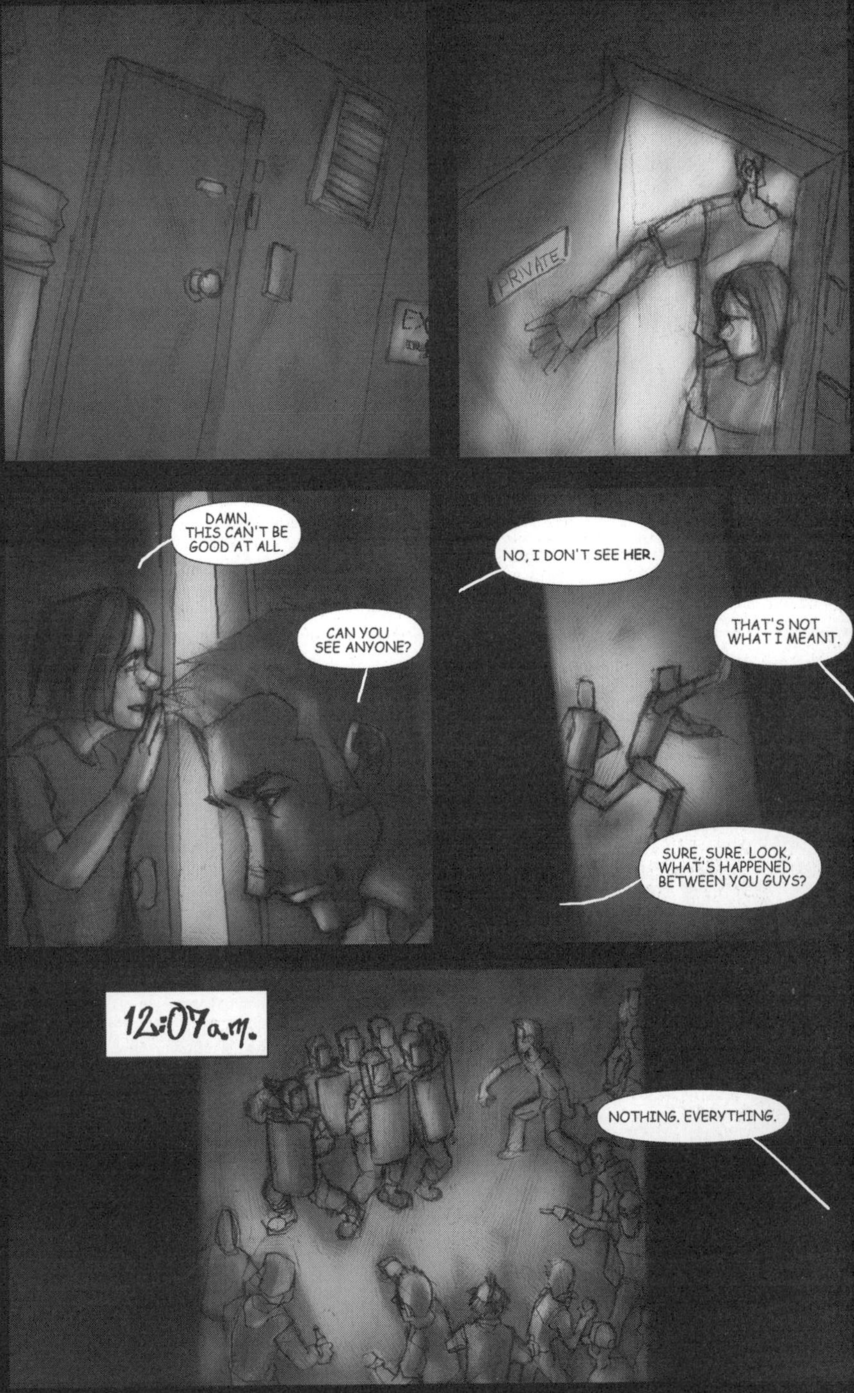
DAMN, THIS CAN'T BE GOOD AT ALL.
CAN YOU SEE ANYONE?
NO, I DON'T SEE HER.
THAT'S NOT WHAT I MEANT.
SURE, SURE. LOOK, WHAT'S HAPPENED BETWEEN YOU GUYS?
12:07a.m.
NOTHING. EVERYTHING.

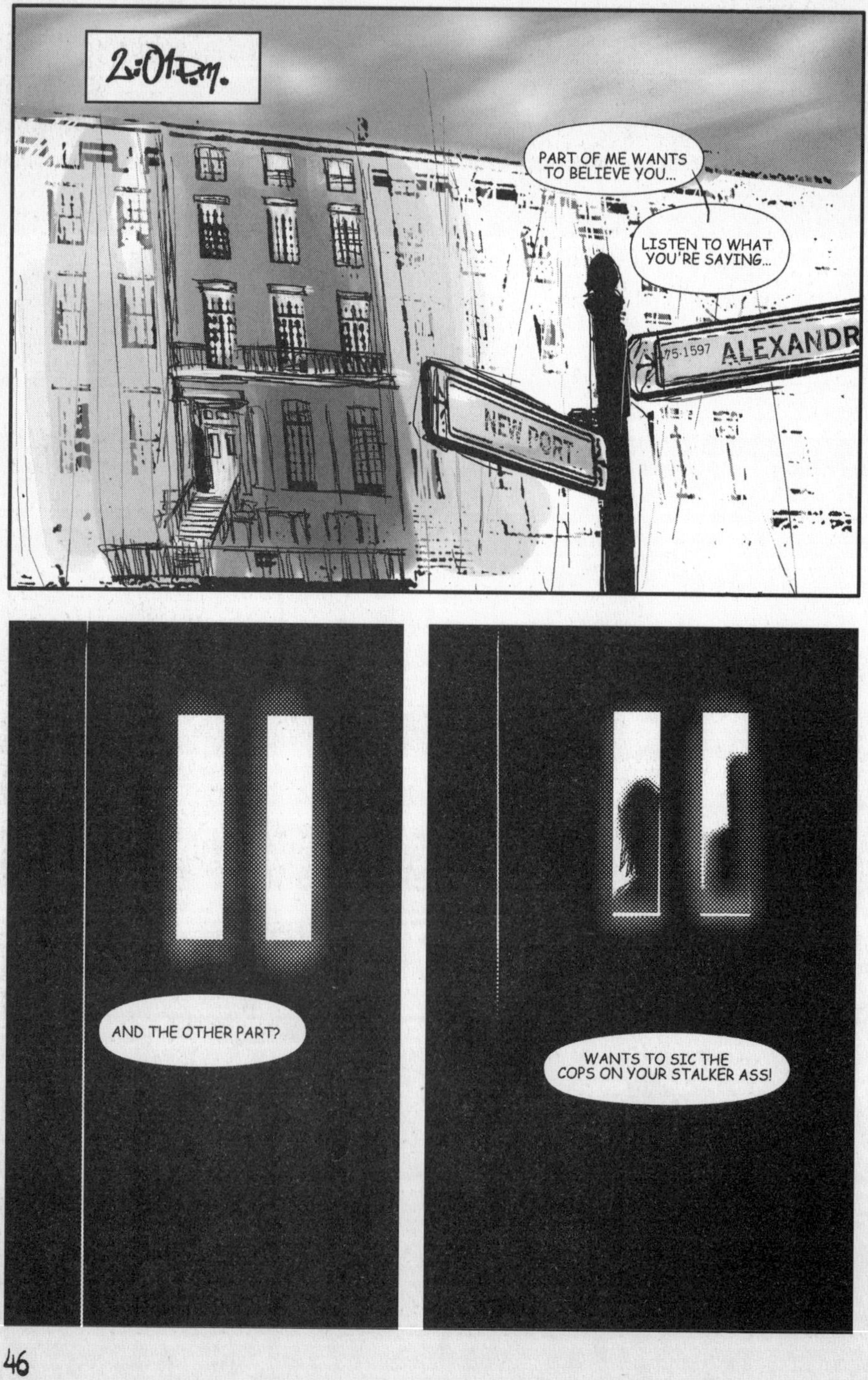
2:01 P.M.
PART OF ME WANTS TO BELIEVE YOU...
LISTEN TO WHAT YOU'RE SAYING...
75-1597 ALEXANDR
NEW PORT
AND THE OTHER PART?
WANTS TO SIC THE COPS ON YOUR STALKER ASS!

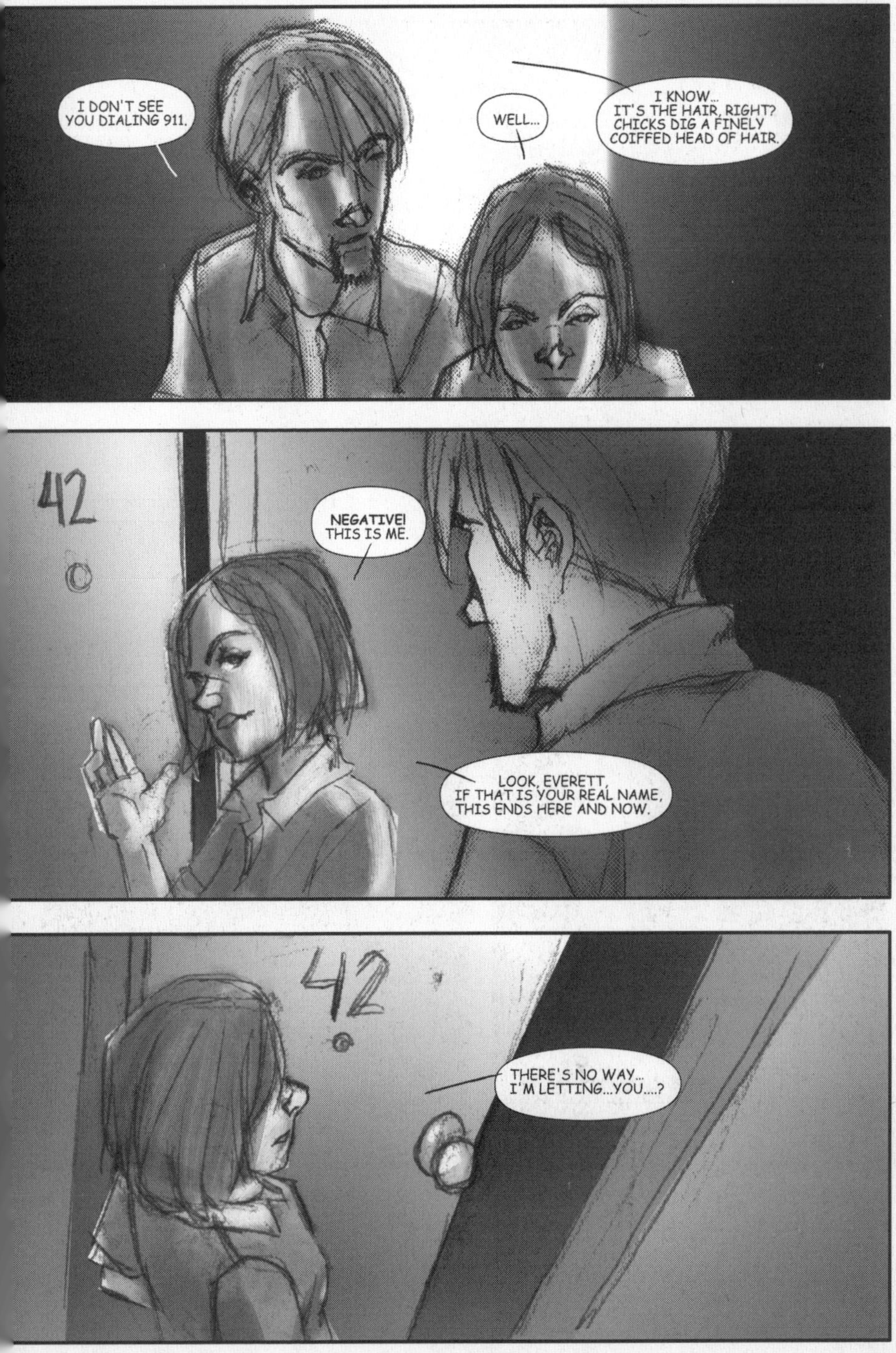
I DON'T SEE YOU DIALING 911.
WELL...
I KNOW... IT'S THE HAIR, RIGHT? CHICKS DIG A FINELY COIFFED HEAD OF HAIR.
NEGATIVE! THIS IS ME.
LOOK, EVERETT, IF THAT IS YOUR REAL NAME, THIS ENDS HERE AND NOW.
THERE'S NO WAY... I'M LETTING...YOU....?

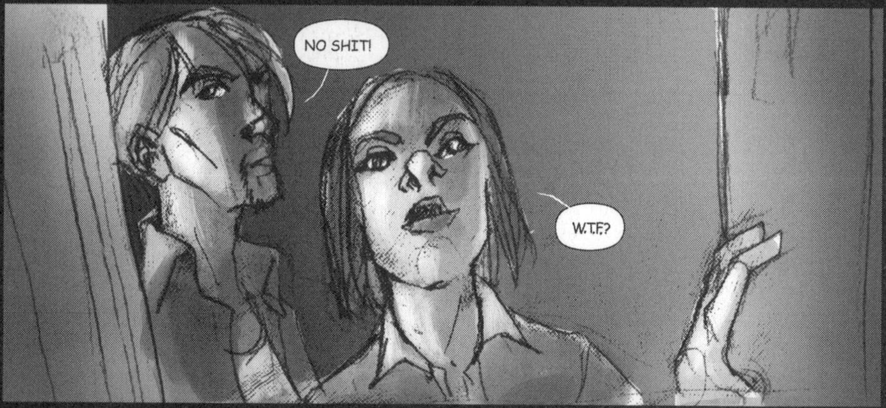
NO SHIT!
W.T.F.?

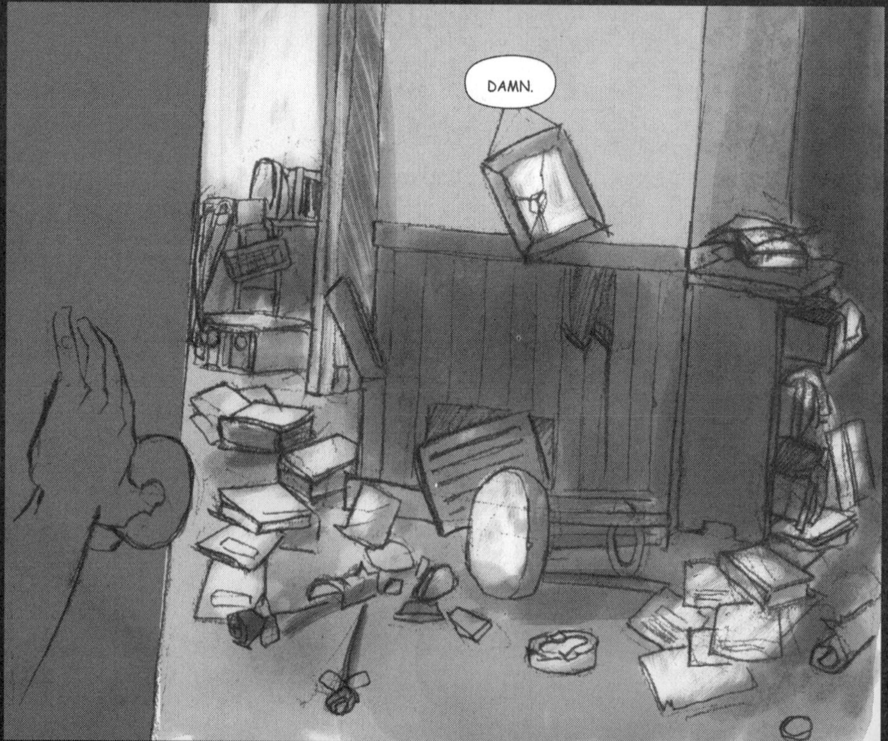
DAMN.

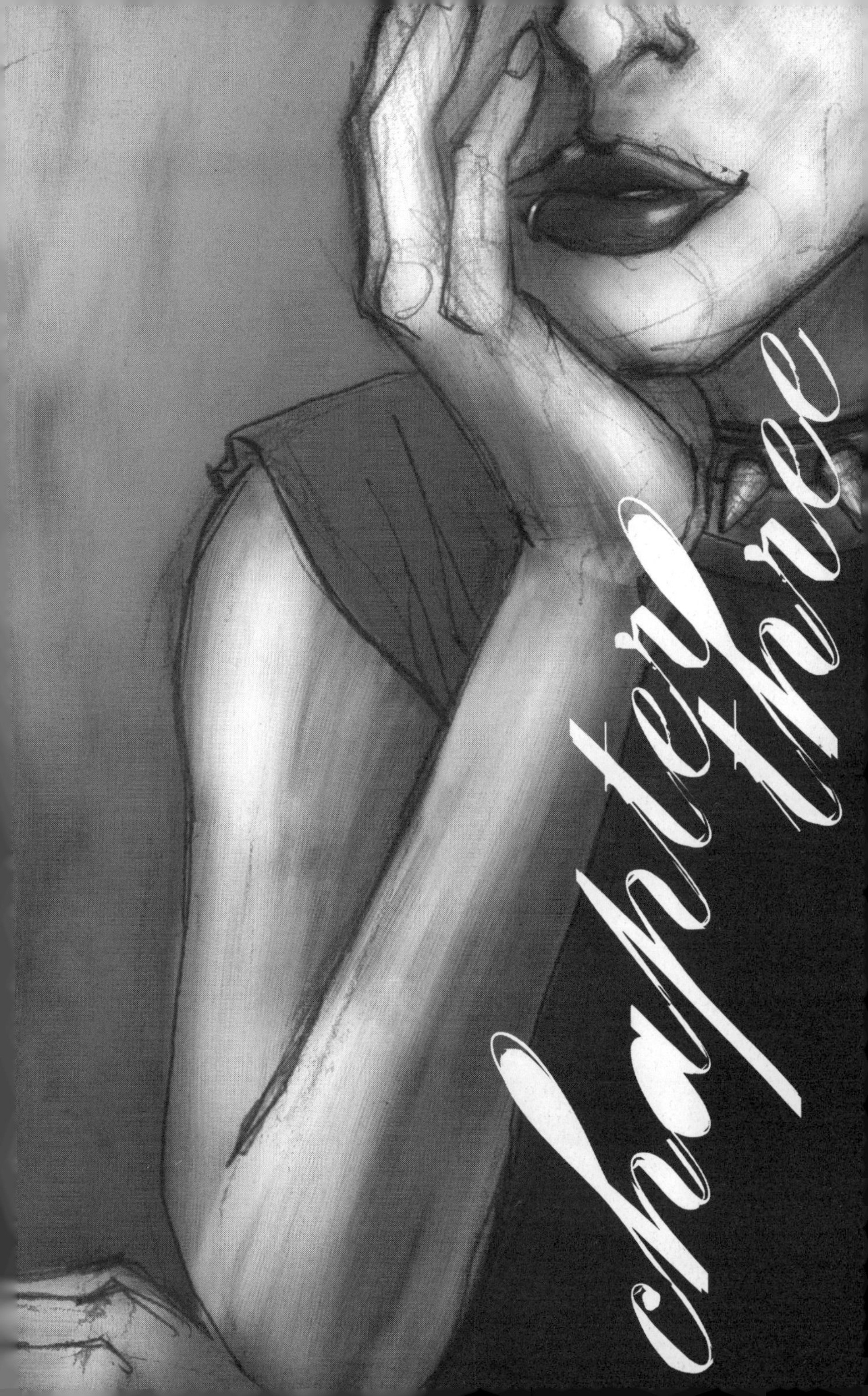
chapter three

just as no two people are alike
no two kisses are alike.

WHERE ARE THEY?!

TIME'S TICKING...

WE STILL HAVE A FEW MINUTES BEFORE IT'S TOO LATE.

ONCE THEY SHOW UP, WE'RE OUT OF HERE!

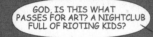

GOD, IS THIS WHAT PASSES FOR ART? A NIGHTCLUB FULL OF RIOTING KIDS?

SOMEONE ONCE SAID ART IS EITHER PLAGIARISM OR REVOLUTION.

HEH, TAKE YOUR PICK.

ERIC, WE'RE NOT GETTING OUT OF HERE ALIVE.

PRIVATE

12:10 a.m.

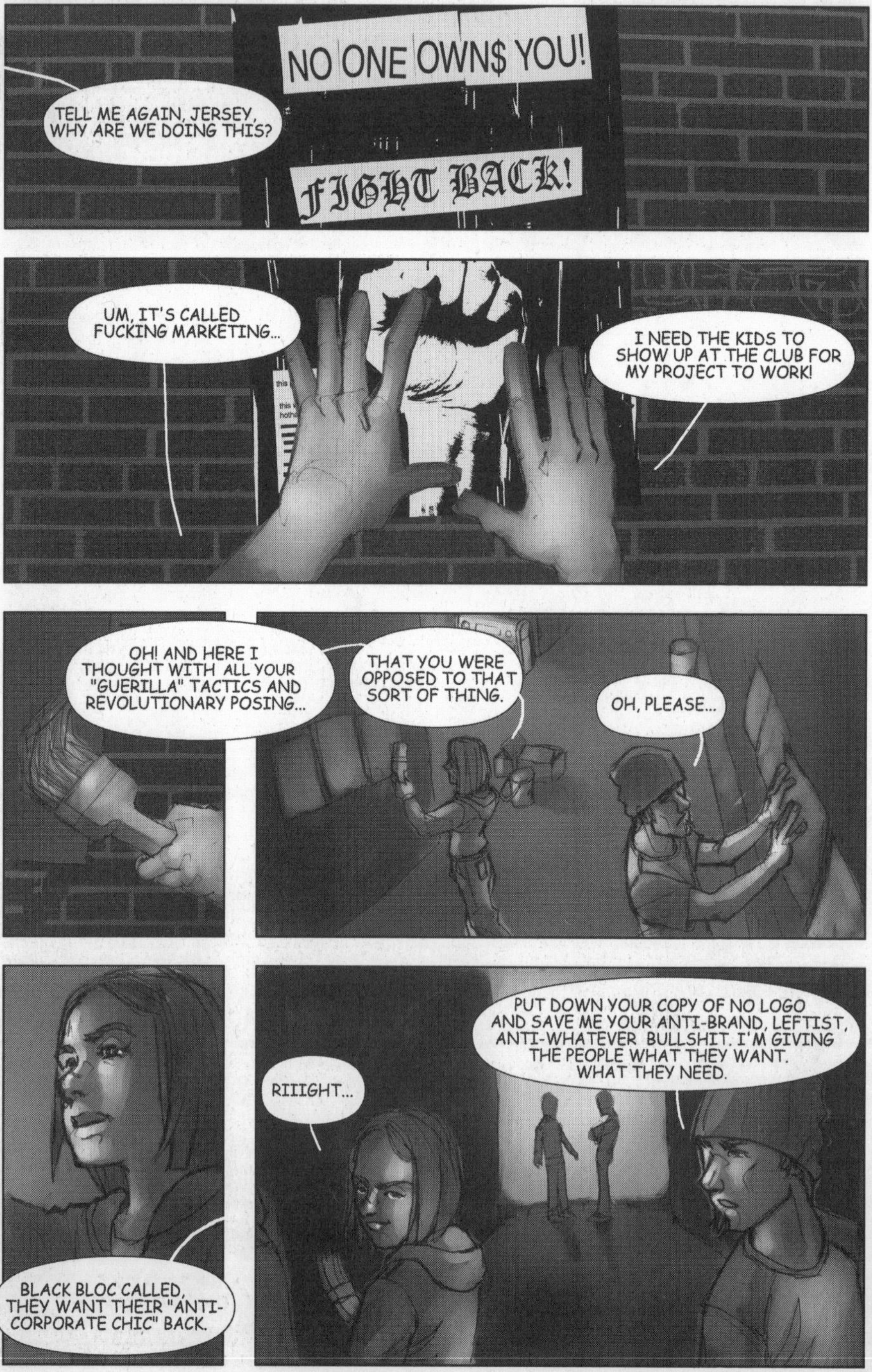
NO ONE OWN$ YOU!
TELL ME AGAIN, JERSEY, WHY ARE WE DOING THIS?
FIGHT BACK!
UM, IT'S CALLED FUCKING MARKETING...
I NEED THE KIDS TO SHOW UP AT THE CLUB FOR MY PROJECT TO WORK!
OH! AND HERE I THOUGHT WITH ALL YOUR "GUERILLA" TACTICS AND REVOLUTIONARY POSING...
THAT YOU WERE OPPOSED TO THAT SORT OF THING.
OH, PLEASE...
BLACK BLOC CALLED, THEY WANT THEIR "ANTI-CORPORATE CHIC" BACK.
RIIIGHT...
PUT DOWN YOUR COPY OF NO LOGO AND SAVE ME YOUR ANTI-BRAND, LEFTIST, ANTI-WHATEVER BULLSHIT. I'M GIVING THE PEOPLE WHAT THEY WANT. WHAT THEY NEED.

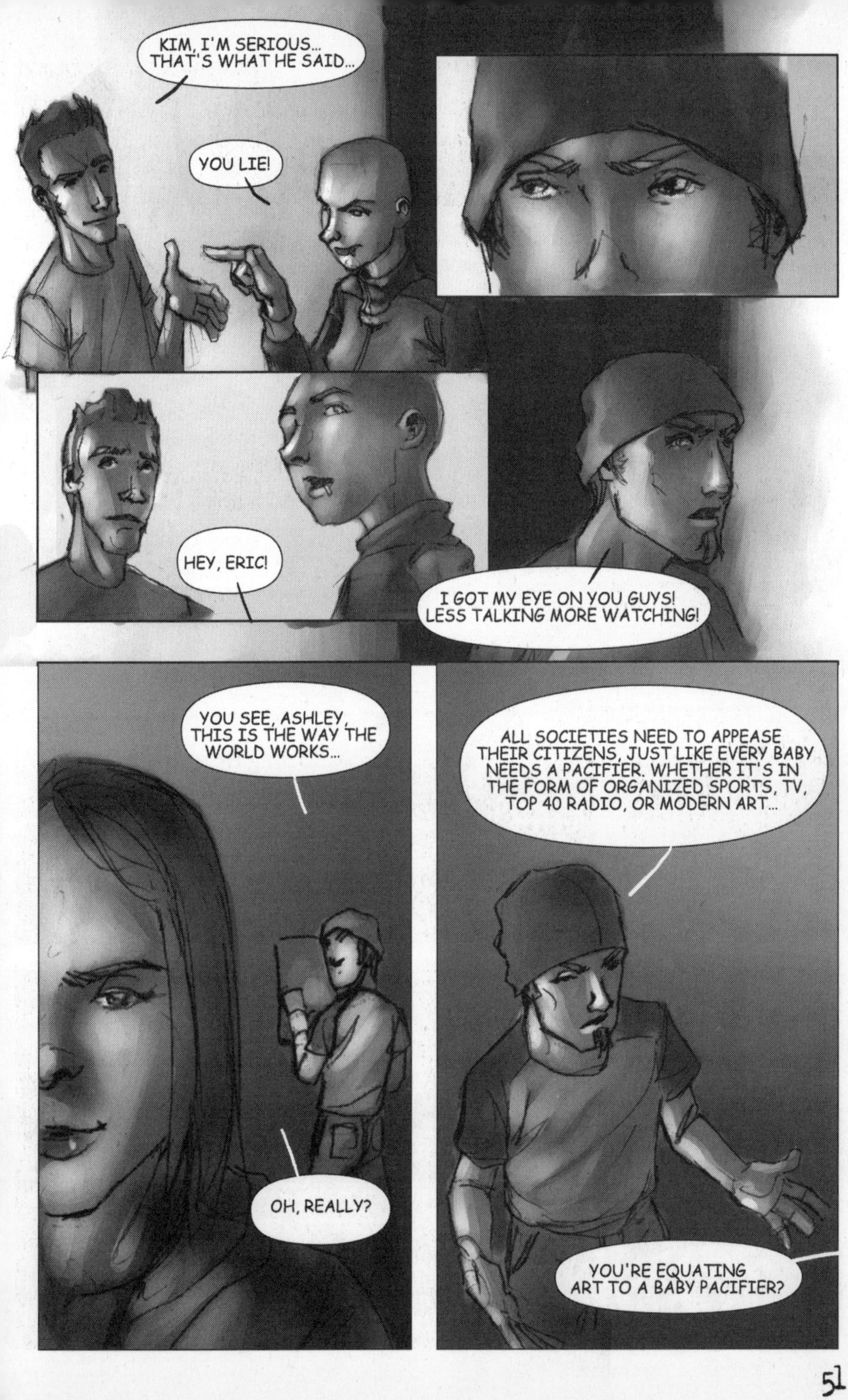
KIM, I'M SERIOUS... THAT'S WHAT HE SAID...
YOU LIE!
HEY, ERIC!
I GOT MY EYE ON YOU GUYS! LESS TALKING MORE WATCHING!
YOU SEE, ASHLEY, THIS IS THE WAY THE WORLD WORKS...
OH, REALLY?
ALL SOCIETIES NEED TO APPEASE THEIR CITIZENS, JUST LIKE EVERY BABY NEEDS A PACIFIER. WHETHER IT'S IN THE FORM OF ORGANIZED SPORTS, TV, TOP 40 RADIO, OR MODERN ART...
YOU'RE EQUATING ART TO A BABY PACIFIER?

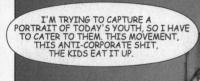

I'M TRYING TO CAPTURE A PORTRAIT OF TODAY'S YOUTH, SO I HAVE TO CATER TO THEM. THIS MOVEMENT, THIS ANTI-CORPORATE SHIT, THE KIDS EAT IT UP.

THEY THINK THEY ARE FIGHTING THE SYSTEM, ALL THE WHILE THEY ARE JUST BECOMING ANOTHER DEMOGRAPHIC FOR THAT SYSTEM TO EXPLOIT. THEY FEEL SAFE WHEN THEY THINK THEY ARE BEING REBELS. IT'S A SECURITY BLANKET, LIKE LINUS OR SOME SHIT.

BUT IT'S NOT REAL! THE IDEA OF REBELLION HAS BEEN A RITE OF PASSAGE FOR YOUTH FOREVER, AND ALL THIS REVOLUTIONARY POSTURING IS JUST ANOTHER WAY FOR KIDS TO ACT OUT THAT REBELLION.

UHH... I MISSED THAT, COULD YOU REPEAT WHAT YOU JUST SAID.

FUCK OFF!

DUDE, YOU'RE GOING TO POSTER OVER THERE? IT SAYS POST NO BILLS.

POST NO BILL

P   NO BIL

FUCK THAT SHIT, MAN, I'M AN ARTIST, THIS IS WHAT I DO.

WELL, AREN'T YOU ON PROBATION OR SOMETHING FOR BURNING THAT FLAG A FEW DAYS AGO?

HEY, I SUFFER FOR MY ART. AND BESIDES, IT'LL GIVE ME A LITTLE MORE NOTORIETY...

SO THIS IS WHAT PASSES FOR ART?

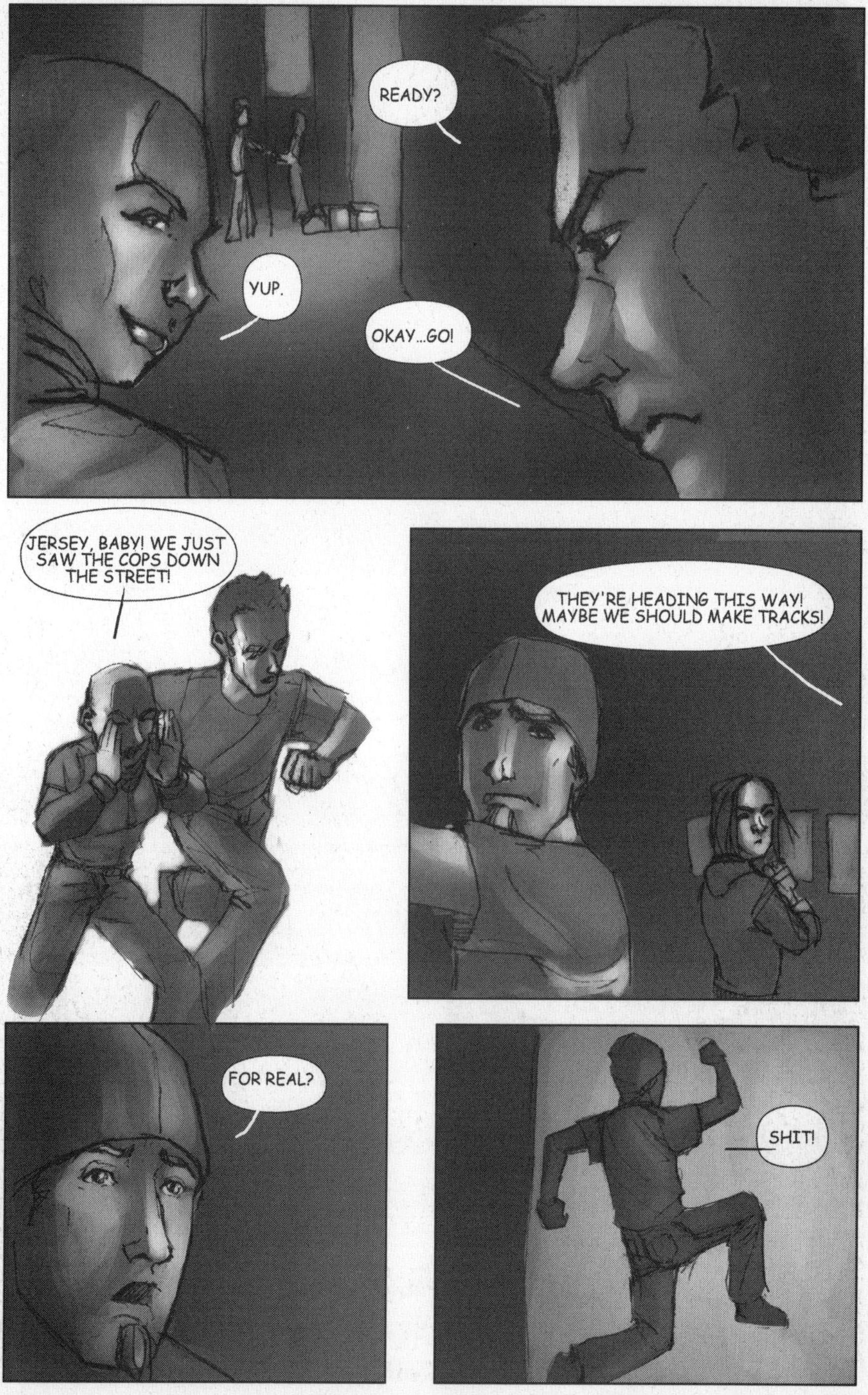
READY?
YUP.
OKAY...GO!
JERSEY, BABY! WE JUST SAW THE COPS DOWN THE STREET!
THEY'RE HEADING THIS WAY! MAYBE WE SHOULD MAKE TRACKS!
FOR REAL?
SHIT!

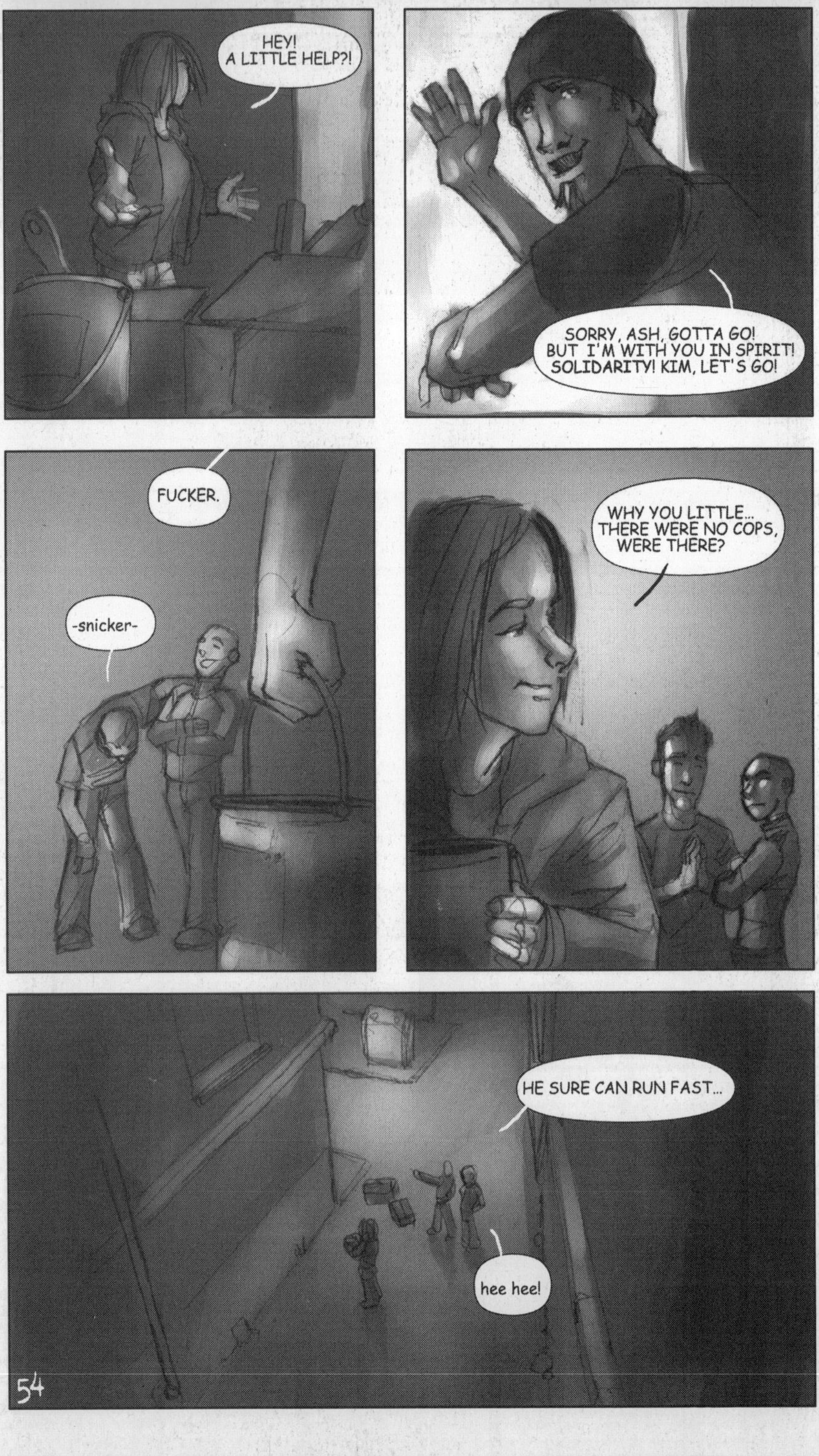
HEY!
A LITTLE HELP?!
SORRY, ASH, GOTTA GO!
BUT I'M WITH YOU IN SPIRIT!
SOLIDARITY! KIM, LET'S GO!
FUCKER.
-snicker-
WHY YOU LITTLE...
THERE WERE NO COPS,
WERE THERE?
HE SURE CAN RUN FAST...
hee hee!

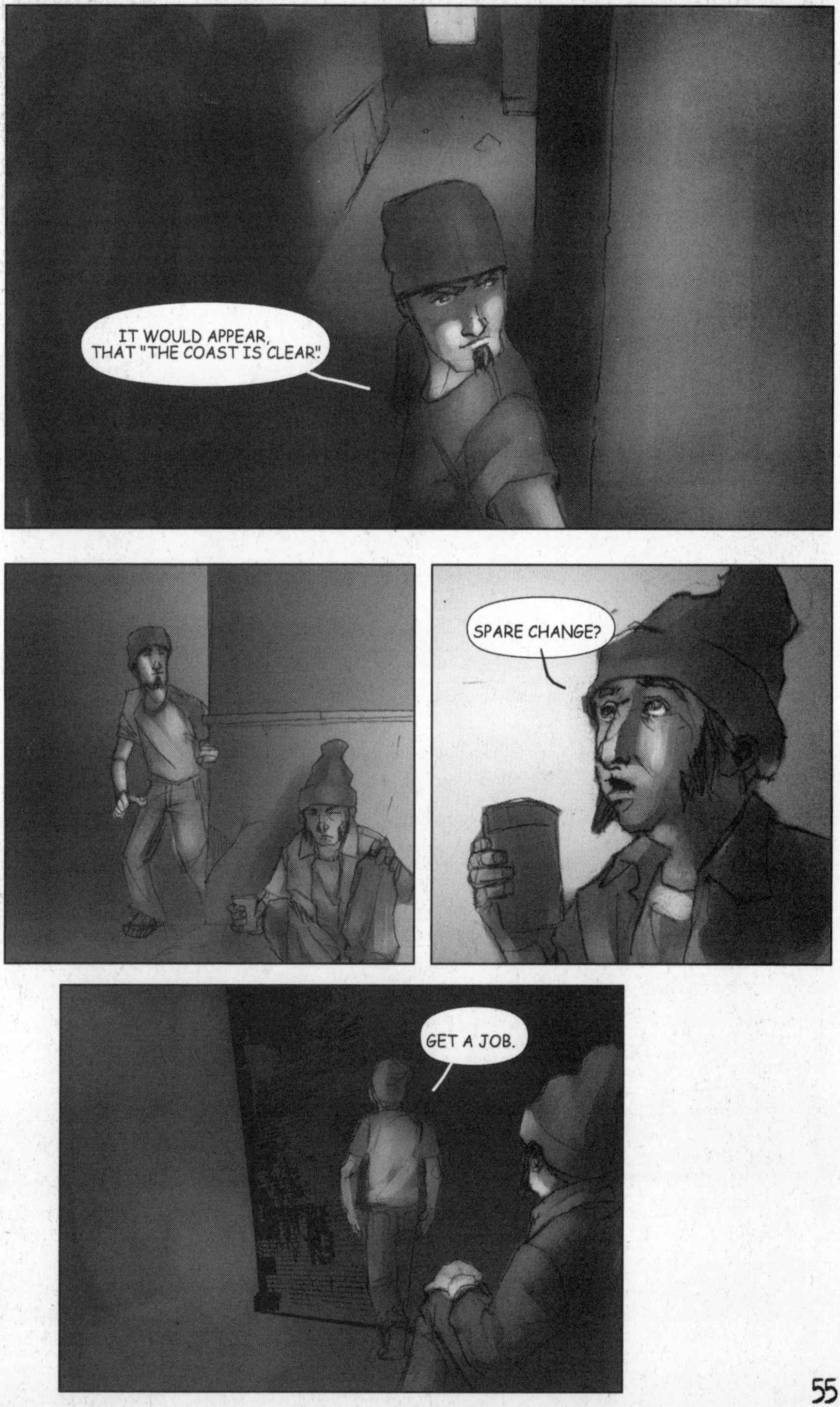
IT WOULD APPEAR, THAT "THE COAST IS CLEAR".
SPARE CHANGE?
GET A JOB.

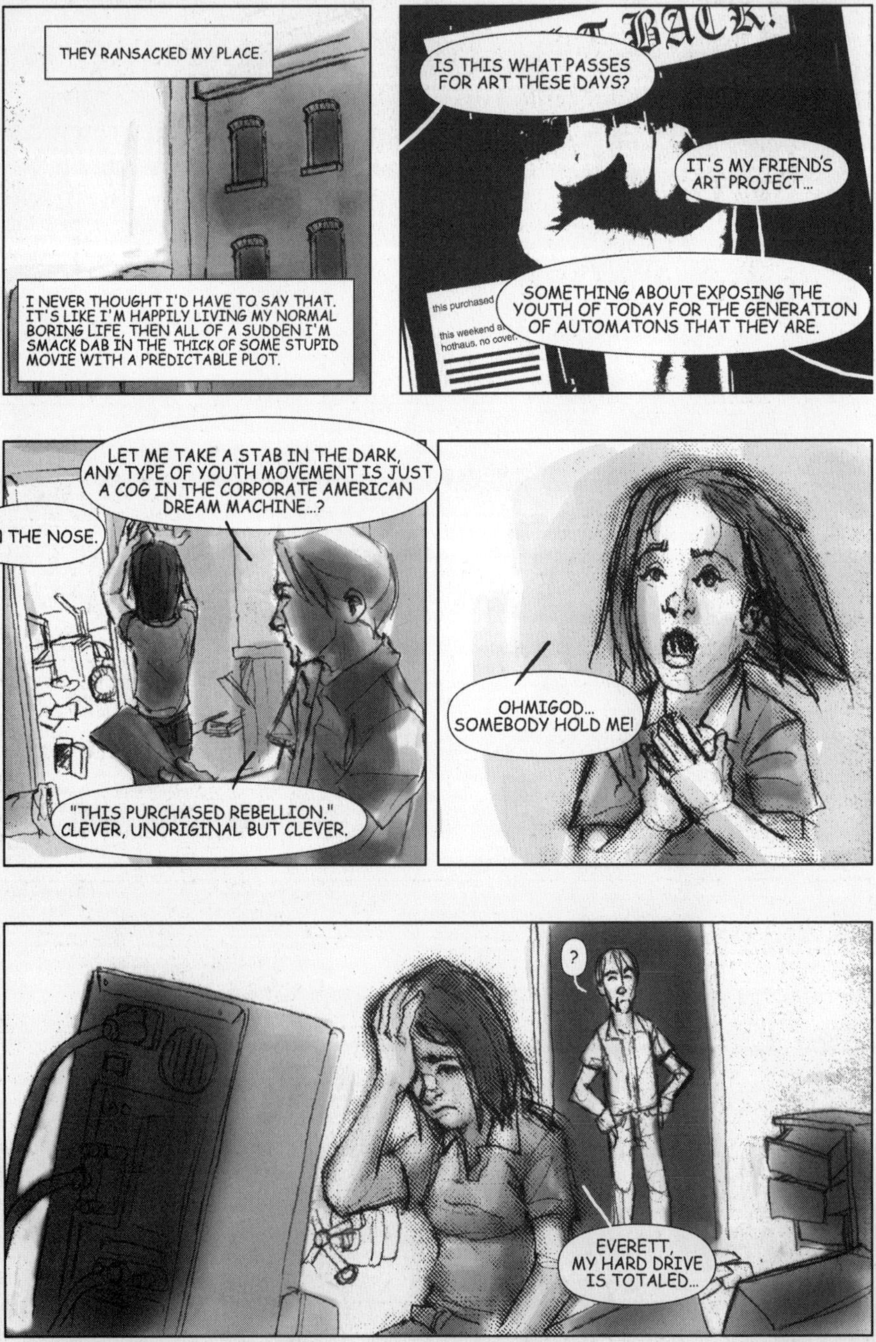
THEY RANSACKED MY PLACE.
I NEVER THOUGHT I'D HAVE TO SAY THAT. IT'S LIKE I'M HAPPILY LIVING MY NORMAL BORING LIFE, THEN ALL OF A SUDDEN I'M SMACK DAB IN THE THICK OF SOME STUPID MOVIE WITH A PREDICTABLE PLOT.
IS THIS WHAT PASSES FOR ART THESE DAYS?
IT'S MY FRIEND'S ART PROJECT...
this purchased
hothaus, no cover.
SOMETHING ABOUT EXPOSING THE YOUTH OF TODAY FOR THE GENERATION OF AUTOMATONS THAT THEY ARE.
LET ME TAKE A STAB IN THE DARK, ANY TYPE OF YOUTH MOVEMENT IS JUST A COG IN THE CORPORATE AMERICAN DREAM MACHINE...?
ON THE NOSE.
"THIS PURCHASED REBELLION." CLEVER, UNORIGINAL BUT CLEVER.
OHMIGOD... SOMEBODY HOLD ME!
?
EVERETT, MY HARD DRIVE IS TOTALED...

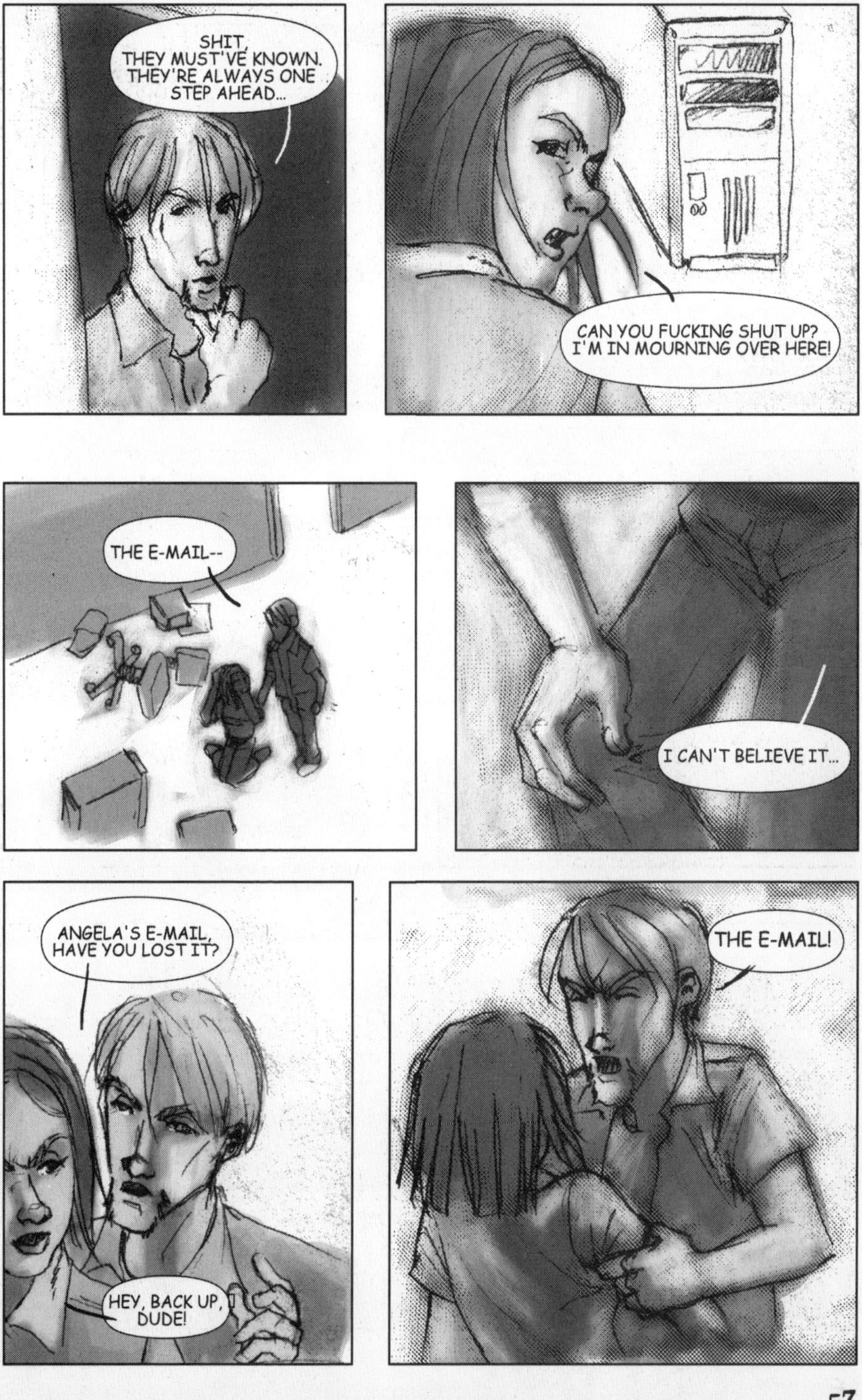
SHIT, THEY MUST'VE KNOWN. THEY'RE ALWAYS ONE STEP AHEAD...
CAN YOU FUCKING SHUT UP? I'M IN MOURNING OVER HERE!
THE E-MAIL--
I CAN'T BELIEVE IT...
ANGELA'S E-MAIL, HAVE YOU LOST IT?
HEY, BACK UP, DUDE!
THE E-MAIL!

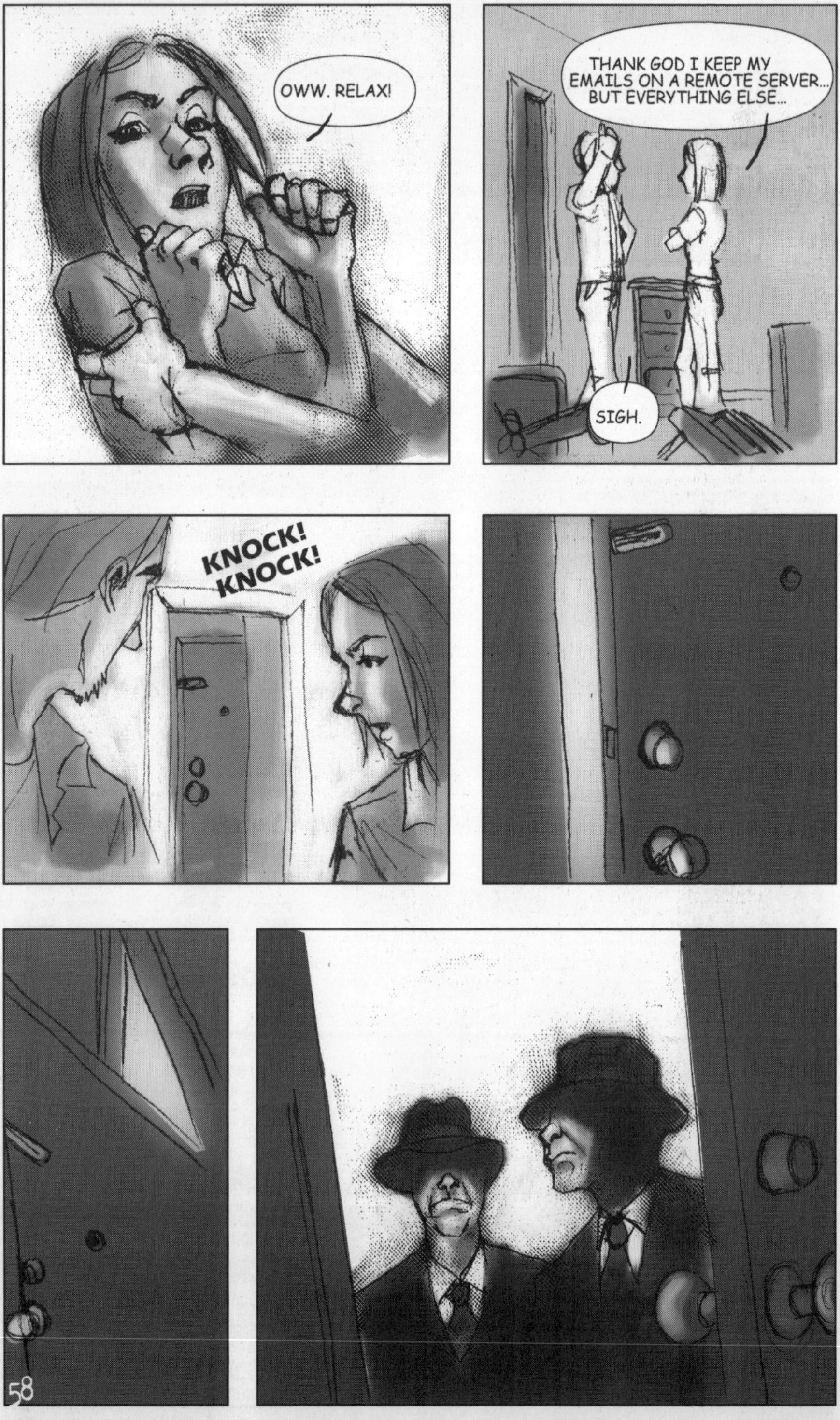
OWW. RELAX!
THANK GOD I KEEP MY EMAILS ON A REMOTE SERVER... BUT EVERYTHING ELSE...
SIGH.
KNOCK! KNOCK!

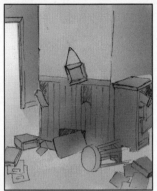

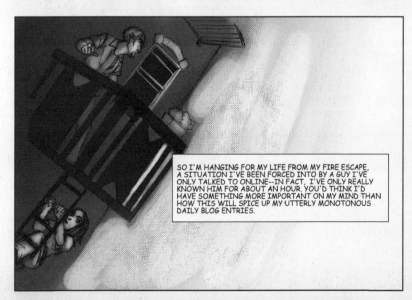

SO I'M HANGING FOR MY LIFE FROM MY FIRE ESCAPE, A SITUATION I'VE BEEN FORCED INTO BY A GUY I'VE ONLY TALKED TO ONLINE--IN FACT, I'VE ONLY REALLY KNOWN HIM FOR ABOUT AN HOUR. YOU'D THINK I'D HAVE SOMETHING MORE IMPORTANT ON MY MIND THAN HOW THIS WILL SPICE UP MY UTTERLY MONOTONOUS DAILY BLOG ENTRIES.

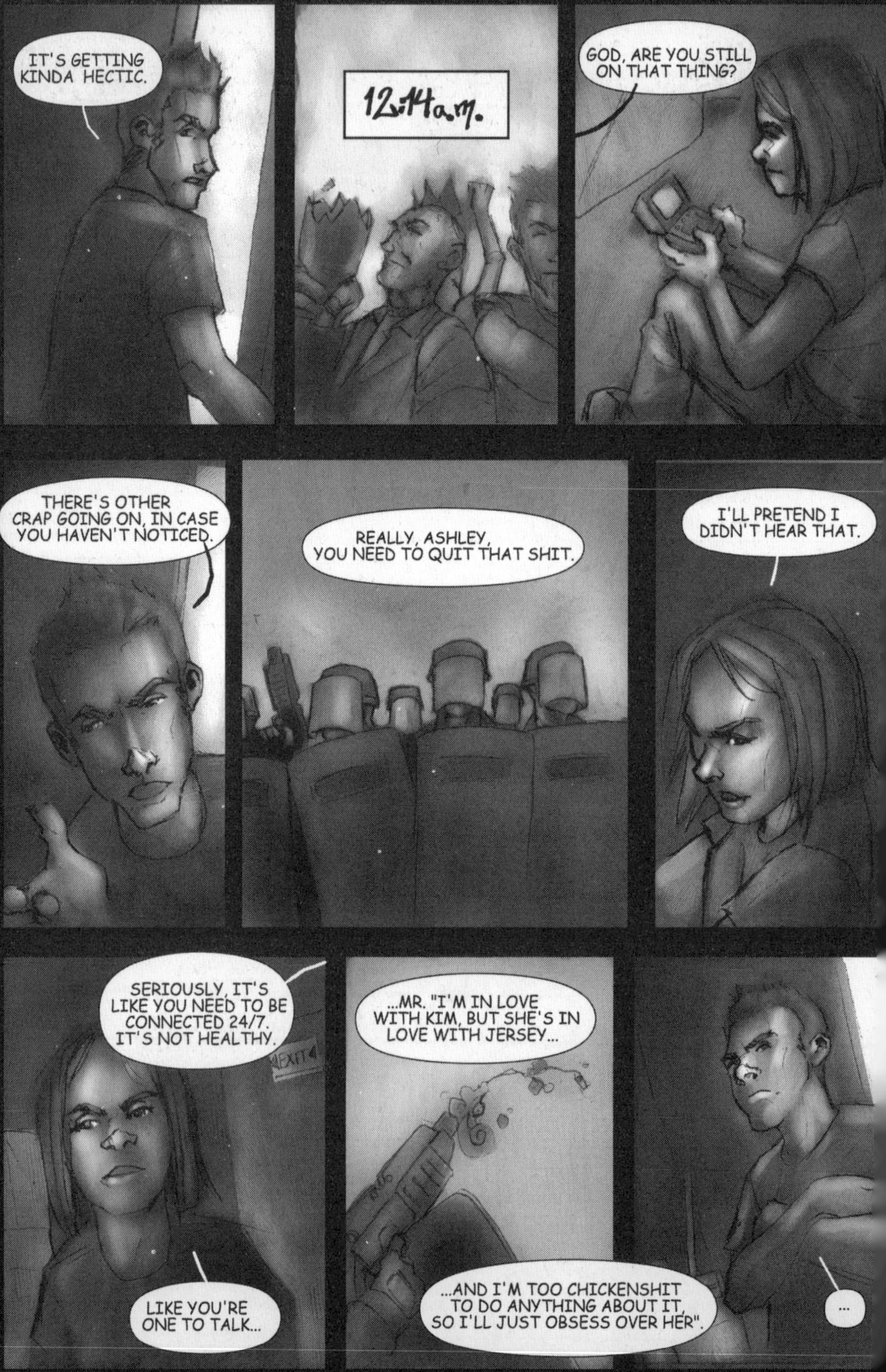
IT'S GETTING KINDA HECTIC.
12:14a.m.
GOD, ARE YOU STILL ON THAT THING?
THERE'S OTHER CRAP GOING ON, IN CASE YOU HAVEN'T NOTICED.
REALLY, ASHLEY, YOU NEED TO QUIT THAT SHIT.
I'LL PRETEND I DIDN'T HEAR THAT.
SERIOUSLY, IT'S LIKE YOU NEED TO BE CONNECTED 24/7. IT'S NOT HEALTHY.
EXIT 4
LIKE YOU'RE ONE TO TALK...
...MR. "I'M IN LOVE WITH KIM, BUT SHE'S IN LOVE WITH JERSEY...
...AND I'M TOO CHICKENSHIT TO DO ANYTHING ABOUT IT, SO I'LL JUST OBSESS OVER HER".
...

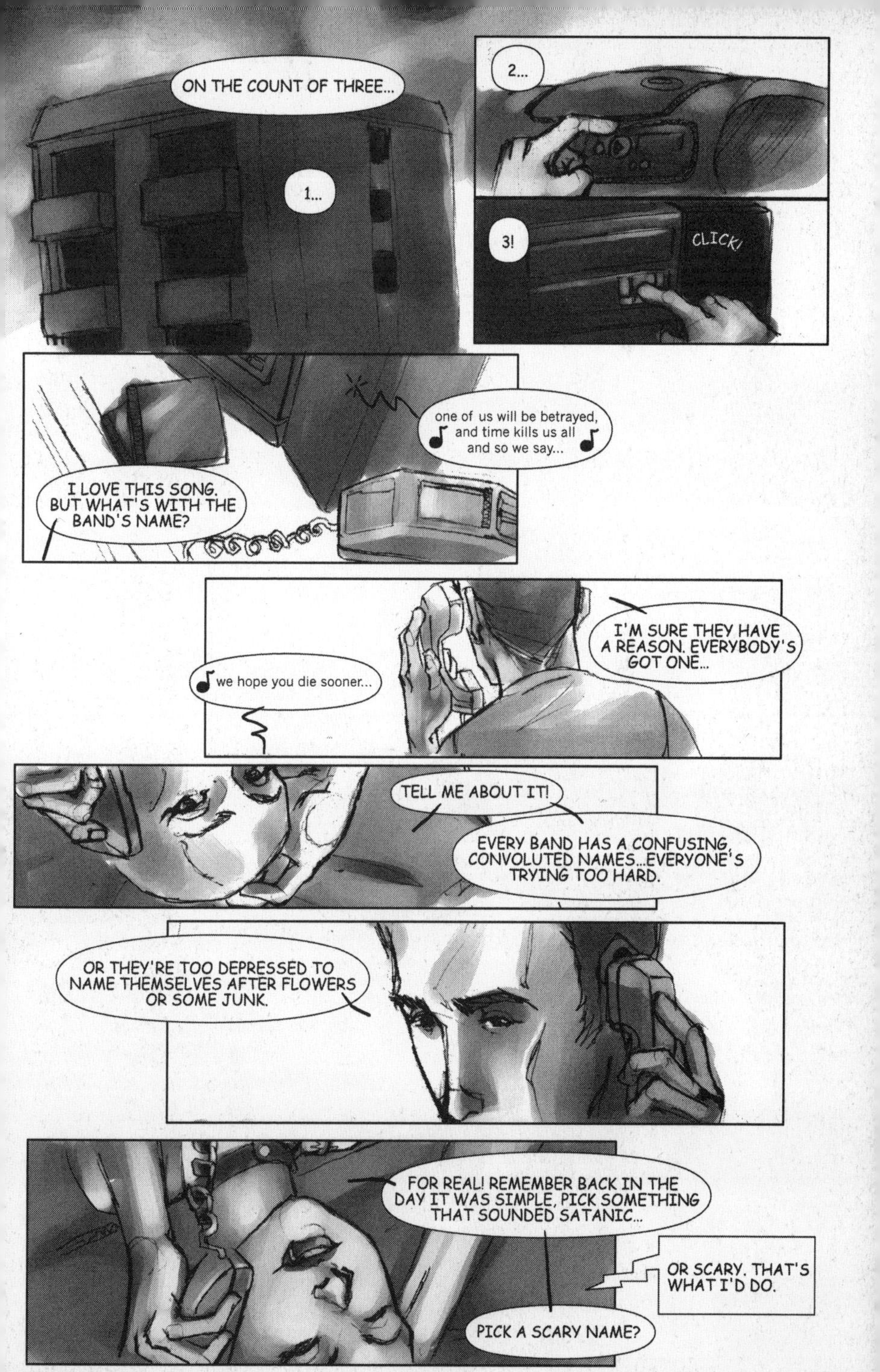
ON THE COUNT OF THREE...
1...
2...
3!
CLICK!
one of us will be betrayed, and time kills us all and so we say...
I LOVE THIS SONG. BUT WHAT'S WITH THE BAND'S NAME?
I'M SURE THEY HAVE A REASON. EVERYBODY'S GOT ONE...
we hope you die sooner...
TELL ME ABOUT IT!
EVERY BAND HAS A CONFUSING, CONVOLUTED NAMES...EVERYONE'S TRYING TOO HARD.
OR THEY'RE TOO DEPRESSED TO NAME THEMSELVES AFTER FLOWERS OR SOME JUNK.
FOR REAL! REMEMBER BACK IN THE DAY IT WAS SIMPLE, PICK SOMETHING THAT SOUNDED SATANIC...
PICK A SCARY NAME?
OR SCARY. THAT'S WHAT I'D DO.

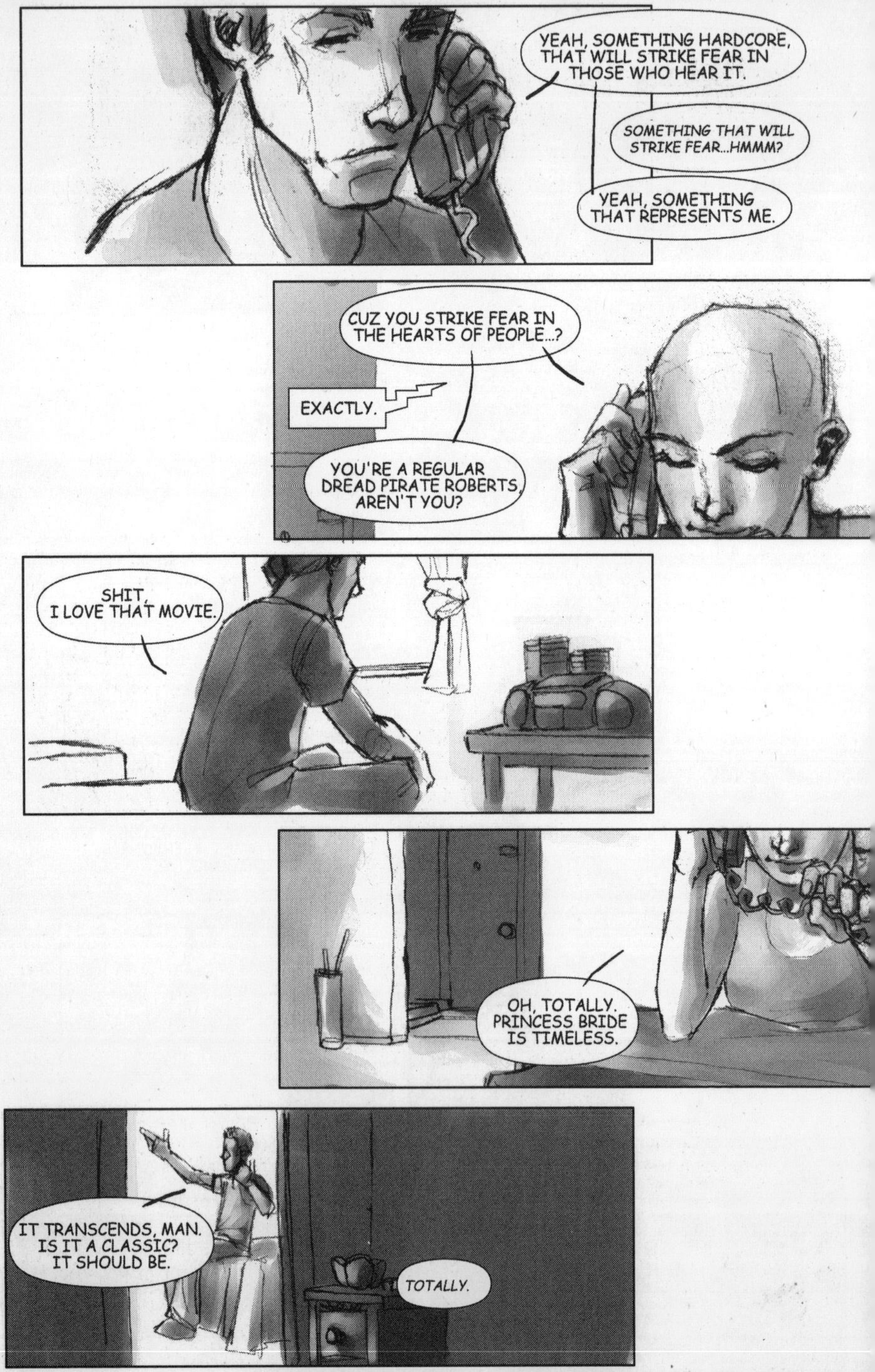
YEAH, SOMETHING HARDCORE, THAT WILL STRIKE FEAR IN THOSE WHO HEAR IT.
SOMETHING THAT WILL STRIKE FEAR...HMMM?
YEAH, SOMETHING THAT REPRESENTS ME.
CUZ YOU STRIKE FEAR IN THE HEARTS OF PEOPLE...?
EXACTLY.
YOU'RE A REGULAR DREAD PIRATE ROBERTS, AREN'T YOU?
SHIT, I LOVE THAT MOVIE.
OH, TOTALLY. PRINCESS BRIDE IS TIMELESS.
IT TRANSCENDS, MAN. IS IT A CLASSIC? IT SHOULD BE.
TOTALLY.

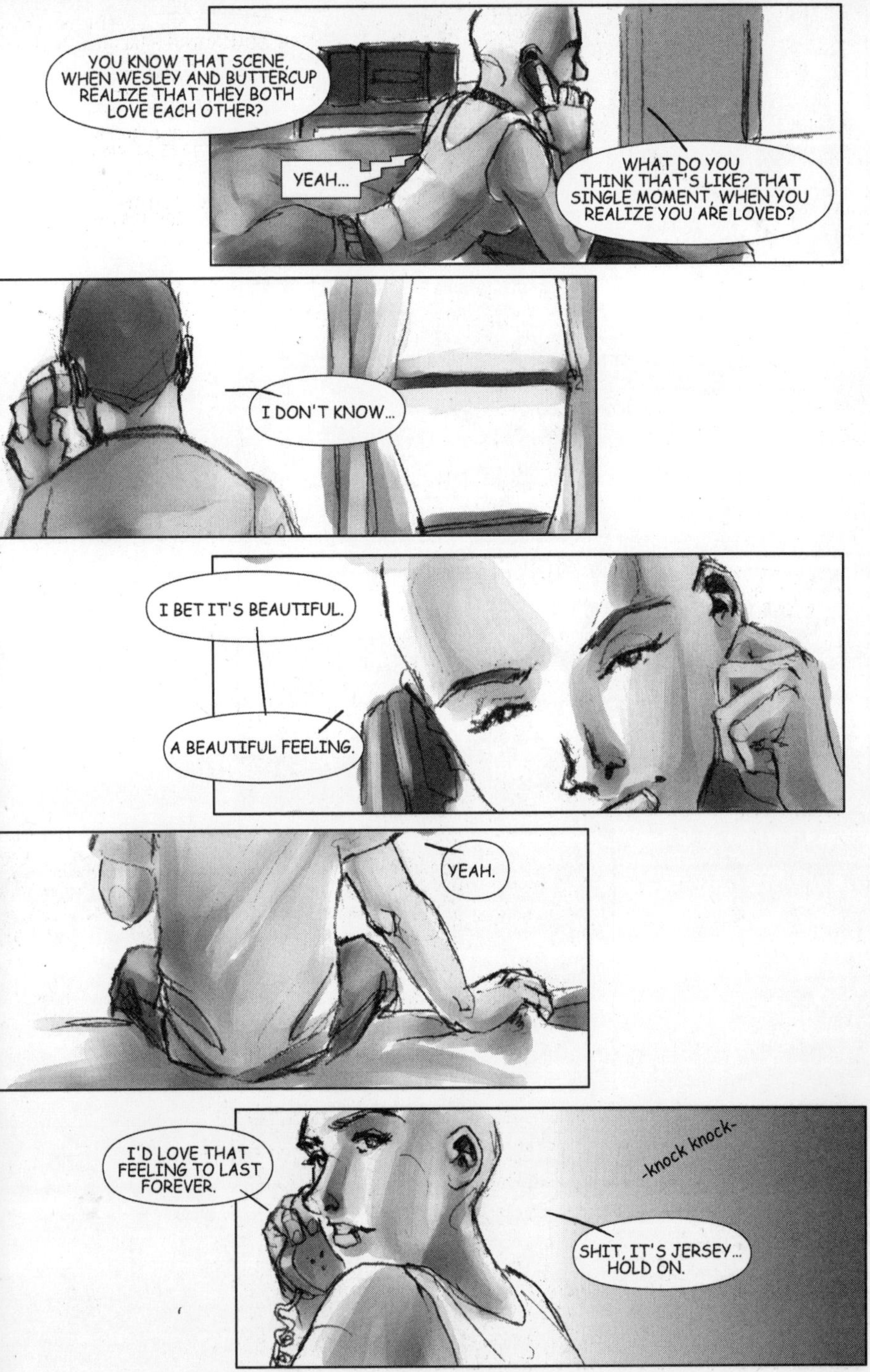
YOU KNOW THAT SCENE, WHEN WESLEY AND BUTTERCUP REALIZE THAT THEY BOTH LOVE EACH OTHER?
YEAH...
WHAT DO YOU THINK THAT'S LIKE? THAT SINGLE MOMENT, WHEN YOU REALIZE YOU ARE LOVED?
I DON'T KNOW...
I BET IT'S BEAUTIFUL.
A BEAUTIFUL FEELING.
YEAH.
I'D LOVE THAT FEELING TO LAST FOREVER.
-knock knock-
SHIT, IT'S JERSEY... HOLD ON.

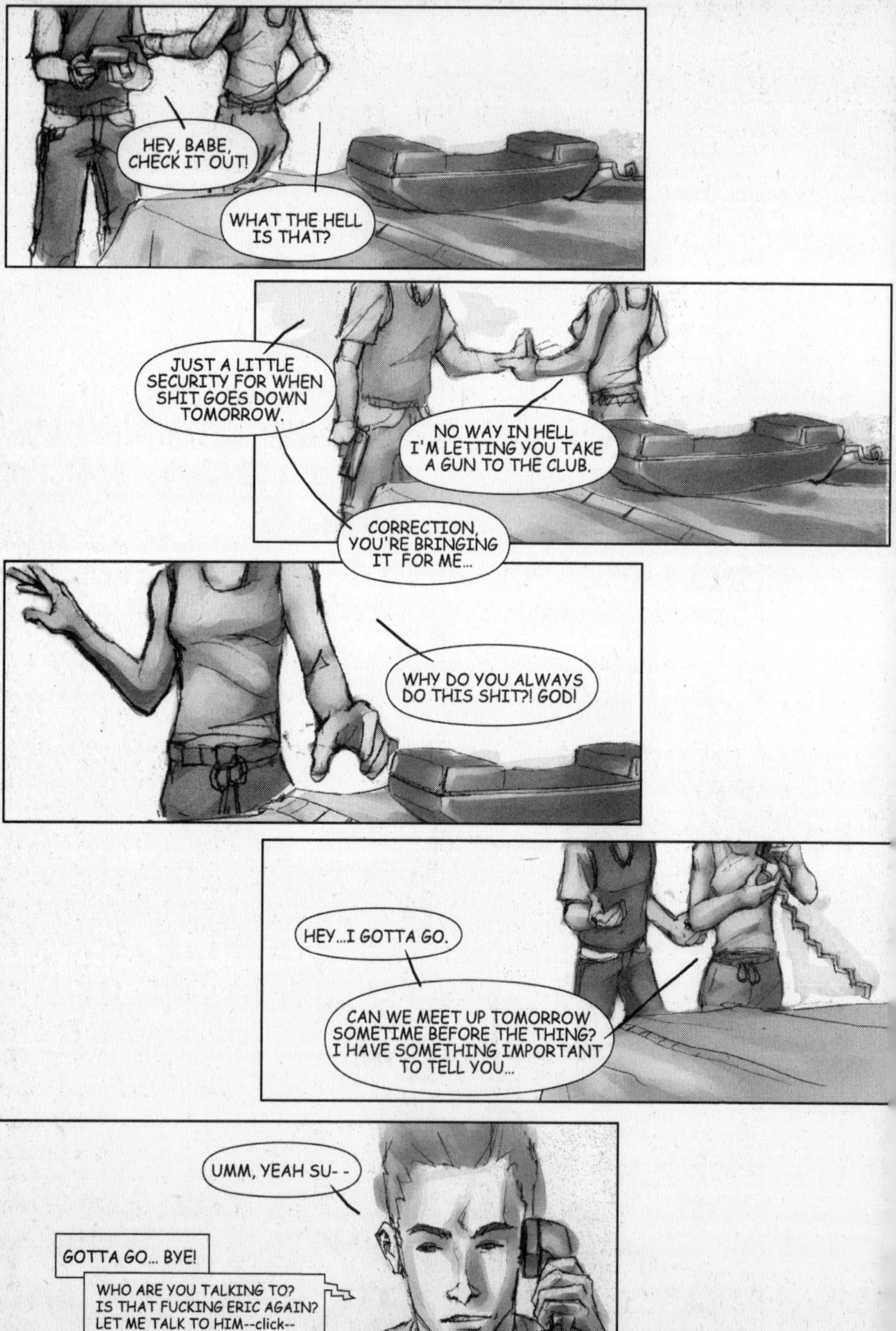
HEY, BABE, CHECK IT OUT!
WHAT THE HELL IS THAT?
JUST A LITTLE SECURITY FOR WHEN SHIT GOES DOWN TOMORROW.
NO WAY IN HELL I'M LETTING YOU TAKE A GUN TO THE CLUB.
CORRECTION, YOU'RE BRINGING IT FOR ME...
WHY DO YOU ALWAYS DO THIS SHIT?! GOD!
HEY...I GOTTA GO.
CAN WE MEET UP TOMORROW SOMETIME BEFORE THE THING? I HAVE SOMETHING IMPORTANT TO TELL YOU...
UMM, YEAH SU- -
GOTTA GO... BYE!
WHO ARE YOU TALKING TO? IS THAT FUCKING ERIC AGAIN? LET ME TALK TO HIM--click--

PRIVATE
SO WHAT HAPPENED BETWEEN YOU AND KIM?
12:17 a.m.
ERIC, IT'S ME... QUIT STALLING.
...
I DON'T KNOW WHAT TO TELL YOU...
C'MON...
I...IT'S JUST, REALLY, NOTHING TO TELL.
UMM, NEGATIVE.
LOOK, WE'VE KNOWN EACH OTHER SINCE WE USED TO CHEAT IN FOUR-SQUARE DURING RECESS.
I'M QUITE AWARE OF ALL YOUR TRICKS. AND YOU'RE NOT TELLING ME SOMETHING.

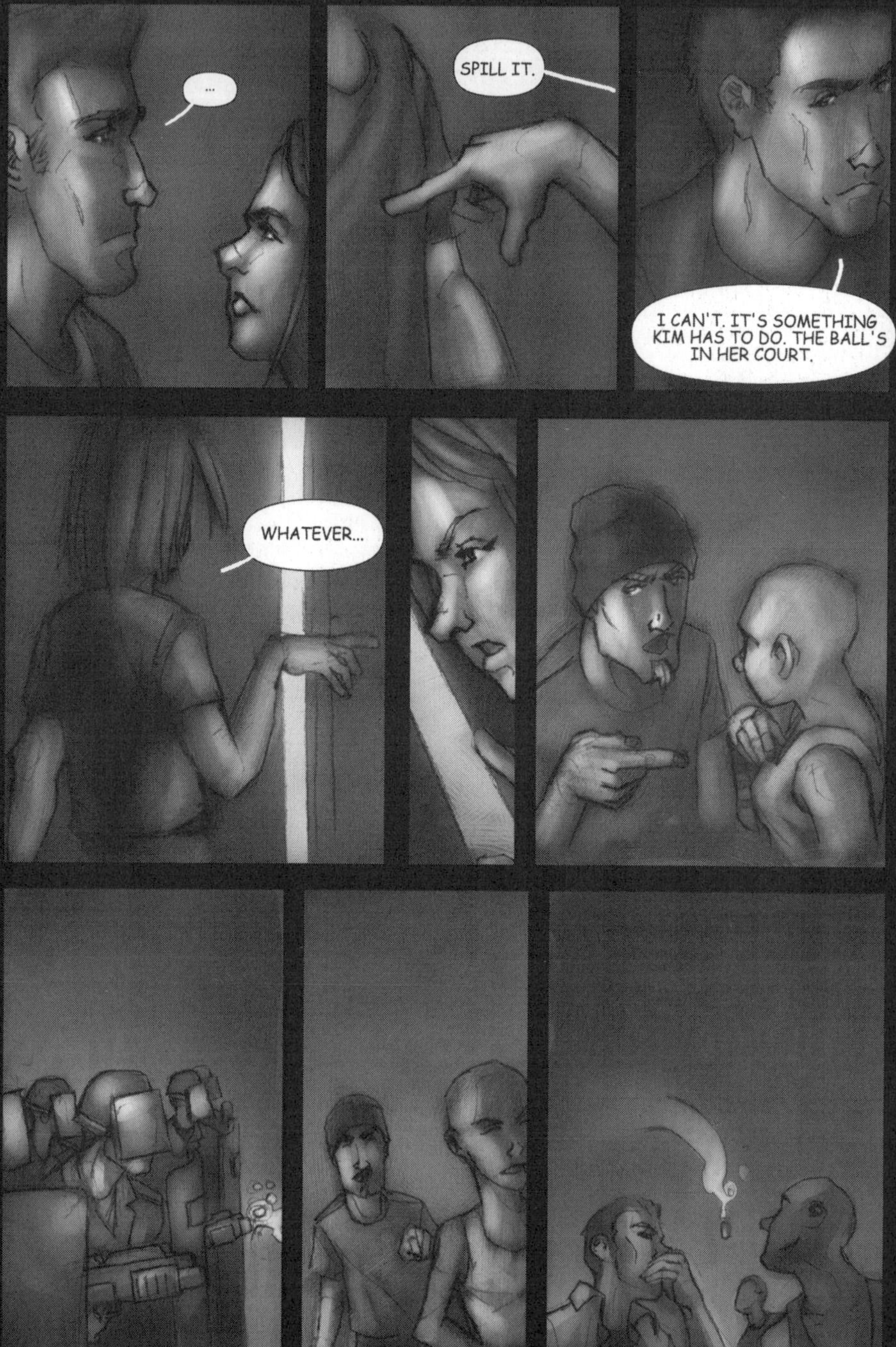
...
SPILL IT.
I CAN'T. IT'S SOMETHING KIM HAS TO DO. THE BALL'S IN HER COURT.
WHATEVER...

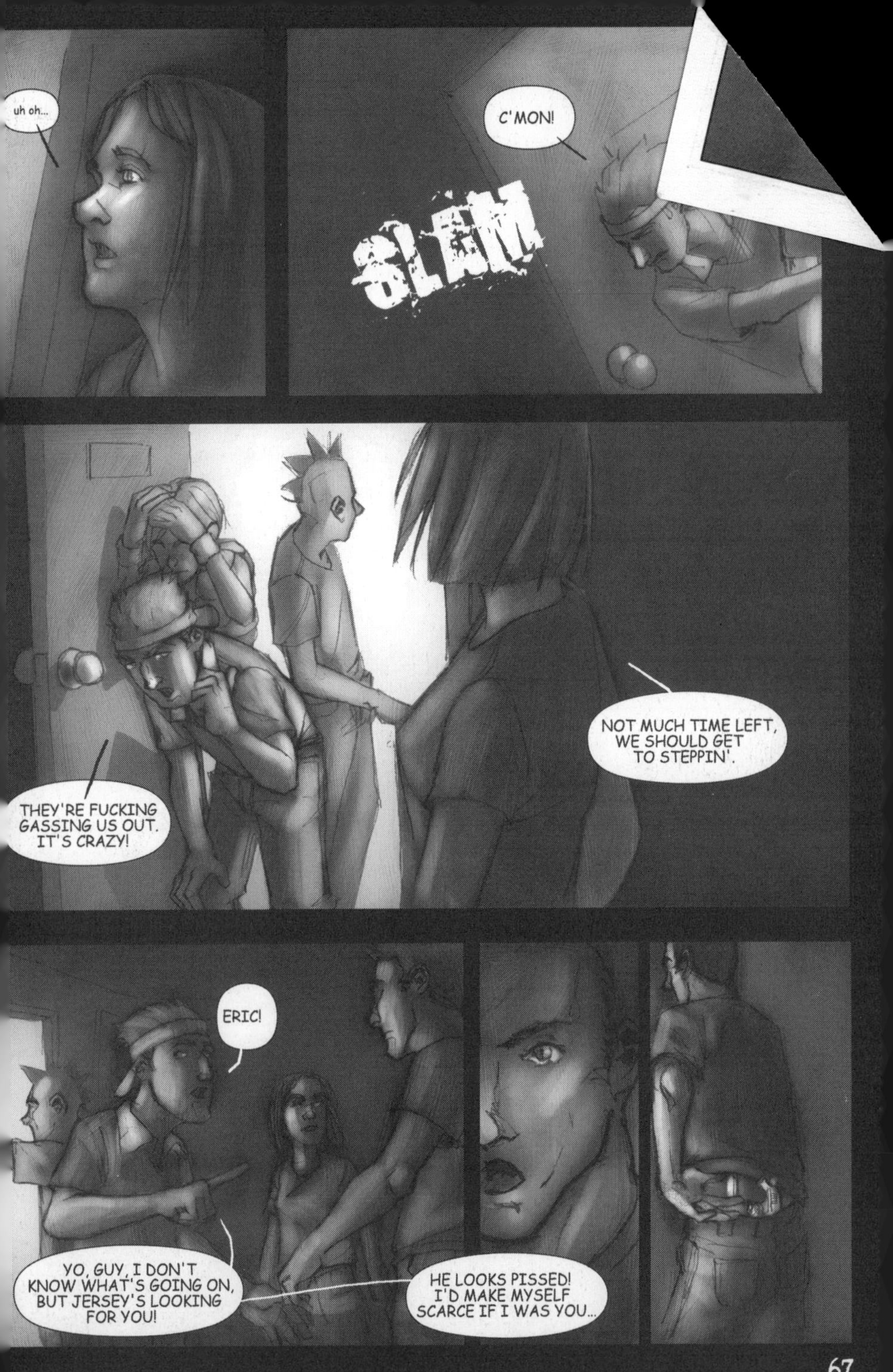
uh oh...
C'MON!
SLAM
THEY'RE FUCKING GASSING US OUT. IT'S CRAZY!
NOT MUCH TIME LEFT, WE SHOULD GET TO STEPPIN'.
ERIC!
YO, GUY, I DON'T KNOW WHAT'S GOING ON, BUT JERSEY'S LOOKING FOR YOU!
HE LOOKS PISSED! I'D MAKE MYSELF SCARCE IF I WAS YOU...

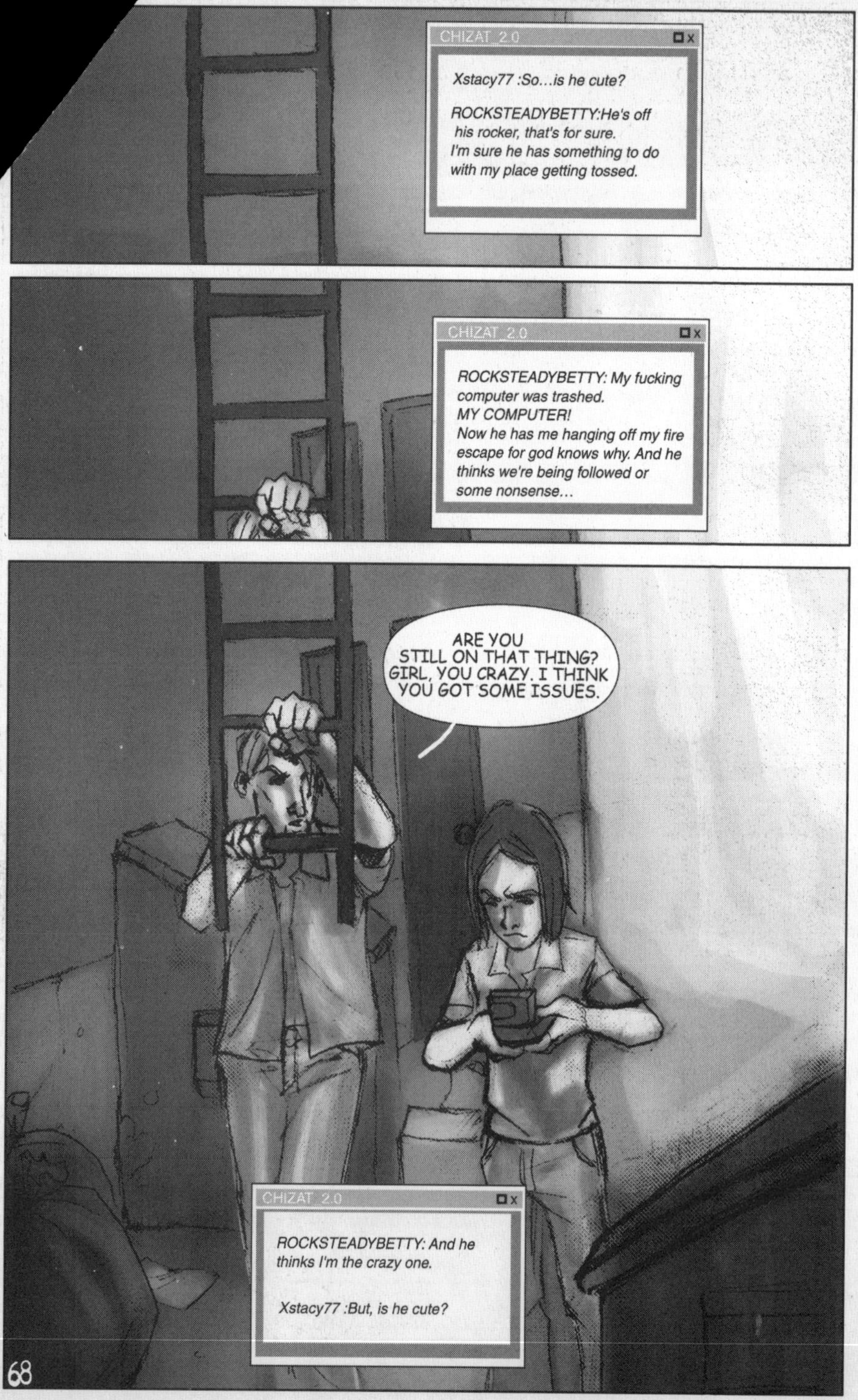

CHIZAT_2.0
Xstacy77 :So…is he cute?
ROCKSTEADYBETTY:He's off his rocker, that's for sure. I'm sure he has something to do with my place getting tossed.
CHIZAT_2.0
ROCKSTEADYBETTY: My fucking computer was trashed. MY COMPUTER! Now he has me hanging off my fire escape for god knows why. And he thinks we're being followed or some nonsense…
ARE YOU STILL ON THAT THING? GIRL, YOU CRAZY. I THINK YOU GOT SOME ISSUES.
CHIZAT_2.0
ROCKSTEADYBETTY: And he thinks I'm the crazy one.
Xstacy77 :But, is he cute?

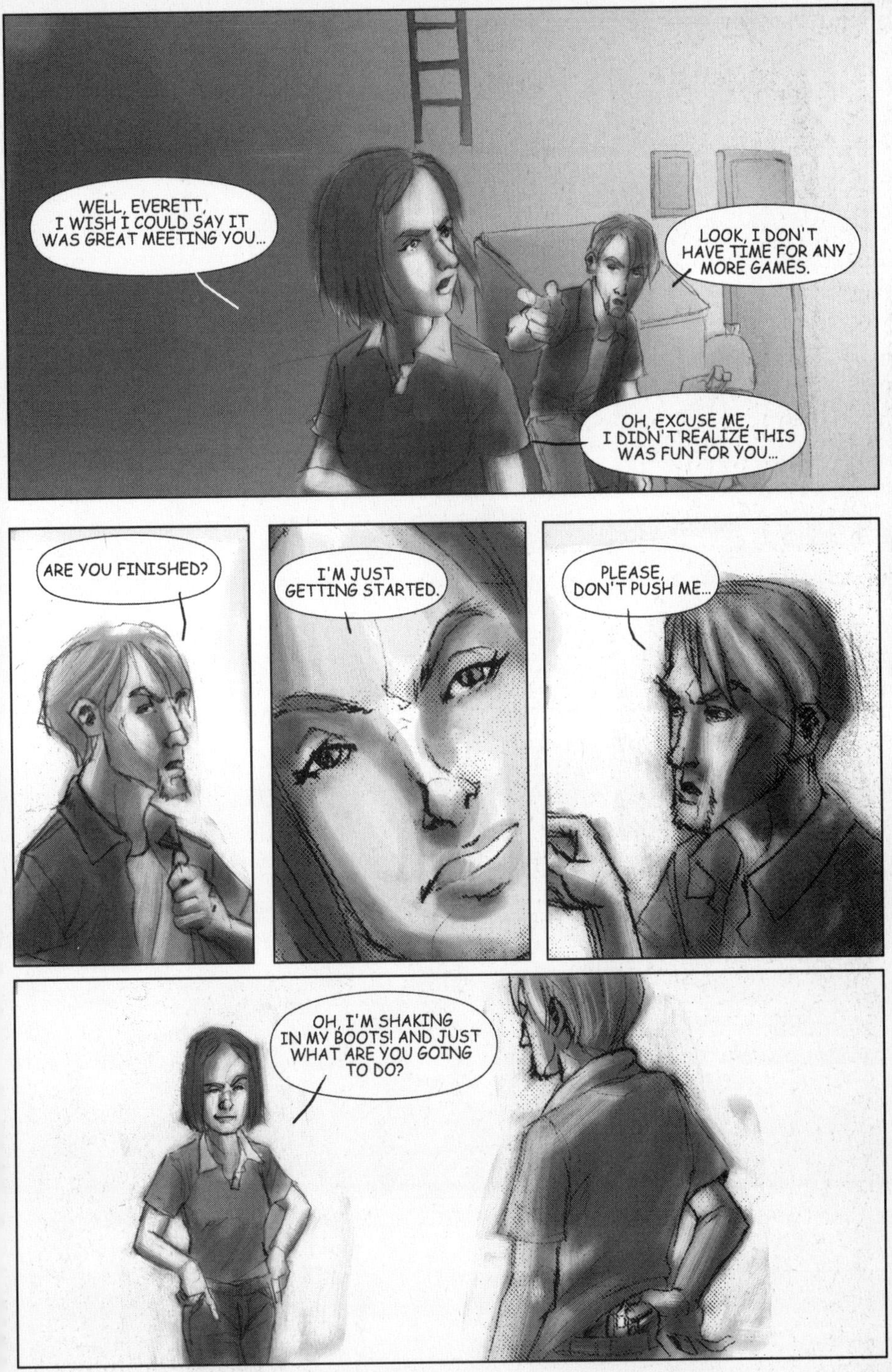
WELL, EVERETT, I WISH I COULD SAY IT WAS GREAT MEETING YOU...
LOOK, I DON'T HAVE TIME FOR ANY MORE GAMES.
OH, EXCUSE ME, I DIDN'T REALIZE THIS WAS FUN FOR YOU...
ARE YOU FINISHED?
I'M JUST GETTING STARTED.
PLEASE, DON'T PUSH ME...
OH, I'M SHAKING IN MY BOOTS! AND JUST WHAT ARE YOU GOING TO DO?

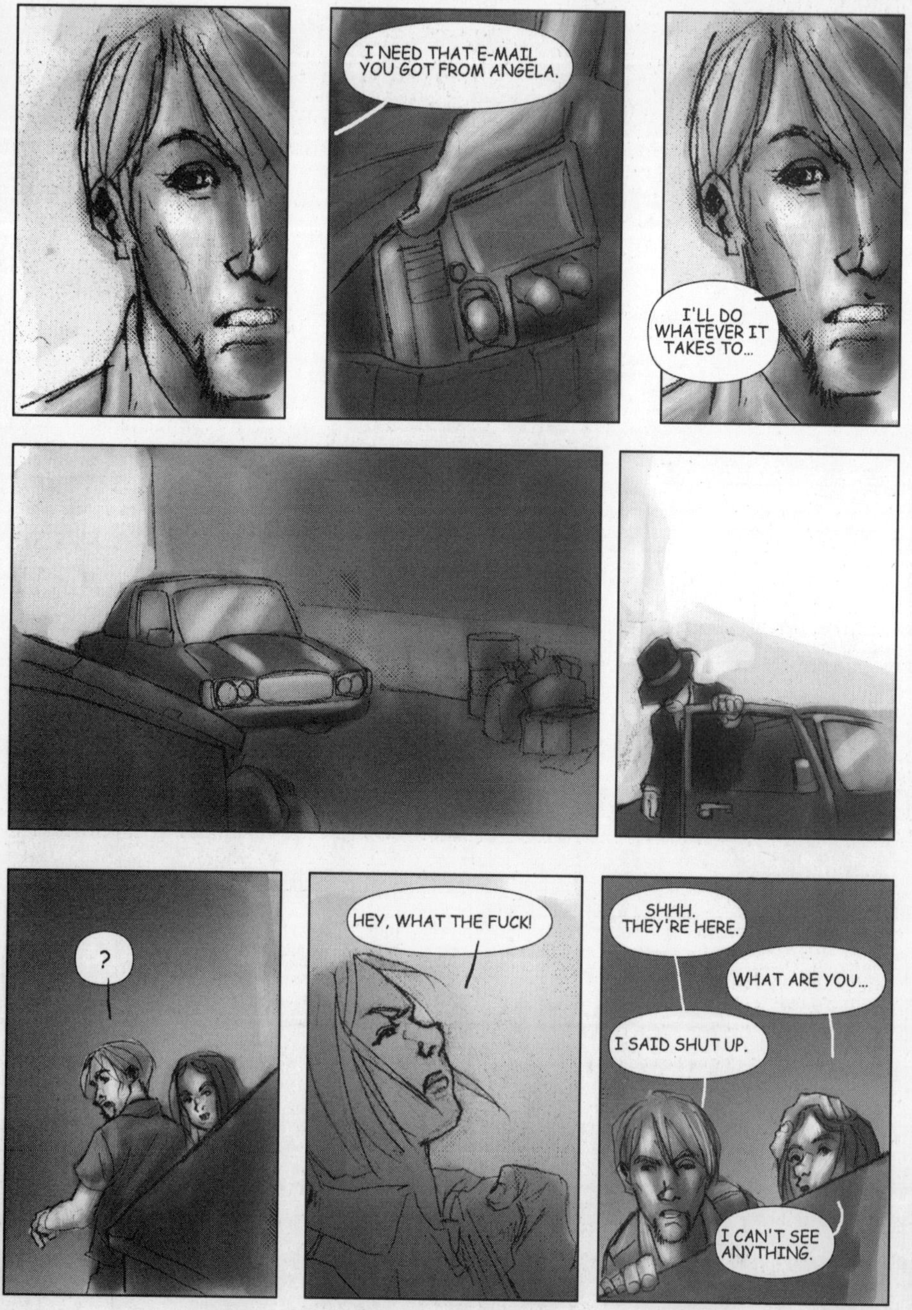
I NEED THAT E-MAIL YOU GOT FROM ANGELA.
I'LL DO WHATEVER IT TAKES TO...
?
HEY, WHAT THE FUCK!
SHHH. THEY'RE HERE.
WHAT ARE YOU...
I SAID SHUT UP.
I CAN'T SEE ANYTHING.

THESE PEOPLE, THEY ARE DANGEROUS.

WHAT PEOPLE?

THEY'RE JUST THE HENCHMEN, CARRYING OUT ORDERS FROM A LARGER ORGANIZATION, WHICH HAS ITS OWN SECRET AGENDA...

WHAT THE HELL ARE YOU BABBLING ABOUT?

THESE MEN ARE THE EYES AND EARS FOR THIS PARENT ORGANIZATION, DOING THEIR DIRTY WORK.

THEY LEAVE NO TRACE, THEY EXIST IN SHADOW.

OHHHKAY... I THINK YOU'VE SEEN ONE TOO MANY SHITTY MOVIES.

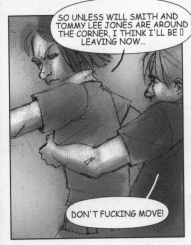

SO UNLESS WILL SMITH AND TOMMY LEE JONES ARE AROUND THE CORNER, I THINK I'LL BE LEAVING NOW...

DON'T FUCKING MOVE!

HAVEN'T YOU BEEN PAYING ATTENTION? THEY'VE BEEN HERE EVERY STEP OF THE WAY, AND IF THEY SEE YOU, IT'S ALL OVER.

71

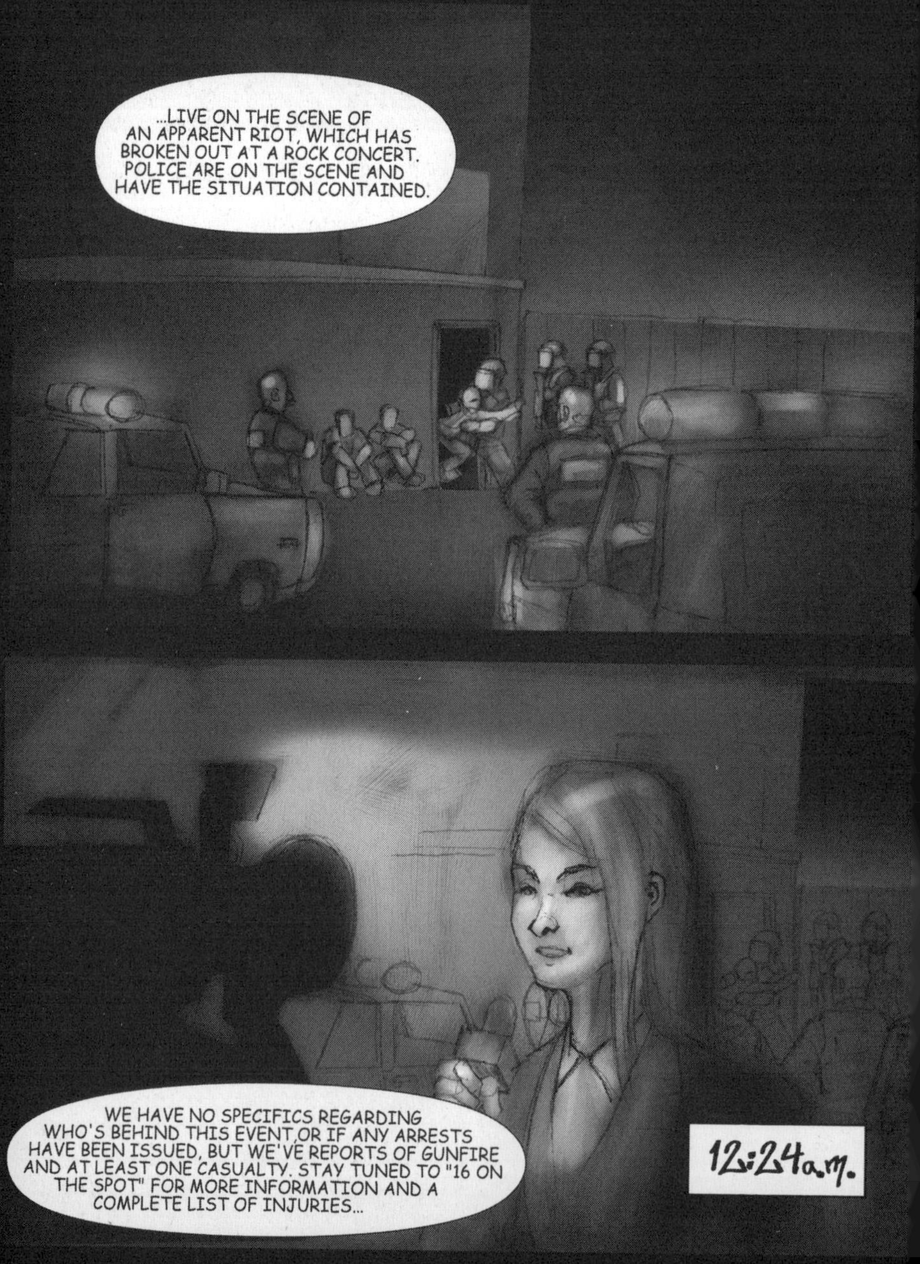
...LIVE ON THE SCENE OF AN APPARENT RIOT, WHICH HAS BROKEN OUT AT A ROCK CONCERT. POLICE ARE ON THE SCENE AND HAVE THE SITUATION CONTAINED.
WE HAVE NO SPECIFICS REGARDING WHO'S BEHIND THIS EVENT,OR IF ANY ARRESTS HAVE BEEN ISSUED, BUT WE'VE REPORTS OF GUNFIRE AND AT LEAST ONE CASUALTY. STAY TUNED TO "16 ON THE SPOT" FOR MORE INFORMATION AND A COMPLETE LIST OF INJURIES...
12:24a.m.

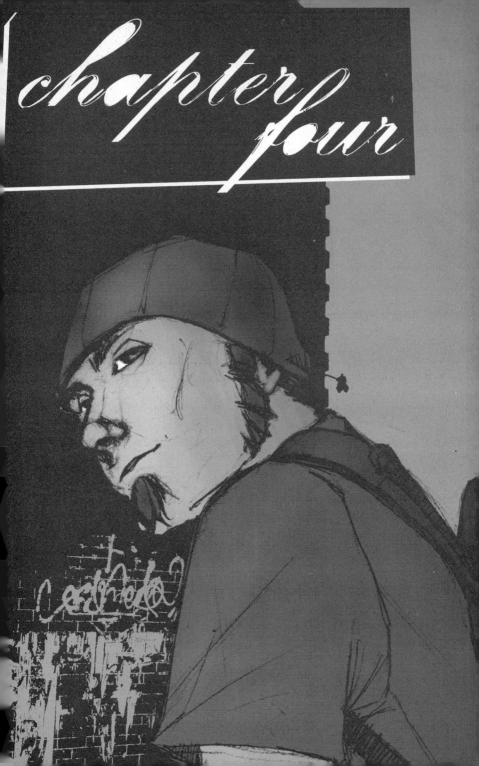

chapter four

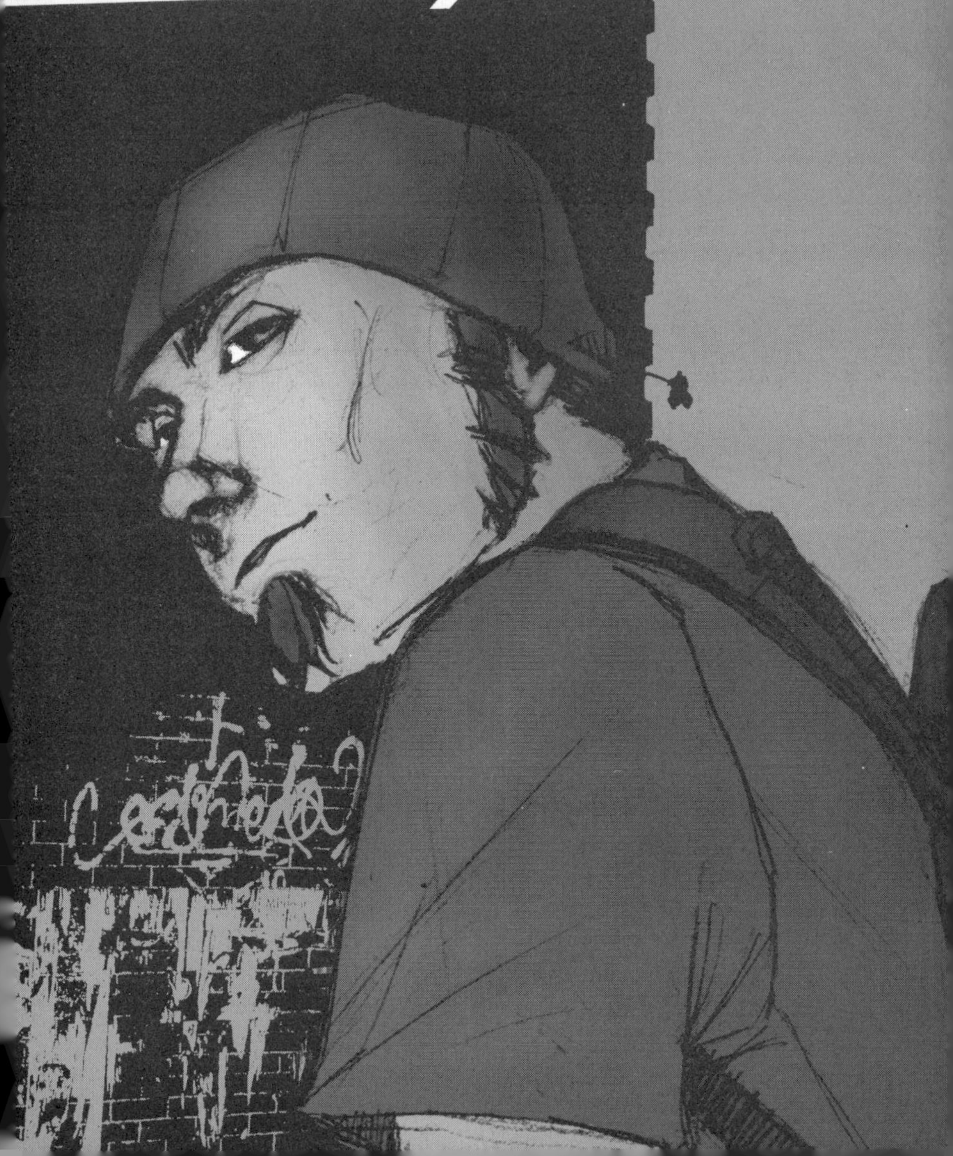

it is people who make kisses...

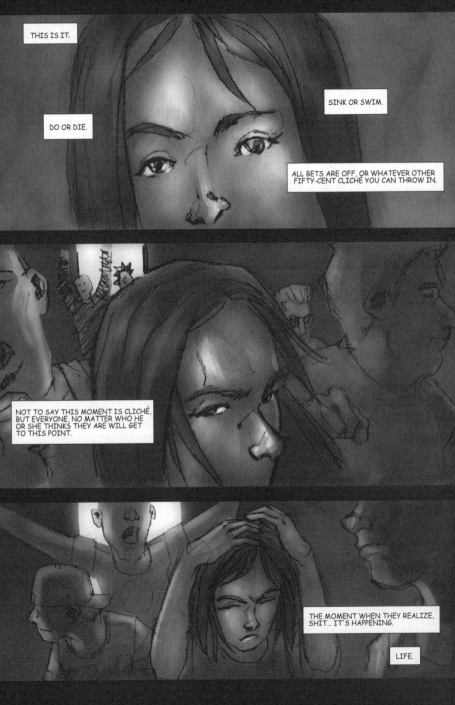

THIS IS IT.

SINK OR SWIM.

DO OR DIE.

ALL BETS ARE OFF, OR WHATEVER OTHER
FIFTY-CENT CLICHÉ YOU CAN THROW IN.

NOT TO SAY THIS MOMENT IS CLICHÉ,
BUT EVERYONE, NO MATTER WHO HE
OR SHE THINKS THEY ARE WILL GET
TO THIS POINT.

THE MOMENT WHEN THEY REALIZE,
SHIT... IT'S HAPPENING.

LIFE.

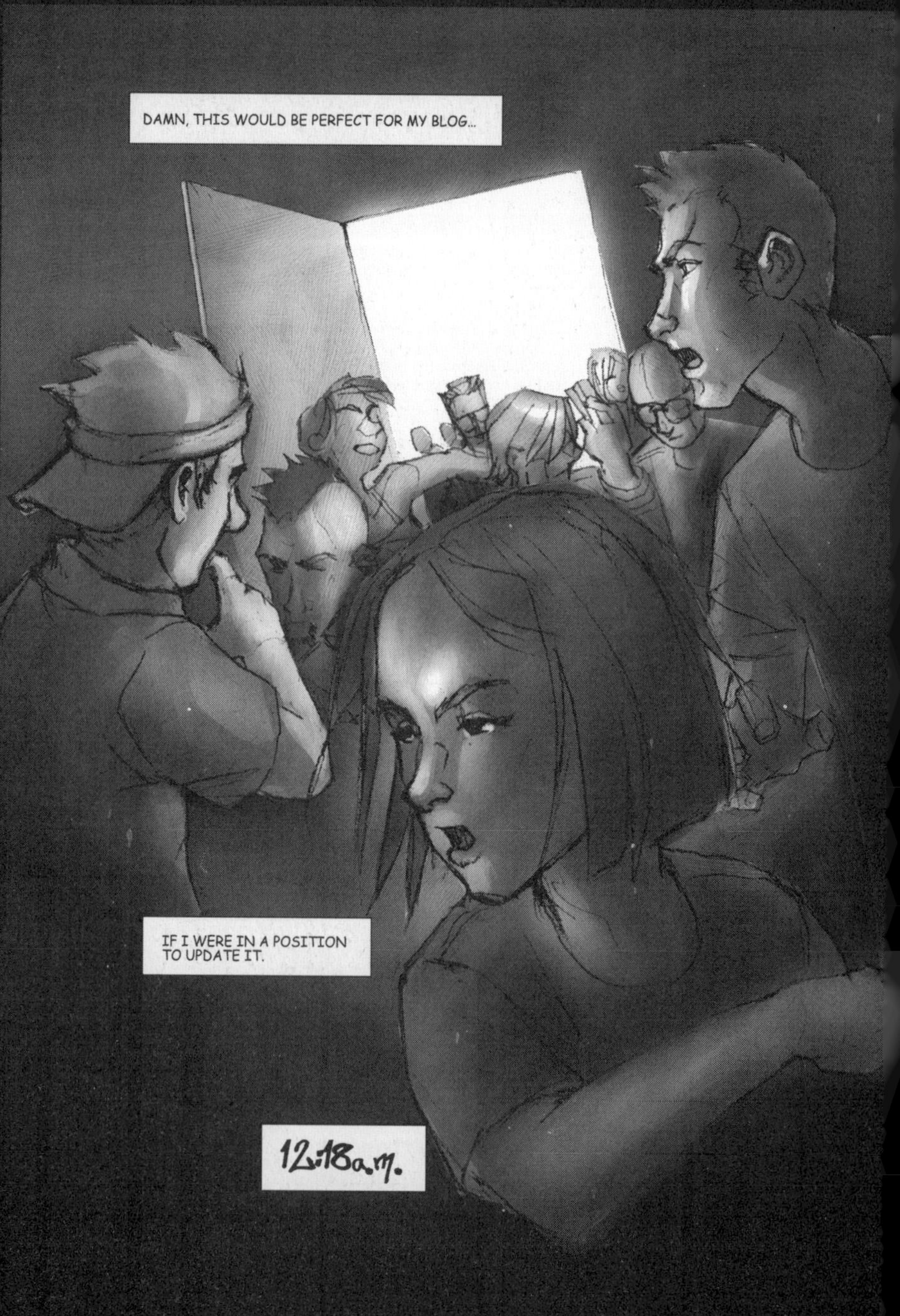
DAMN, THIS WOULD BE PERFECT FOR MY BLOG...
IF I WERE IN A POSITION TO UPDATE IT.
12:18a.m.

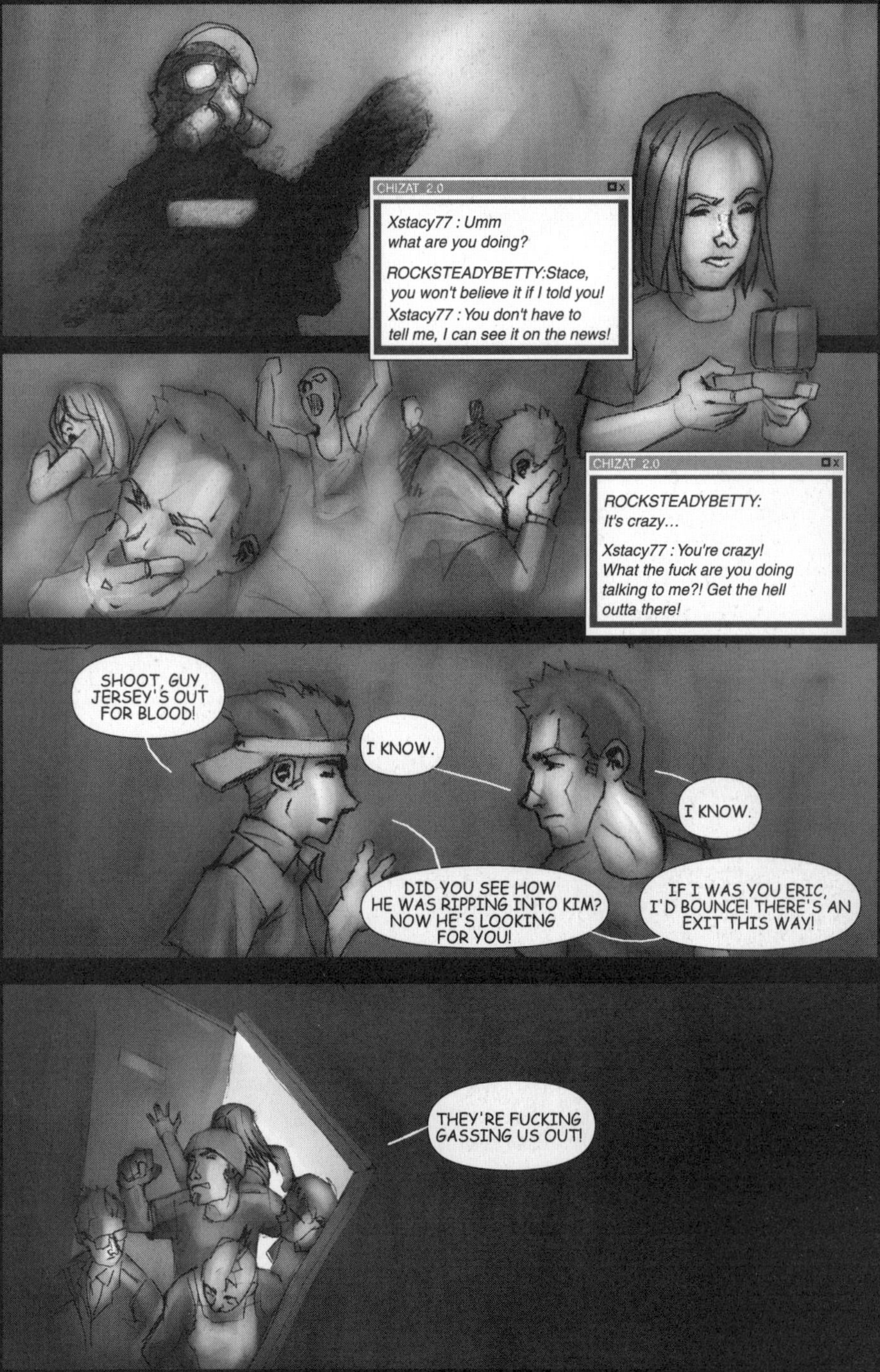
CHIZAT 2.0
Xstacy77 : Umm what are you doing?
ROCKSTEADYBETTY:Stace, you won't believe it if I told you!
Xstacy77 : You don't have to tell me, I can see it on the news!
CHIZAT 2.0
ROCKSTEADYBETTY: It's crazy…
Xstacy77 : You're crazy! What the fuck are you doing talking to me?! Get the hell outta there!
SHOOT, GUY, JERSEY'S OUT FOR BLOOD!
I KNOW.
I KNOW.
DID YOU SEE HOW HE WAS RIPPING INTO KIM? NOW HE'S LOOKING FOR YOU!
IF I WAS YOU ERIC, I'D BOUNCE! THERE'S AN EXIT THIS WAY!
THEY'RE FUCKING GASSING US OUT!

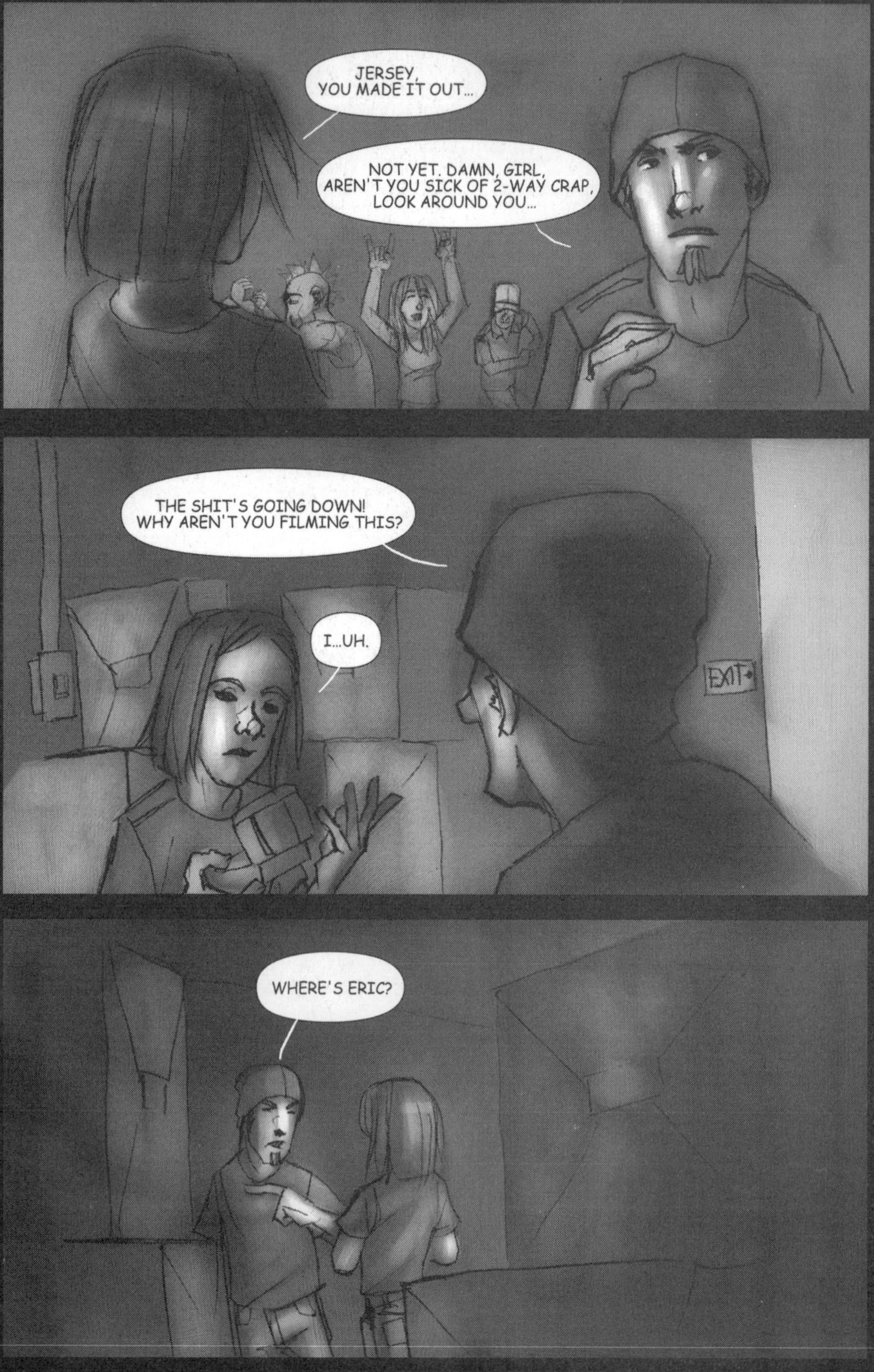
JERSEY, YOU MADE IT OUT...
NOT YET. DAMN, GIRL, AREN'T YOU SICK OF 2-WAY CRAP, LOOK AROUND YOU...
THE SHIT'S GOING DOWN! WHY AREN'T YOU FILMING THIS?
I...UH.
EXIT
WHERE'S ERIC?

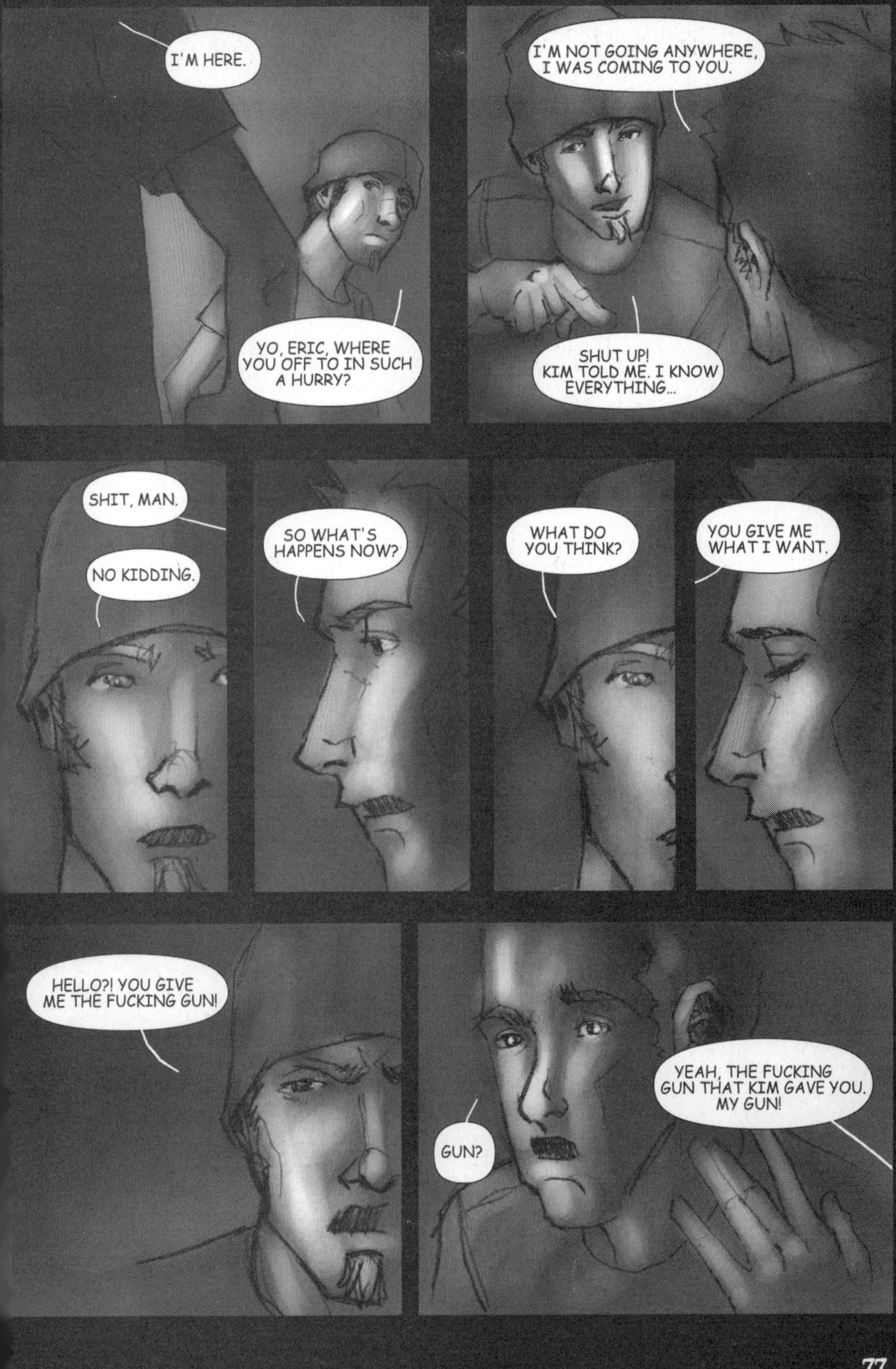
I'M HERE.
YO, ERIC, WHERE YOU OFF TO IN SUCH A HURRY?
I'M NOT GOING ANYWHERE, I WAS COMING TO YOU.
SHUT UP! KIM TOLD ME. I KNOW EVERYTHING...
SHIT, MAN.
NO KIDDING.
SO WHAT'S HAPPENS NOW?
WHAT DO YOU THINK?
YOU GIVE ME WHAT I WANT.
HELLO?! YOU GIVE ME THE FUCKING GUN!
GUN?
YEAH, THE FUCKING GUN THAT KIM GAVE YOU. MY GUN!

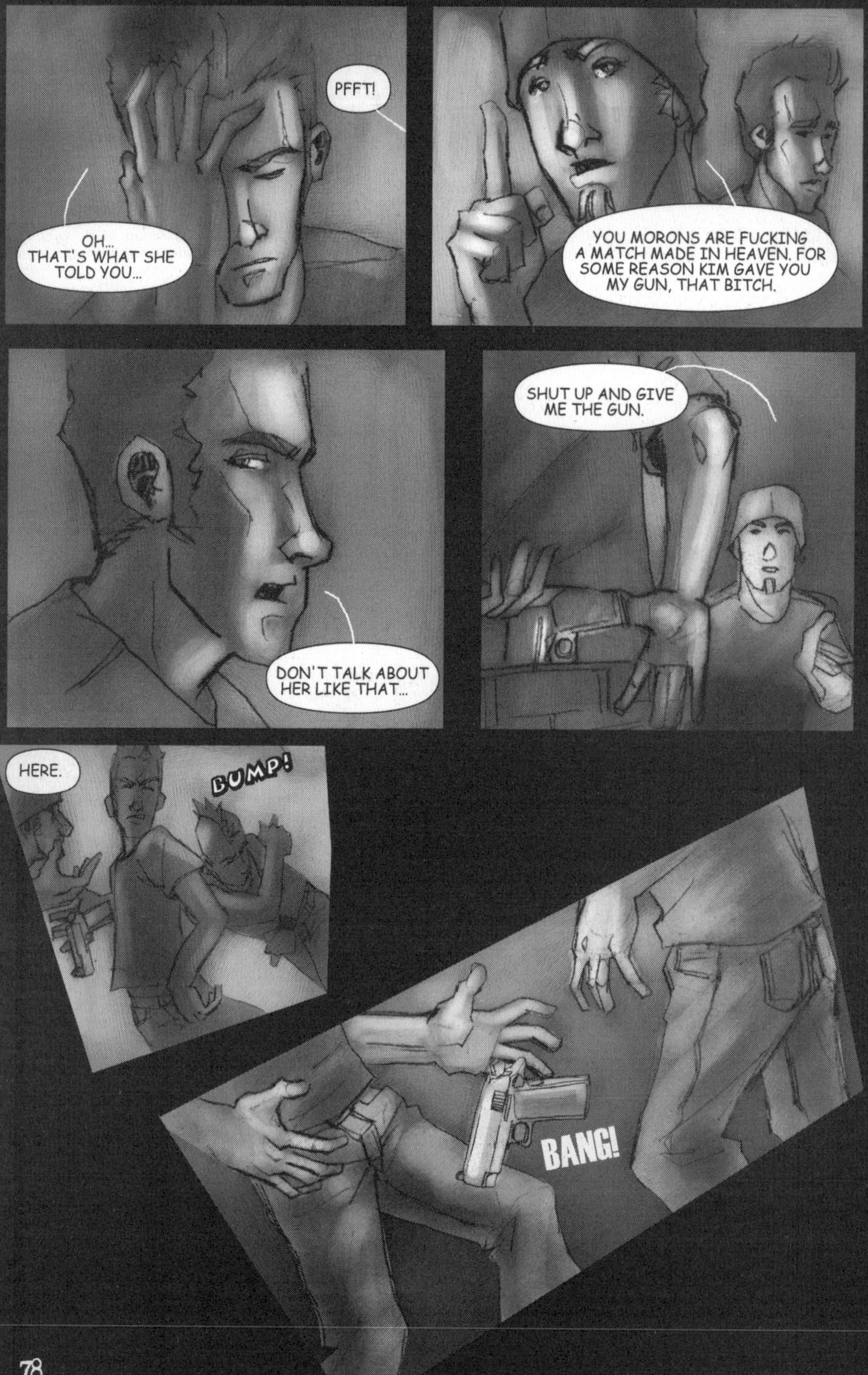
PFFT!
OH... THAT'S WHAT SHE TOLD YOU...
YOU MORONS ARE FUCKING A MATCH MADE IN HEAVEN. FOR SOME REASON KIM GAVE YOU MY GUN, THAT BITCH.
DON'T TALK ABOUT HER LIKE THAT...
SHUT UP AND GIVE ME THE GUN.
HERE.
BUMP!
BANG!

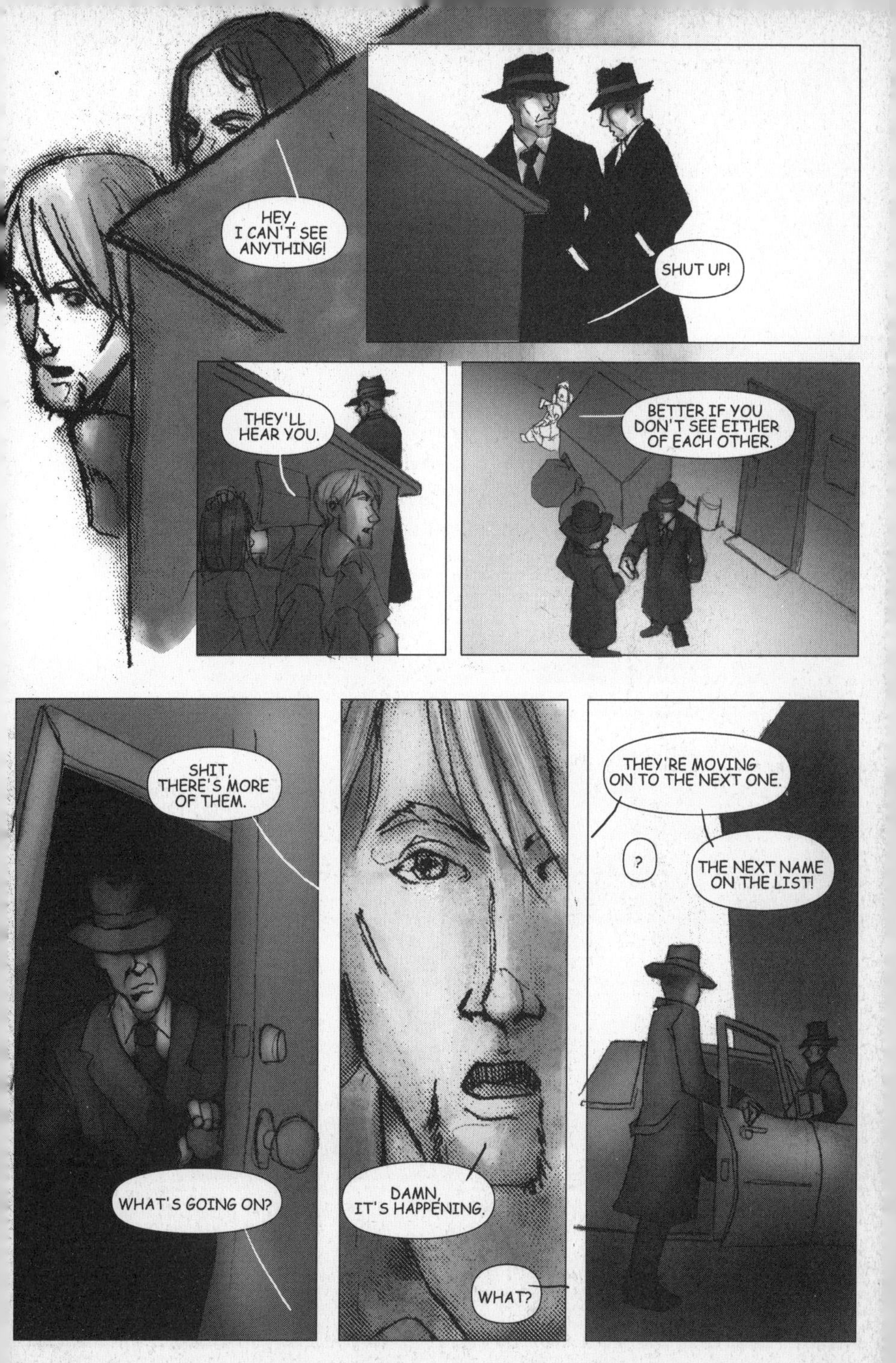
HEY, I CAN'T SEE ANYTHING!
SHUT UP!
THEY'LL HEAR YOU.
BETTER IF YOU DON'T SEE EITHER OF EACH OTHER.
SHIT, THERE'S MORE OF THEM.
WHAT'S GOING ON?
DAMN, IT'S HAPPENING.
WHAT?
THEY'RE MOVING ON TO THE NEXT ONE.
?
THE NEXT NAME ON THE LIST!

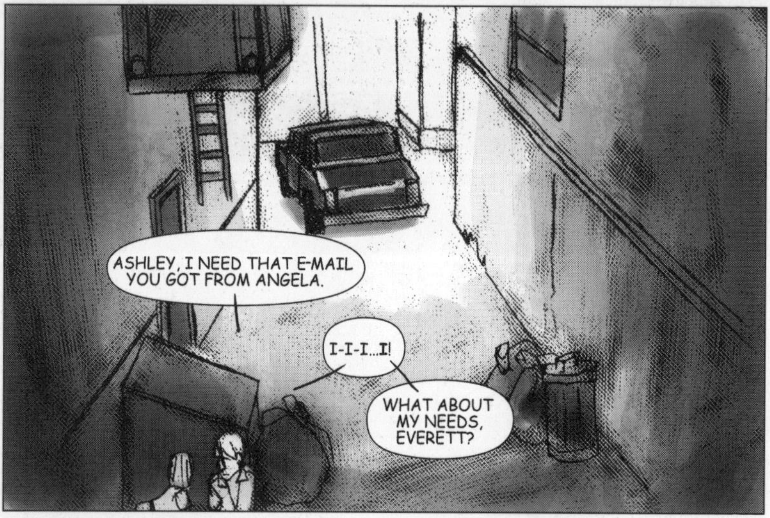
ASHLEY, I NEED THAT E-MAIL YOU GOT FROM ANGELA.
I-I-I...I!
WHAT ABOUT MY NEEDS, EVERETT?

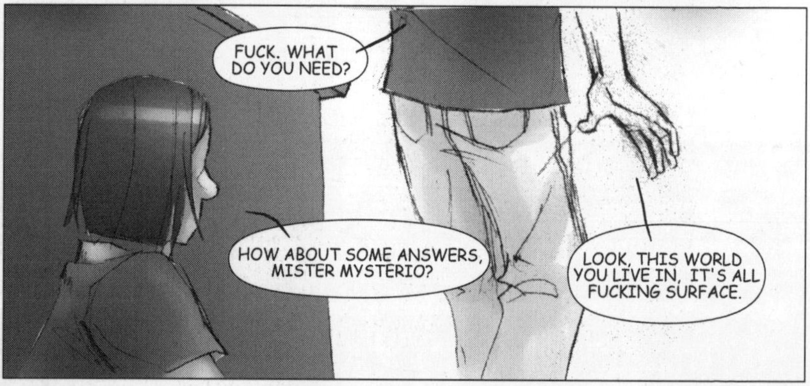
FUCK. WHAT DO YOU NEED?
HOW ABOUT SOME ANSWERS, MISTER MYSTERIO?
LOOK, THIS WORLD YOU LIVE IN, IT'S ALL FUCKING SURFACE.

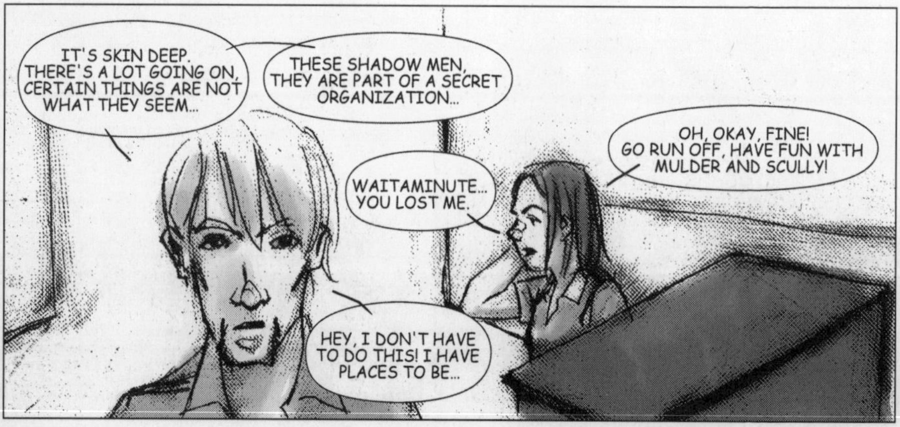
IT'S SKIN DEEP. THERE'S A LOT GOING ON, CERTAIN THINGS ARE NOT WHAT THEY SEEM...
THESE SHADOW MEN, THEY ARE PART OF A SECRET ORGANIZATION...
OH, OKAY, FINE! GO RUN OFF, HAVE FUN WITH MULDER AND SCULLY!
WAITAMINUTE... YOU LOST ME.
HEY, I DON'T HAVE TO DO THIS! I HAVE PLACES TO BE...

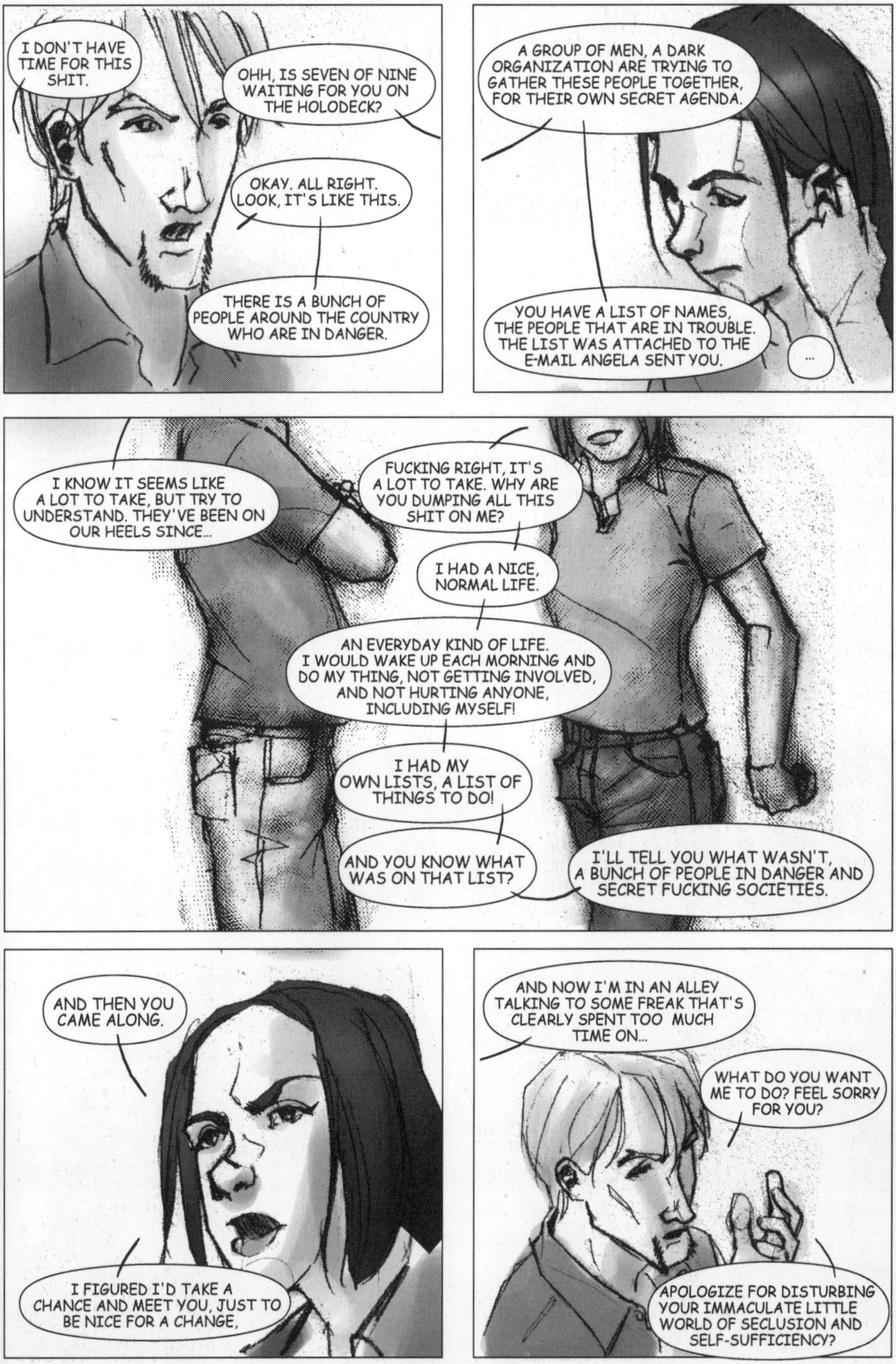
I DON'T HAVE TIME FOR THIS SHIT.
OHH, IS SEVEN OF NINE WAITING FOR YOU ON THE HOLODECK?
OKAY. ALL RIGHT. LOOK, IT'S LIKE THIS.
THERE IS A BUNCH OF PEOPLE AROUND THE COUNTRY WHO ARE IN DANGER.
A GROUP OF MEN, A DARK ORGANIZATION ARE TRYING TO GATHER THESE PEOPLE TOGETHER, FOR THEIR OWN SECRET AGENDA.
YOU HAVE A LIST OF NAMES, THE PEOPLE THAT ARE IN TROUBLE. THE LIST WAS ATTACHED TO THE E-MAIL ANGELA SENT YOU.
...
I KNOW IT SEEMS LIKE A LOT TO TAKE, BUT TRY TO UNDERSTAND. THEY'VE BEEN ON OUR HEELS SINCE...
FUCKING RIGHT, IT'S A LOT TO TAKE. WHY ARE YOU DUMPING ALL THIS SHIT ON ME?
I HAD A NICE, NORMAL LIFE.
AN EVERYDAY KIND OF LIFE. I WOULD WAKE UP EACH MORNING AND DO MY THING, NOT GETTING INVOLVED, AND NOT HURTING ANYONE, INCLUDING MYSELF!
I HAD MY OWN LISTS, A LIST OF THINGS TO DO!
AND YOU KNOW WHAT WAS ON THAT LIST?
I'LL TELL YOU WHAT WASN'T, A BUNCH OF PEOPLE IN DANGER AND SECRET FUCKING SOCIETIES.
AND THEN YOU CAME ALONG.
I FIGURED I'D TAKE A CHANCE AND MEET YOU, JUST TO BE NICE FOR A CHANGE,
AND NOW I'M IN AN ALLEY TALKING TO SOME FREAK THAT'S CLEARLY SPENT TOO MUCH TIME ON...
WHAT DO YOU WANT ME TO DO? FEEL SORRY FOR YOU?
APOLOGIZE FOR DISTURBING YOUR IMMACULATE LITTLE WORLD OF SECLUSION AND SELF-SUFFICIENCY?

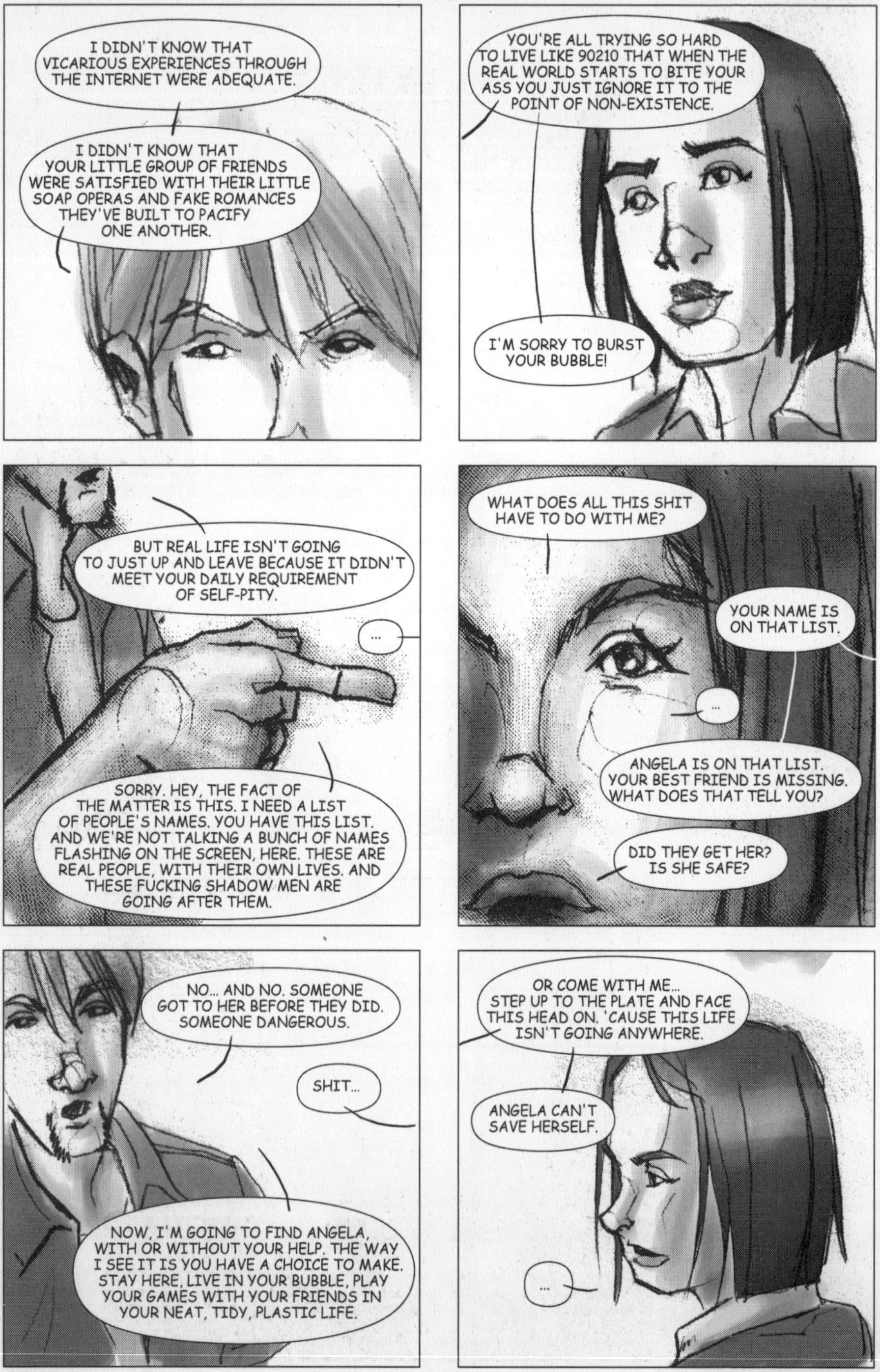
I DIDN'T KNOW THAT VICARIOUS EXPERIENCES THROUGH THE INTERNET WERE ADEQUATE.
I DIDN'T KNOW THAT YOUR LITTLE GROUP OF FRIENDS WERE SATISFIED WITH THEIR LITTLE SOAP OPERAS AND FAKE ROMANCES THEY'VE BUILT TO PACIFY ONE ANOTHER.
YOU'RE ALL TRYING SO HARD TO LIVE LIKE 90210 THAT WHEN THE REAL WORLD STARTS TO BITE YOUR ASS YOU JUST IGNORE IT TO THE POINT OF NON-EXISTENCE.
I'M SORRY TO BURST YOUR BUBBLE!
BUT REAL LIFE ISN'T GOING TO JUST UP AND LEAVE BECAUSE IT DIDN'T MEET YOUR DAILY REQUIREMENT OF SELF-PITY.
...
SORRY. HEY, THE FACT OF THE MATTER IS THIS. I NEED A LIST OF PEOPLE'S NAMES. YOU HAVE THIS LIST. AND WE'RE NOT TALKING A BUNCH OF NAMES FLASHING ON THE SCREEN, HERE. THESE ARE REAL PEOPLE, WITH THEIR OWN LIVES. AND THESE FUCKING SHADOW MEN ARE GOING AFTER THEM.
WHAT DOES ALL THIS SHIT HAVE TO DO WITH ME?
YOUR NAME IS ON THAT LIST.
...
ANGELA IS ON THAT LIST. YOUR BEST FRIEND IS MISSING. WHAT DOES THAT TELL YOU?
DID THEY GET HER? IS SHE SAFE?
NO... AND NO. SOMEONE GOT TO HER BEFORE THEY DID. SOMEONE DANGEROUS.
SHIT...
NOW, I'M GOING TO FIND ANGELA, WITH OR WITHOUT YOUR HELP. THE WAY I SEE IT IS YOU HAVE A CHOICE TO MAKE. STAY HERE, LIVE IN YOUR BUBBLE, PLAY YOUR GAMES WITH YOUR FRIENDS IN YOUR NEAT, TIDY, PLASTIC LIFE.
OR COME WITH ME... STEP UP TO THE PLATE AND FACE THIS HEAD ON. 'CAUSE THIS LIFE ISN'T GOING ANYWHERE.
ANGELA CAN'T SAVE HERSELF.
...

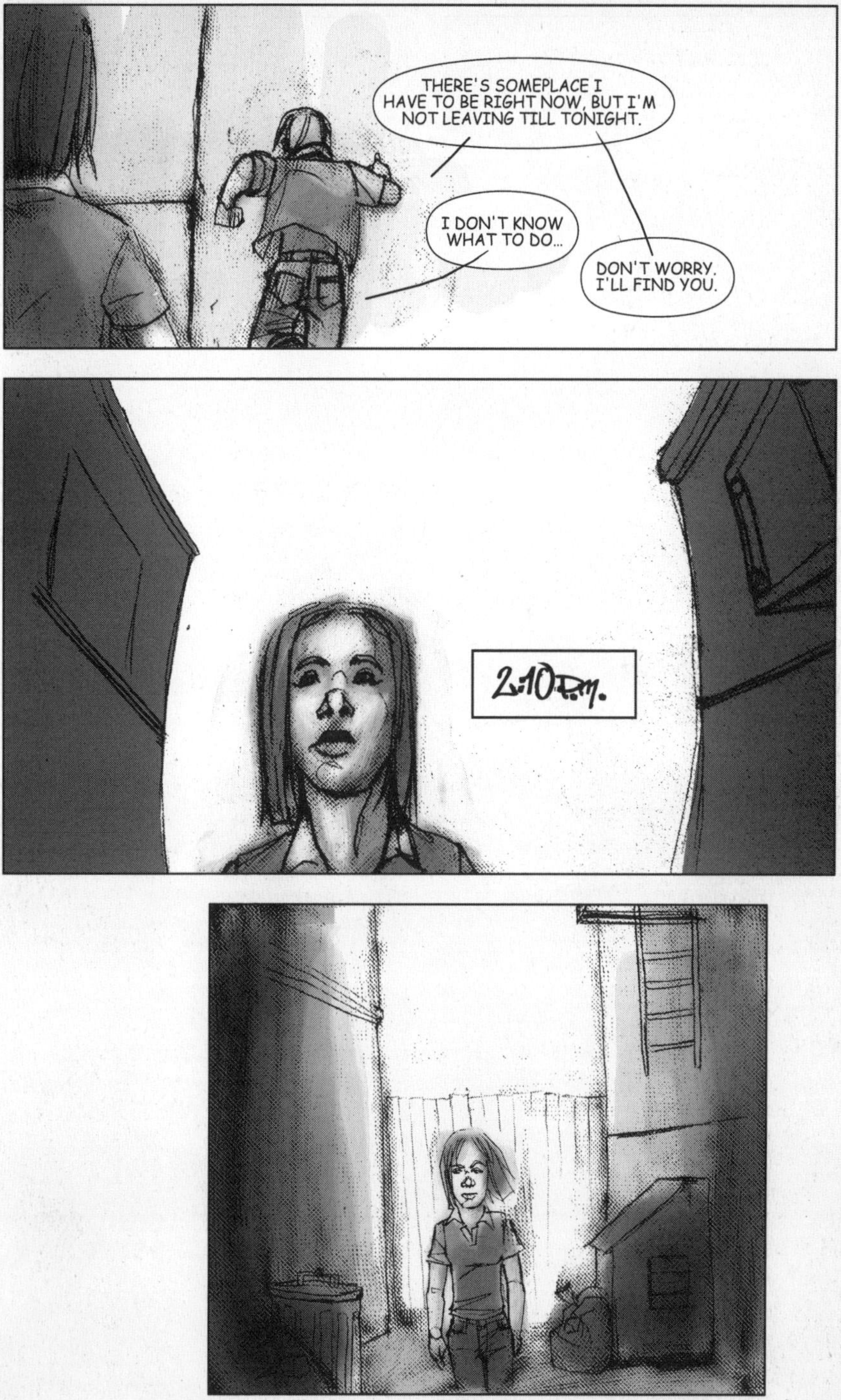
THERE'S SOMEPLACE I HAVE TO BE RIGHT NOW, BUT I'M NOT LEAVING TILL TONIGHT.
I DON'T KNOW WHAT TO DO...
DON'T WORRY. I'LL FIND YOU.
2:10 P.M.

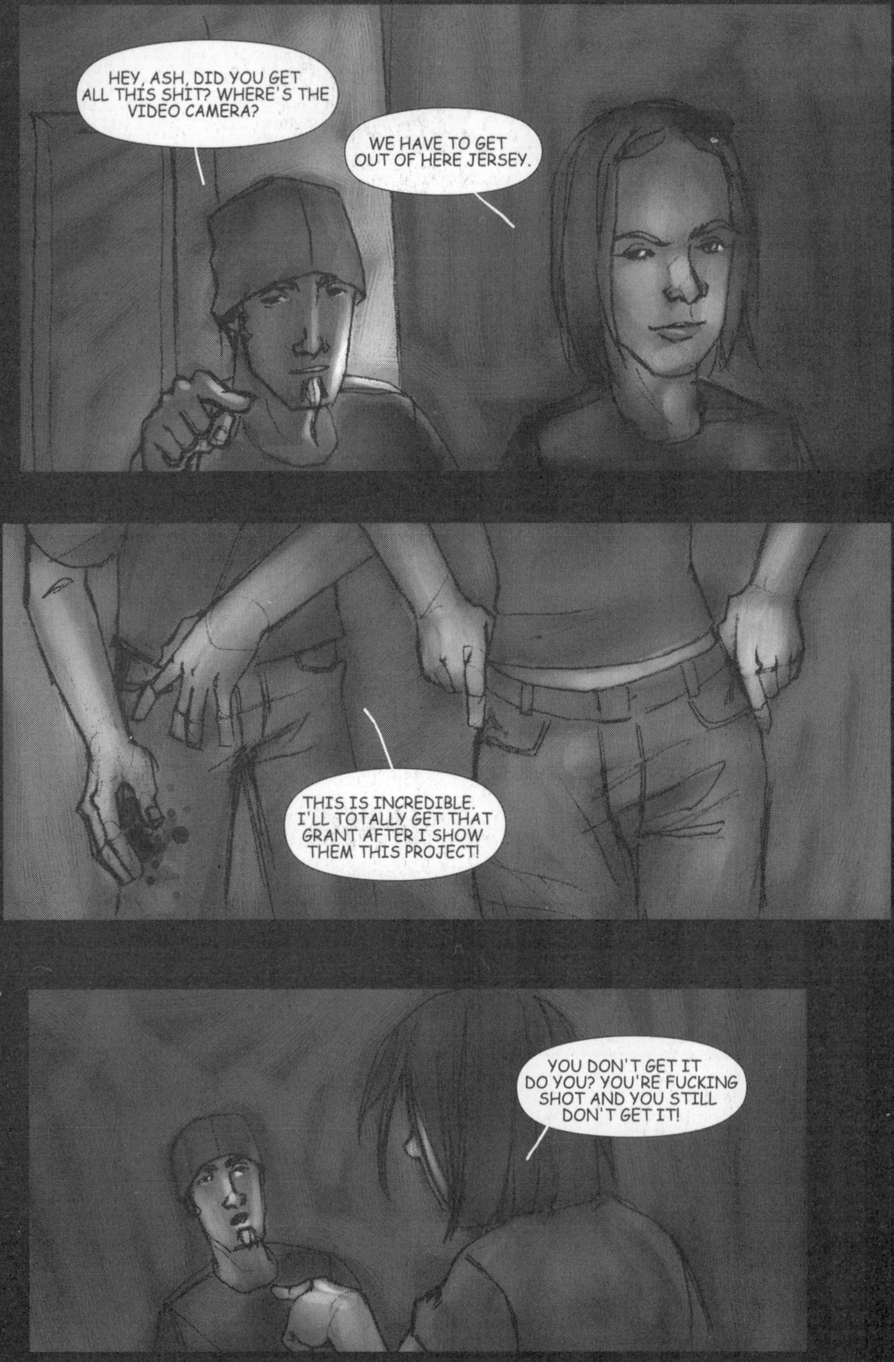
HEY, ASH, DID YOU GET ALL THIS SHIT? WHERE'S THE VIDEO CAMERA?
WE HAVE TO GET OUT OF HERE JERSEY.
THIS IS INCREDIBLE. I'LL TOTALLY GET THAT GRANT AFTER I SHOW THEM THIS PROJECT!
YOU DON'T GET IT DO YOU? YOU'RE FUCKING SHOT AND YOU STILL DON'T GET IT!

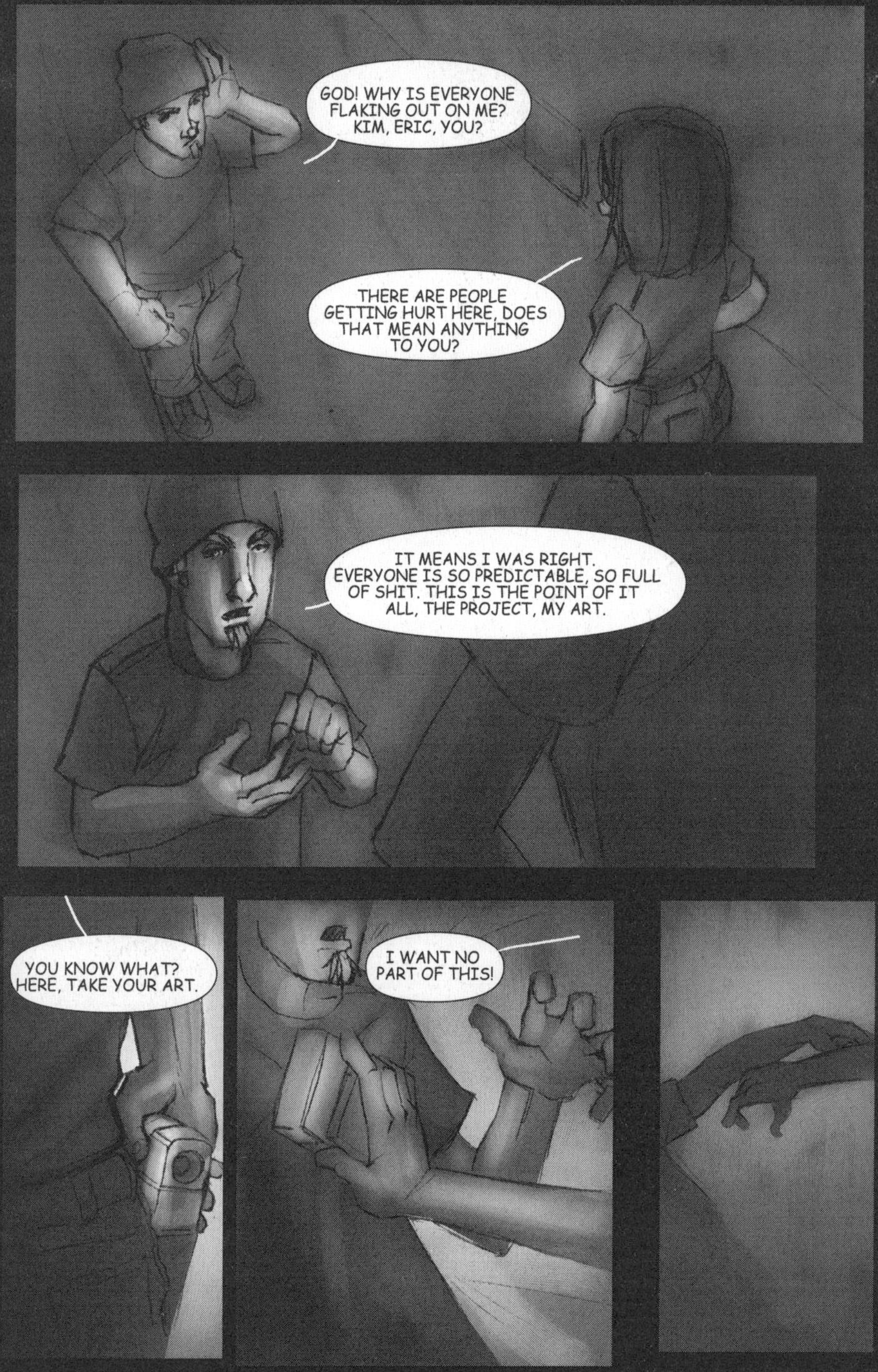
GOD! WHY IS EVERYONE FLAKING OUT ON ME? KIM, ERIC, YOU?
THERE ARE PEOPLE GETTING HURT HERE, DOES THAT MEAN ANYTHING TO YOU?
IT MEANS I WAS RIGHT. EVERYONE IS SO PREDICTABLE, SO FULL OF SHIT. THIS IS THE POINT OF IT ALL, THE PROJECT, MY ART.
YOU KNOW WHAT? HERE, TAKE YOUR ART.
I WANT NO PART OF THIS!

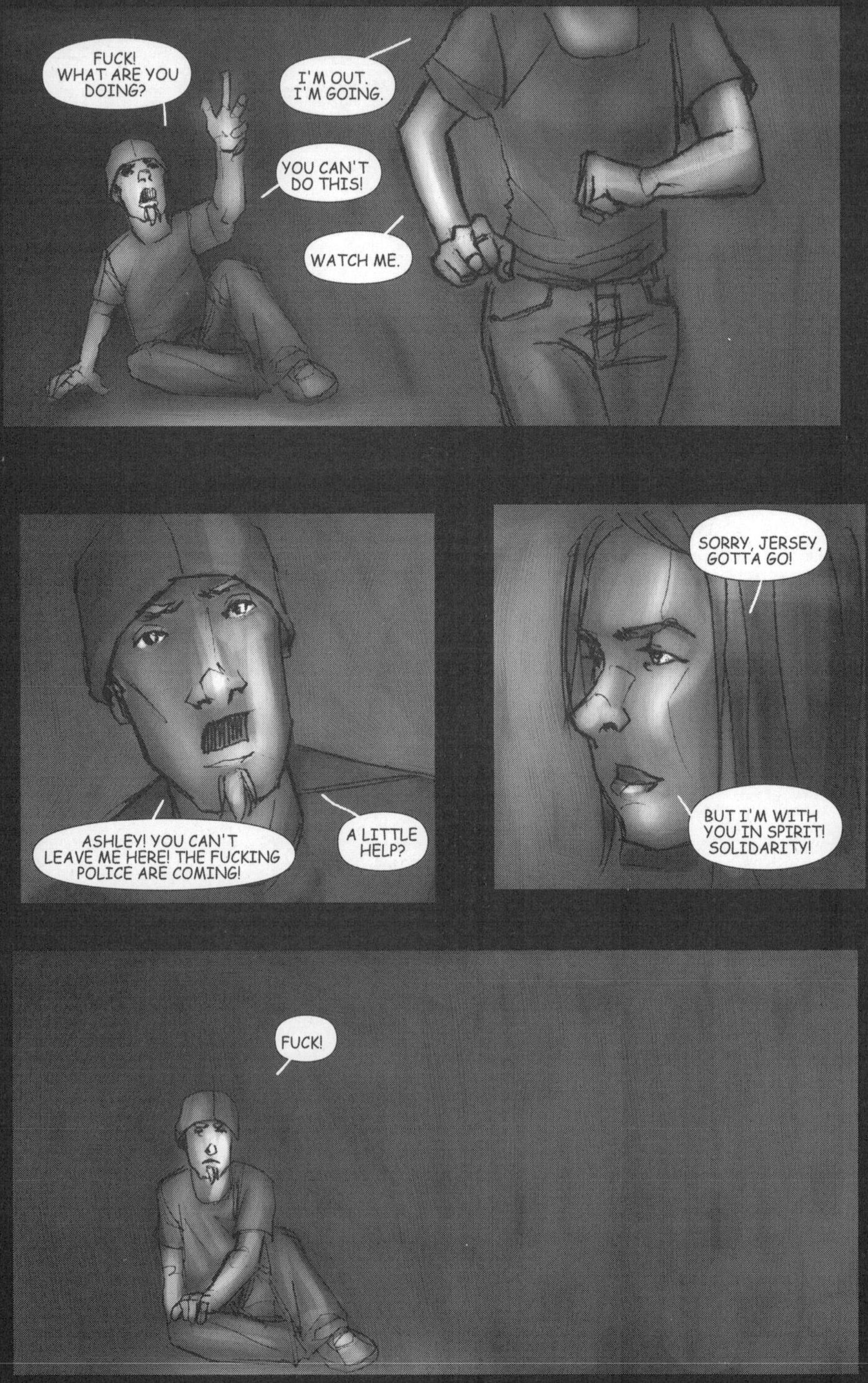
FUCK! WHAT ARE YOU DOING?
I'M OUT. I'M GOING.
YOU CAN'T DO THIS!
WATCH ME.
ASHLEY! YOU CAN'T LEAVE ME HERE! THE FUCKING POLICE ARE COMING!
A LITTLE HELP?
SORRY, JERSEY, GOTTA GO!
BUT I'M WITH YOU IN SPIRIT! SOLIDARITY!
FUCK!

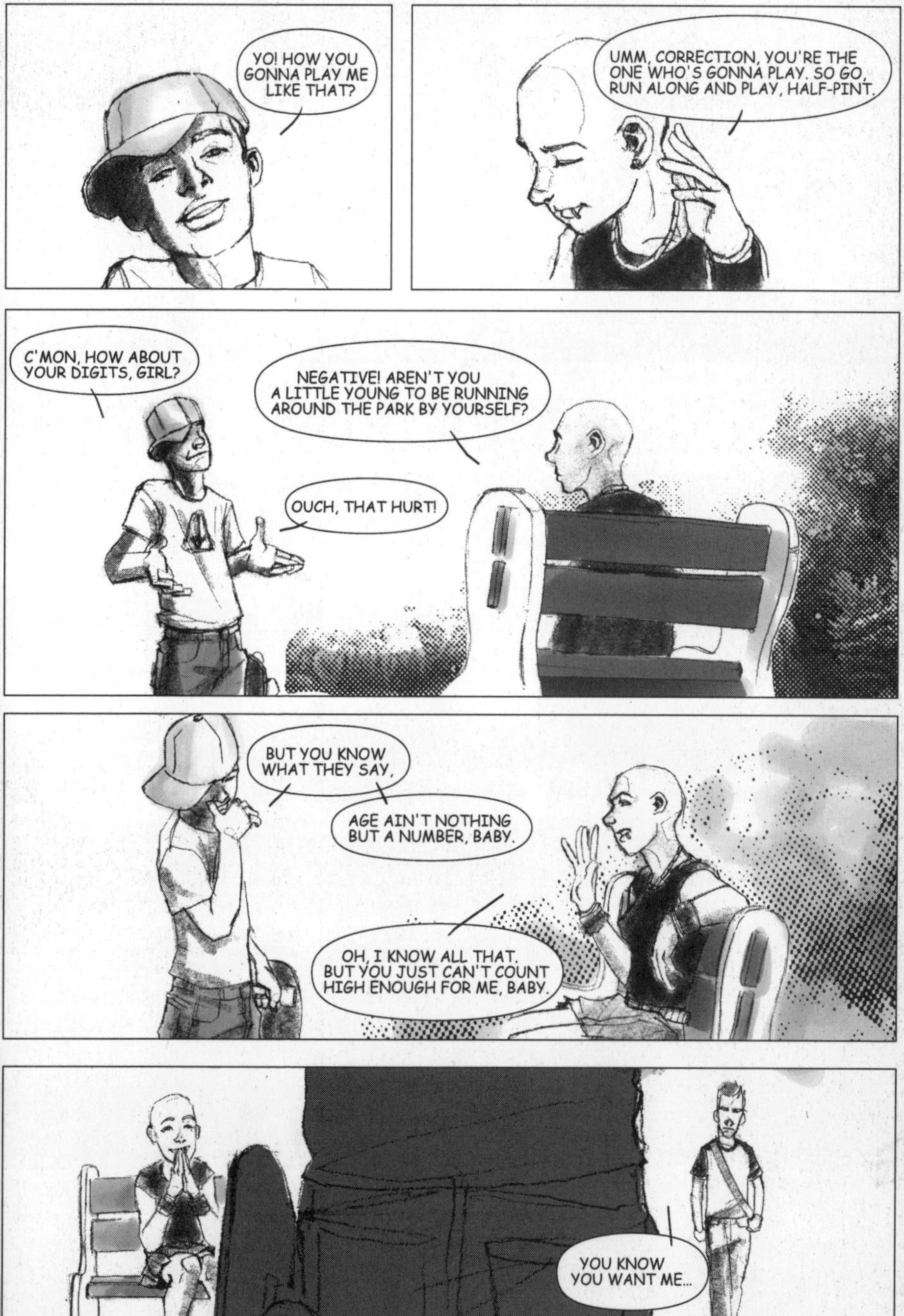
YO! HOW YOU GONNA PLAY ME LIKE THAT?
UMM, CORRECTION, YOU'RE THE ONE WHO'S GONNA PLAY. SO GO, RUN ALONG AND PLAY, HALF-PINT.
C'MON, HOW ABOUT YOUR DIGITS, GIRL?
NEGATIVE! AREN'T YOU A LITTLE YOUNG TO BE RUNNING AROUND THE PARK BY YOURSELF?
OUCH, THAT HURT!
BUT YOU KNOW WHAT THEY SAY,
AGE AIN'T NOTHING BUT A NUMBER, BABY.
OH, I KNOW ALL THAT. BUT YOU JUST CAN'T COUNT HIGH ENOUGH FOR ME, BABY.
YOU KNOW YOU WANT ME...

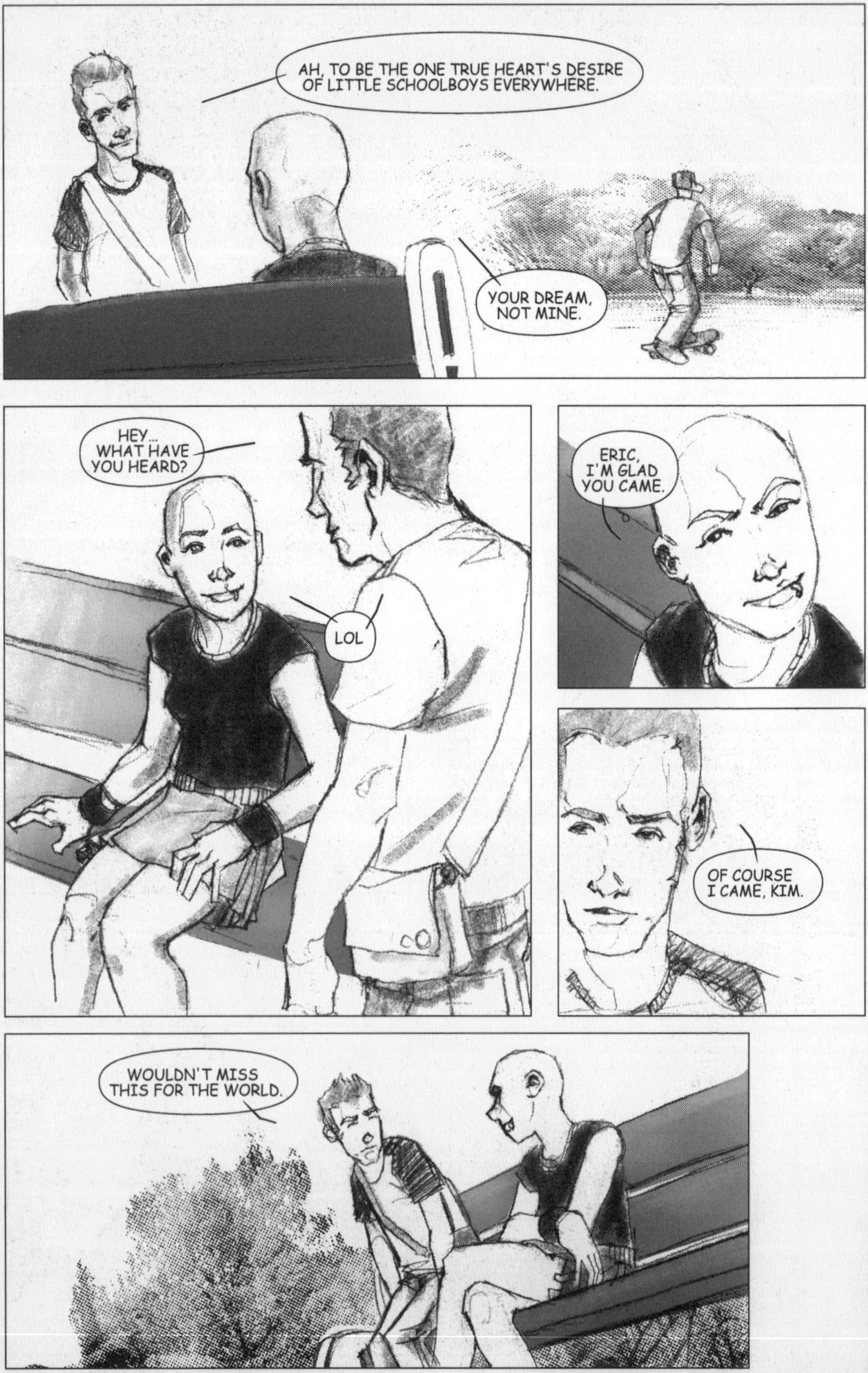
AH, TO BE THE ONE TRUE HEART'S DESIRE OF LITTLE SCHOOLBOYS EVERYWHERE.
YOUR DREAM, NOT MINE.
HEY... WHAT HAVE YOU HEARD?
LOL
ERIC, I'M GLAD YOU CAME.
OF COURSE I CAME, KIM.
WOULDN'T MISS THIS FOR THE WORLD.

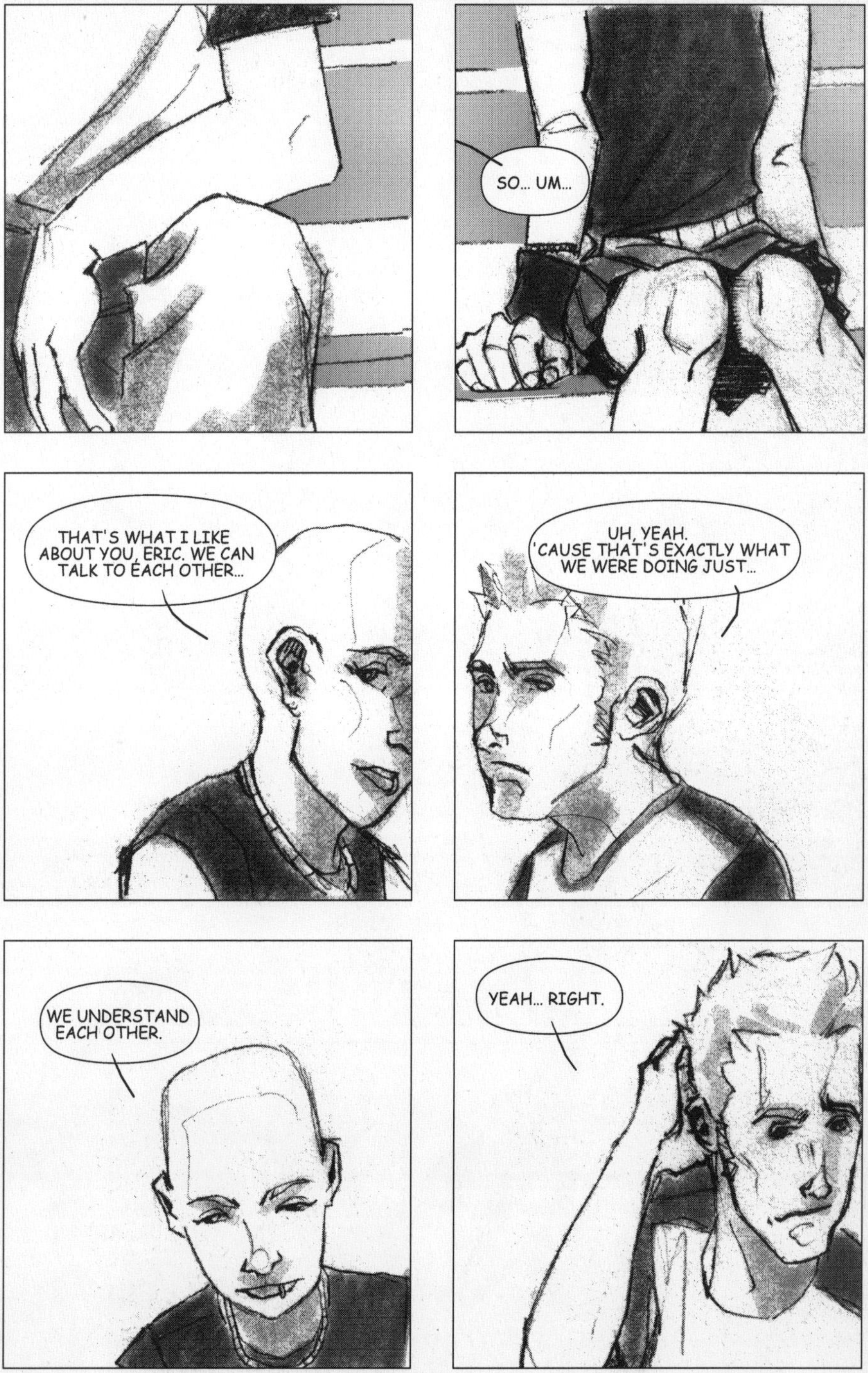
SO... UM...
THAT'S WHAT I LIKE ABOUT YOU, ERIC. WE CAN TALK TO EACH OTHER...
UH, YEAH. 'CAUSE THAT'S EXACTLY WHAT WE WERE DOING JUST...
WE UNDERSTAND EACH OTHER.
YEAH... RIGHT.

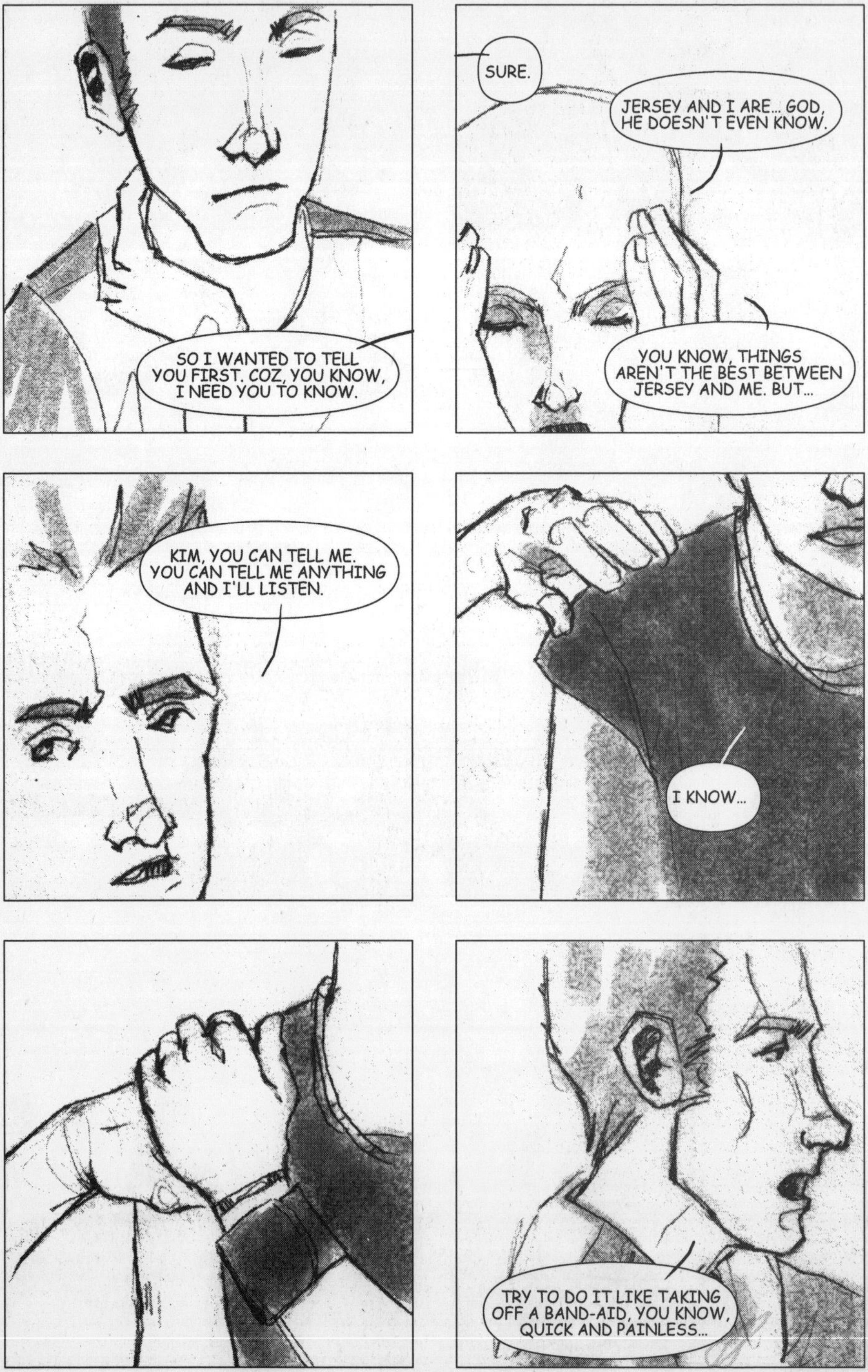
SO I WANTED TO TELL YOU FIRST. COZ, YOU KNOW, I NEED YOU TO KNOW.
SURE.
JERSEY AND I ARE... GOD, HE DOESN'T EVEN KNOW.
YOU KNOW, THINGS AREN'T THE BEST BETWEEN JERSEY AND ME. BUT...
KIM, YOU CAN TELL ME. YOU CAN TELL ME ANYTHING AND I'LL LISTEN.
I KNOW...
TRY TO DO IT LIKE TAKING OFF A BAND-AID, YOU KNOW, QUICK AND PAINLESS...

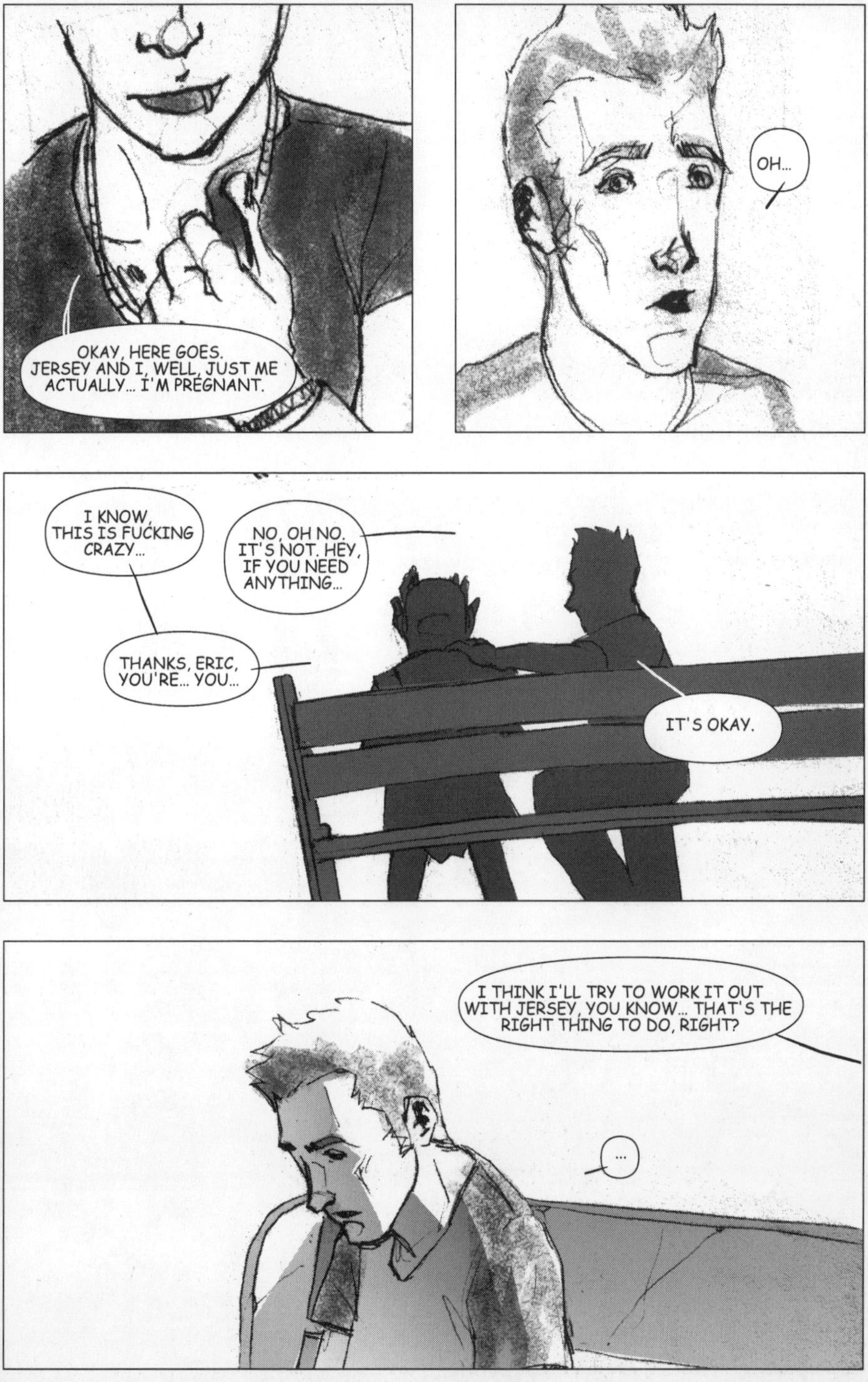
OKAY, HERE GOES. JERSEY AND I, WELL, JUST ME ACTUALLY... I'M PREGNANT.
OH...
I KNOW, THIS IS FUCKING CRAZY...
NO, OH NO. IT'S NOT. HEY, IF YOU NEED ANYTHING...
THANKS, ERIC, YOU'RE... YOU...
IT'S OKAY.
I THINK I'LL TRY TO WORK IT OUT WITH JERSEY, YOU KNOW... THAT'S THE RIGHT THING TO DO, RIGHT?
...

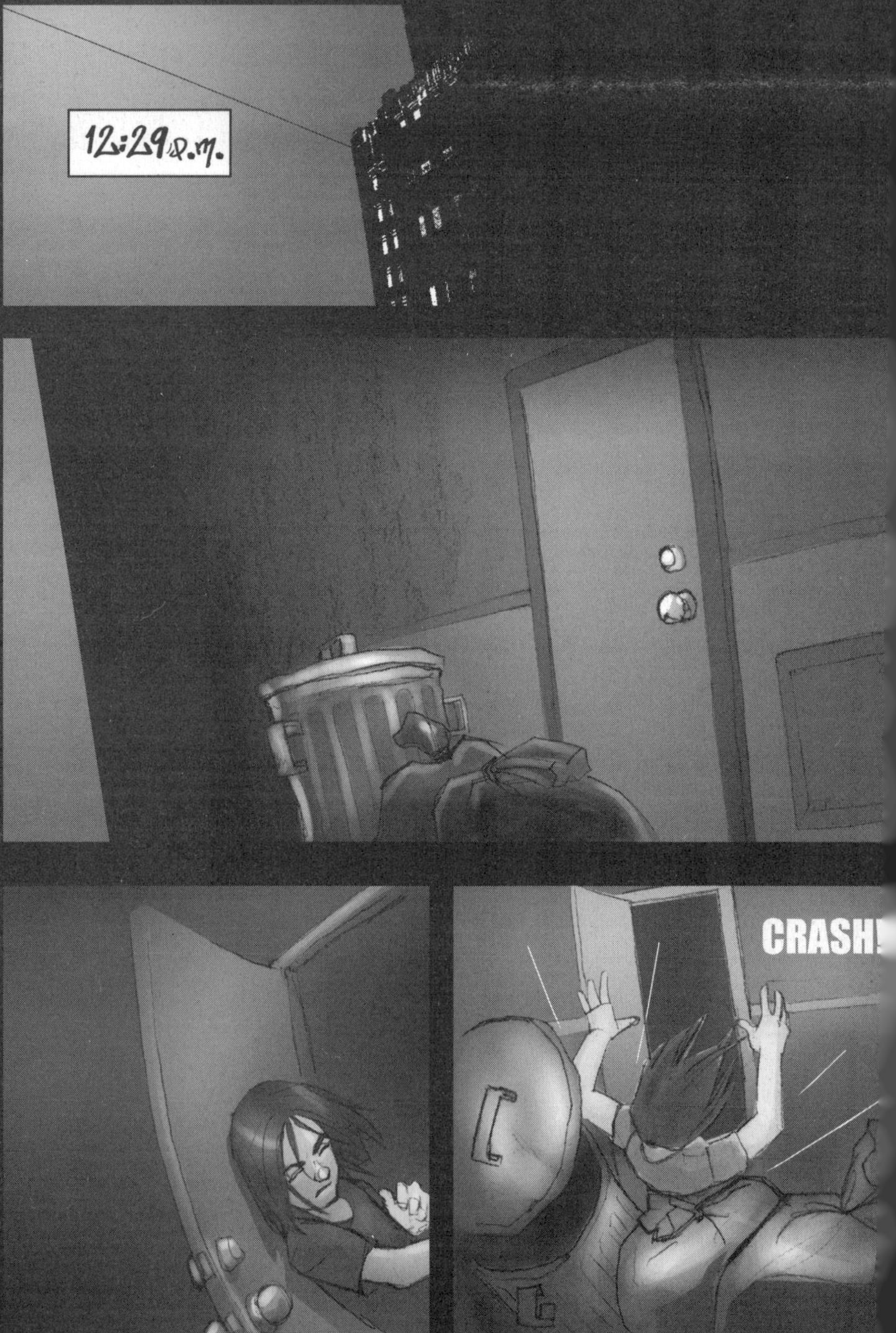
12:29 a.m.
CRASH!

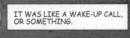
IT WAS LIKE A WAKE-UP CALL, OR SOMETHING.

IT'S LIKE AT THAT MOMENT, I REALIZED THAT I'VE PASSED THE BREAKING POINT, THAT I CAN NO LONGER SIT IDLE WHILE LIFE PASSES ME BY.

THE GUNSHOT, THAT SOUND.

IT WAS MORE LIKE LIFE WOULDN'T TAKE NO FOR AN ANSWER.

I THINK I'M STARTING TO FIGURE SHIT OUT NOW.

IT'S LIKE, I'M COMING OF AGE, OR WHATEVER.

IT WAS LIKE A TOTAL WONDER YEARS MOMENT.

CUE THE OLD-ASS '60S ROCK SOUNDTRACK.

OR WAS IT '70S?

93

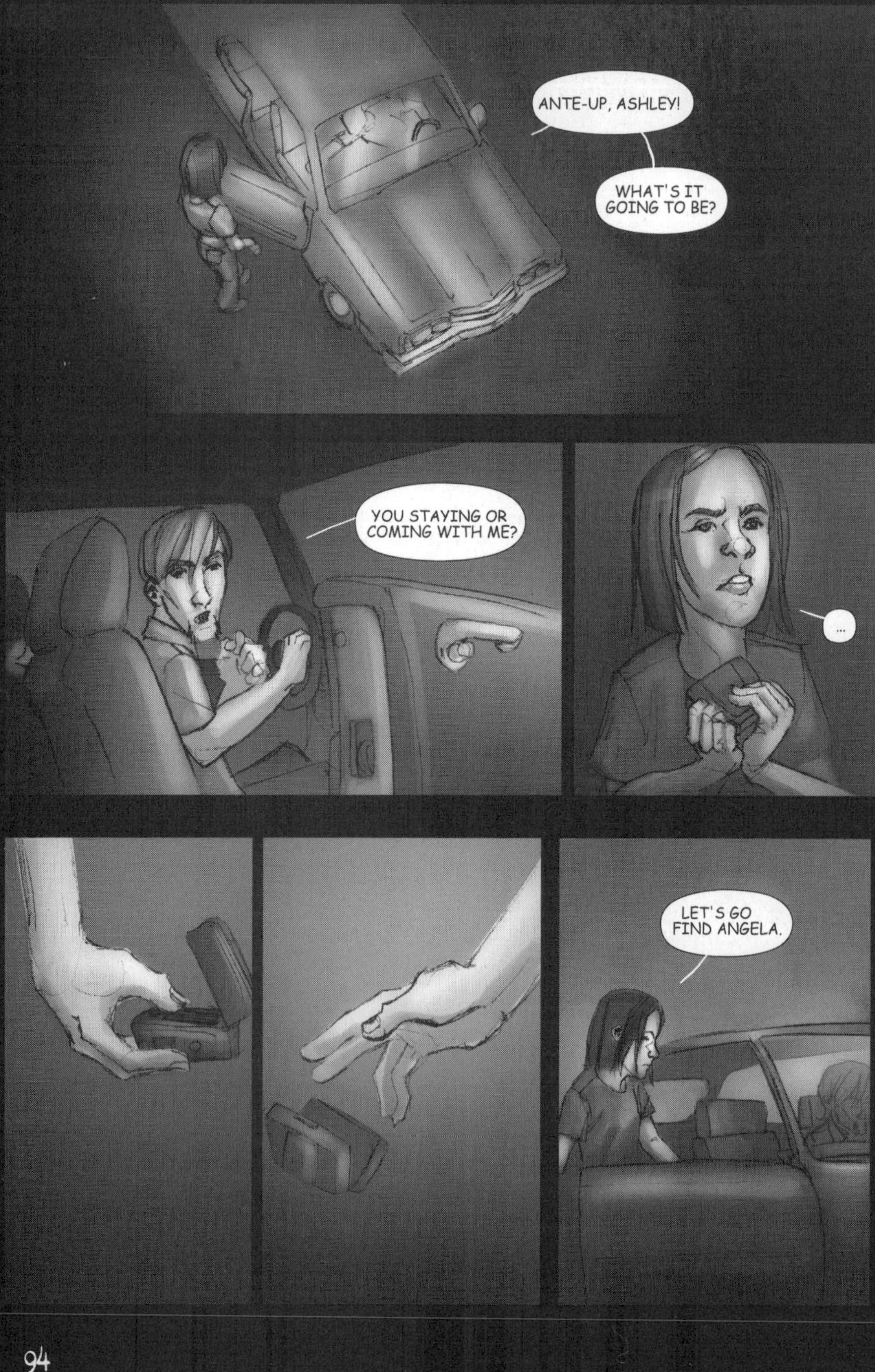
ANTE-UP, ASHLEY!
WHAT'S IT GOING TO BE?
YOU STAYING OR COMING WITH ME?
...
LET'S GO FIND ANGELA.

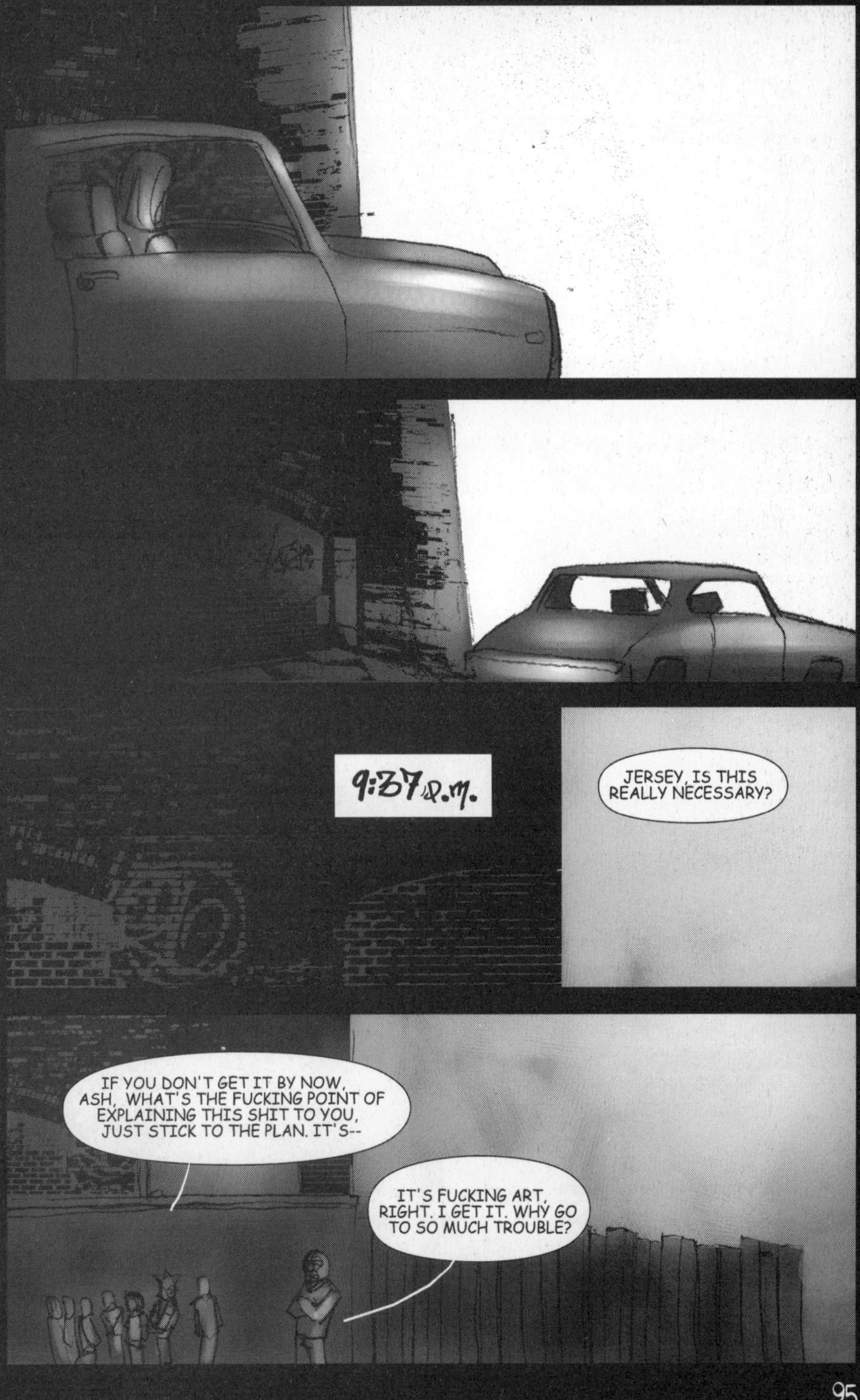
9:37 p.m.
JERSEY, IS THIS REALLY NECESSARY?
IF YOU DON'T GET IT BY NOW, ASH, WHAT'S THE FUCKING POINT OF EXPLAINING THIS SHIT TO YOU, JUST STICK TO THE PLAN. IT'S--
IT'S FUCKING ART, RIGHT. I GET IT. WHY GO TO SO MUCH TROUBLE?

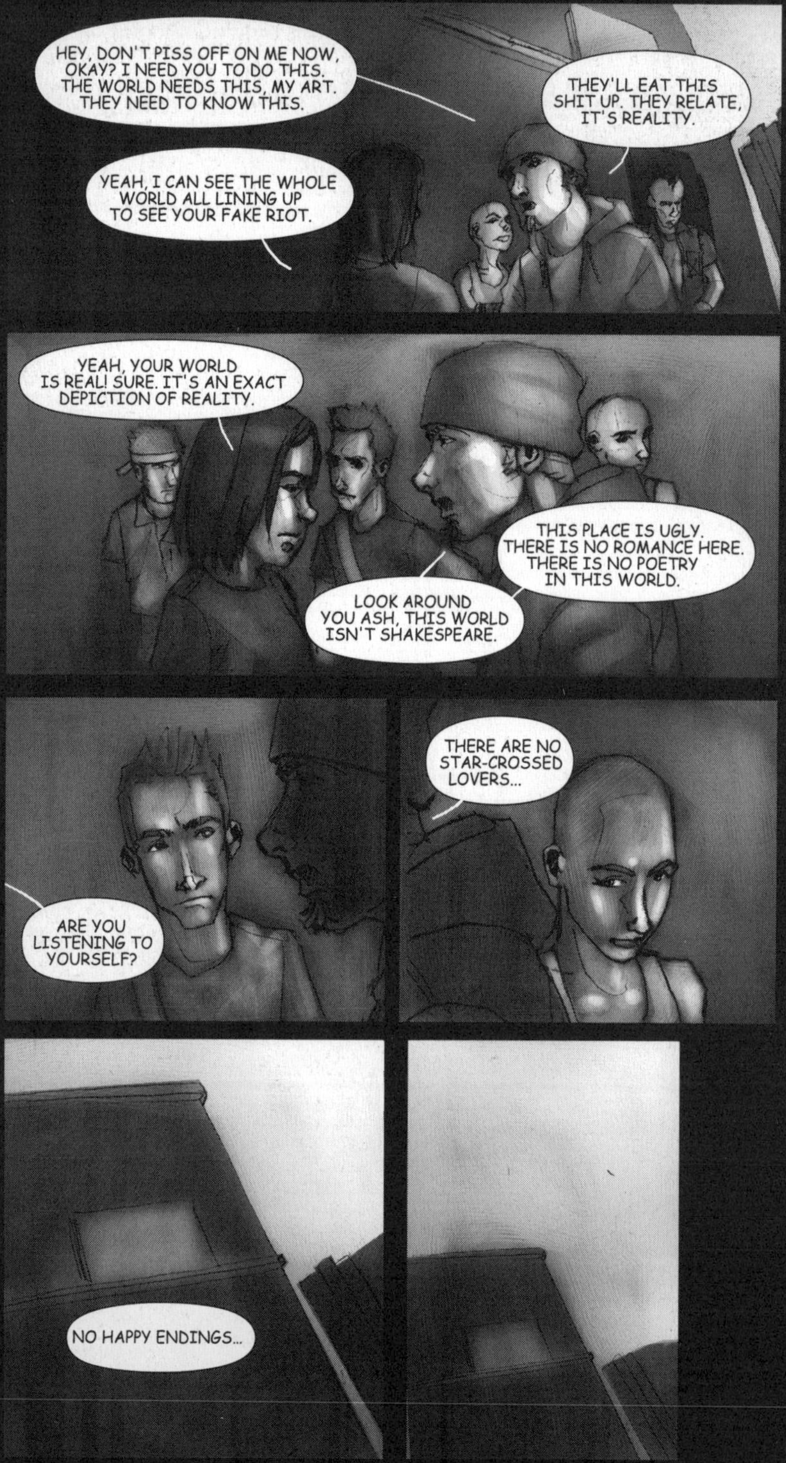
HEY, DON'T PISS OFF ON ME NOW, OKAY? I NEED YOU TO DO THIS. THE WORLD NEEDS THIS, MY ART. THEY NEED TO KNOW THIS.
THEY'LL EAT THIS SHIT UP. THEY RELATE, IT'S REALITY.
YEAH, I CAN SEE THE WHOLE WORLD ALL LINING UP TO SEE YOUR FAKE RIOT.
YEAH, YOUR WORLD IS REAL! SURE. IT'S AN EXACT DEPICTION OF REALITY.
LOOK AROUND YOU ASH, THIS WORLD ISN'T SHAKESPEARE.
THIS PLACE IS UGLY. THERE IS NO ROMANCE HERE. THERE IS NO POETRY IN THIS WORLD.
ARE YOU LISTENING TO YOURSELF?
THERE ARE NO STAR-CROSSED LOVERS...
NO HAPPY ENDINGS...

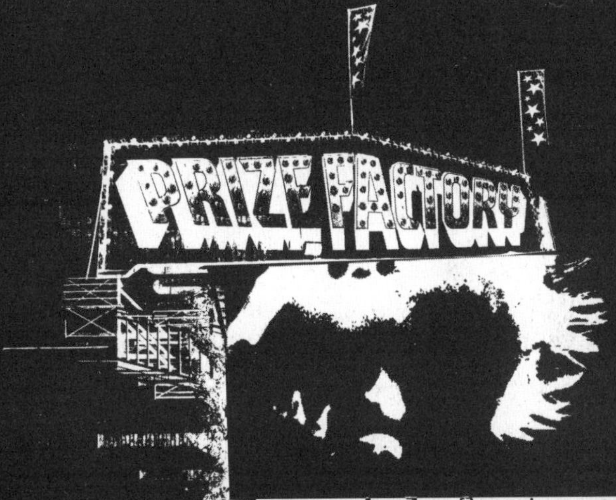
PRIZE FACTORY

special features

-author's notes

-street team gallery

authors notes

-The first reaction I got from fans of the original KC series was "what the hell is going on?" "Where's Angela and Damien?" "It can't be the end of their story, can it?" I guess beginning a "sequel" to an ongoing story with an entirely new cast and situation isn't that common. (Actually, Ashley was mentioned a couple times in the first KC series)

-So with the beloved cast of KC Series One out of the picture, one might ask why do a sequel this way? Why change what people know and love as Kissing Chaos? Well, in my head, NSB is still very much a KC story. The cast and scene have a different feel, but the underlying themes and emotions are very similar.

I've described each story arc of KC as a piece of a puzzle, and when the series has run its course, readers will be able to see the big picture. With each issue fans should be able to put the little clues together. There are a number of clues and plot threads revealed in the first series, NSB, and the 1000 Words one-shot that should give readers an idea of what might be going on. But I'm making the fans work for it, which is hopefully part of the fun of Kissing Chaos. (And hey, Chaos is in the title.)

My goal is to have each KC story give people a different experience than the last. And while there are ongoing plot threads, I think it's really the tones and themes just below the surface that really unify the KC experience.

ISSUE #1

-This series, though a bit more straightforward than the previous, is a lot more complex. There are more characters, with more intricate relationships. With only 24 pages an issue, I had to cram a lot into each scene. For example, in the opening scene I had to establish the very close friendship between Eric and Kim, Kim's relationship with Jersey, set up the premise of the staged riot (the main plot of this book), and hint at Eric's secret love for Kim. All in 4 pages. While this may be all in a day's work for some writers, for someone inexperienced like myself it was challenging and fun! The entire series is pretty much broken down into 4-5 page vignettes.

-Sometimes to get readers interested the characters must be believable, and someone they can relate to. To do so, I try to put some elements of myself and people I know into the characters. For example, Ashley's to-do list is totally what I do. People sometimes ask me if I'm Damien, or Jersey, or Eric, but I think I put a little bit of myself in all the characters. (Except Jersey. ;))

ISSUE #2

-This story jumps back and forth through time, giving the readers little vignettes of the overall plot. It's kind of an overused gimmick, but I think this way there are more possibilities for different kinds of storytelling, and it could be fun to piece it all together bit by bit. (Kind of like the whole concept behind Kissing Chaos.)

-(page27-31)Here's the scene where we have one of the only returning characters from KC series one. Everett, who was chasing Damien, Angela, and Raevyn now shows the same interest in Ashley. Note how they met each other online, and the usage of computers and technology. The laptop seemed to play a role in the first series, as well.

-(page 37) Wang Computers is on Mike's shirt. That's a small joke from The Simpsons. I think that may be the second Simpsons related joke I've tossed into KC just for fun. [Editor's note: Wang is an actual computer company, however.]

-(page 42) Ah, the return of the men in black/shadow men or whatever you call them. Who are they? What do they want? I actually divulge some info on them in this series, but their motives will slowly be unraveled as KC progresses.

ISSUE #3

-this series features a number a scenes where the kid's debate about what passes for art. Unfortunately (or fortunately!) I'm not that pretentious, or skilled enough to wax philosophically on the nature of art, so their conversations merely scratch the surface of the subject.

-I think we all know fashion punks and jerks like Jersey.

-(pages 56-59)I'm the king of broken deadlines and bad time management. Sometimes I spend too much time on the art for certain scene. This wasn't one of them. This scene got rushed so the book wouldn't be too late. Sadly, it shows.

-(page 61-64) This is probably my favorite scene in this entire miniseries. I really wanted to capture one of those moments between two people who are in "like" with each other and are talking on the phone. We've all been there. Hopefully I've recreated it well. I also really wanted the visuals to compliment the back and forth of the conversation between Eric and Kim. I'm pretty happy with how it all came out. And how many books can reference Leftover Crack and The Princess Bride in the same scene? :)

The song lyrics are from a Leftover Crack song. Given the environment and the type of clique these kids could be in, I figured LOC a good choice for the music they would dig.

KC is rife with subtle references to music I like, from the Elvis Costello nod in KC series one, to the LOC reference and the SKA poster in Ashley's room. Just reading over the series again reminds me of all the little things I put in that come from songs or what not. Even the title Kissing Chaos is from a song. I challenge anyone to find them all!

-(page68-70) Here's where I drop a bomb of sorts on the readers. I was worried about how people would take the revelations in this scene. In retrospect, it wasn't as huge a deal as I thought. We finally have some sort of bearing on the faceless shadow men, revealing they are just foot soldiers for a larger organization. My apprehension came from wondering how readers would react to the introduction of a big company with a secret agenda in the story. Until this point, though shrouded in mystery, KC has for the most part been solely about teenage politics. Then again, big business butting into a bunch of kids' lives is pretty much a metaphor for what happens in the real world.

At any rate, I figured we might lose some readers at this point, as conspiracy theories aren't everyone's bag. I love Ashley's response, and I like that Men In Black quip. One question you need to ponder, does Ashley actually acknowledge seeing the shadow men?

ISSUE #4

-(page77) in the previous issue, during a flashback, we hinted that Kim was going to tell Eric something. She finally spoke to Eric earlier in the day (the day of this riot). Somehow Jersey found out what Kim told Eric, and this is his reaction. It's apparent that whatever the news was, it affected all three of the kids in this triangle as they seem to act different after Kim and Eric's talk (which occurs later this issue).

-(page80-83) Here's where I drop the rest of the bomb on the readers. I reveal the shadow men are seeking certain individuals for their own "dark agenda". Oooh, scary! And finally, direct ties to KC Series One are made. This list that Everett is searching for, the info that Angela emailed to Ashley, was the list on the laptop computer in the first series. The laptop was originally Everett's, and after two miniseries of searching, he'll finally get his precious information back.

Just what is this list, who are all the people on it, and how are they, Ashley, and Angela all connected? Who are the shadow men, and who employs them? These questions remain to be answered.

-There was another subtle revelation in this scene. Everett says Angela is not safe, and she's with someone dangerous. That someone is Damien, the object of Angela's affection. How can this be? This will be explored in more detail in the KC:1000 Words one-shot and in upcoming miniseries.

-One important thing here was Ashley's reaction. Knowing a lot of fans and readers were expecting some closure, some answers to all the loose ends, I tried to imagine how they would react to everything, if I just explained it to them flat out. I knew some people wouldn't like it, and that there would be some confusion and cynicism. I tried to mirror how readers would react in Ashley's response. All the disbelief, anger, and confusion in Ashley is what I totally expected from those who are reading the book. I really like how the scene played out, and how Everett had to try and break down the situation into simple terms that Ashley would understand. "Your friend is in trouble. Let's help her." Hopefully readers feeling confused or perturbed by the revelations will be able to relate with Ashley, who is going through the exact same thing.

-(page 88-91) Here's the crux of NSB. This love triangle falling apart was the basis of this entire miniseries. I really wanted to capture the heartbreak of a couple that's meant to be, but can't be together due to precipitating circumstances. Eric and Kim are so in love, but it can't happen. Unrequited love, now that's what Kissing Chaos is supposed to be about, right? Right?!

-Ashley decides to join Everett on his quest to save Angela. This scene is basically a set up for what future KC stories may come. Trust me, there is a big picture and all the characters will cross paths again, in this story of teenage politics, dark conspiracies, and unrequited love.

WOLFE IRON
SCRAP
WE SELL-STEEL BEAMS
CDS VIDEOS STREETWARE
VINYL TAPES
LOONIES
ONLY
$1.00

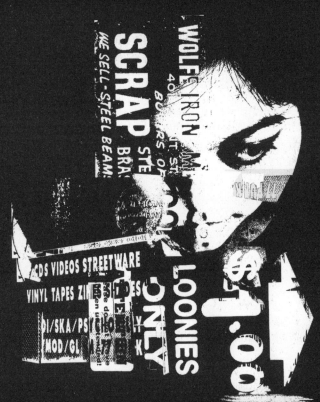

kissing chaos street team

-the following pages feature a collection of the flyers I created for the KC street team

When I was putting this series together, I had not heard of a comic book having a street team. Given the subject matter of KC: NSB, I thought it would be great to experiment with a street team. A number of loyal fans signed up and helped promote Kissing Chaos in their home towns, all across the world. The final page of this section showcases the flyer designed by the winner of the "KC Street team contest".

www.kissingchaos.com

KISSING CHAOS

11/02

www.kissingchaos.com

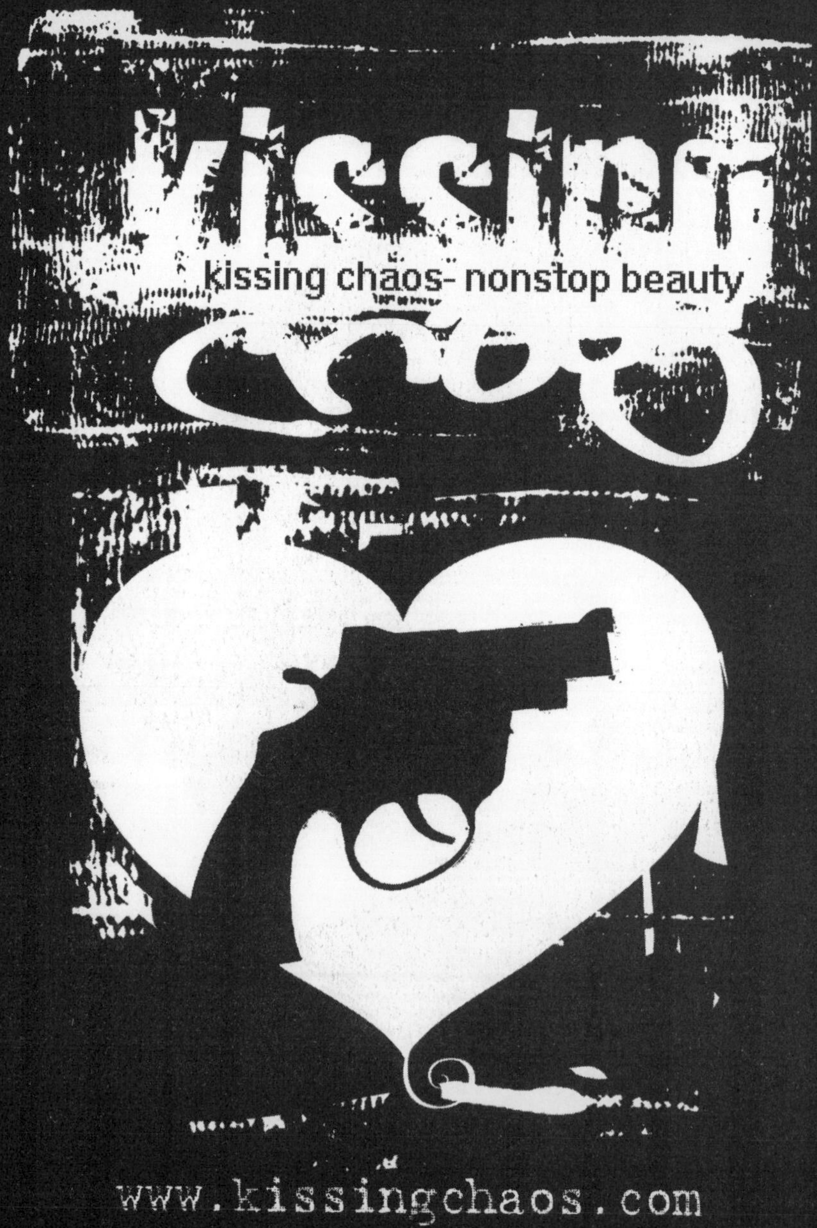
kissing chaos
kissing chaos- nonstop beauty
www.kissingchaos.com

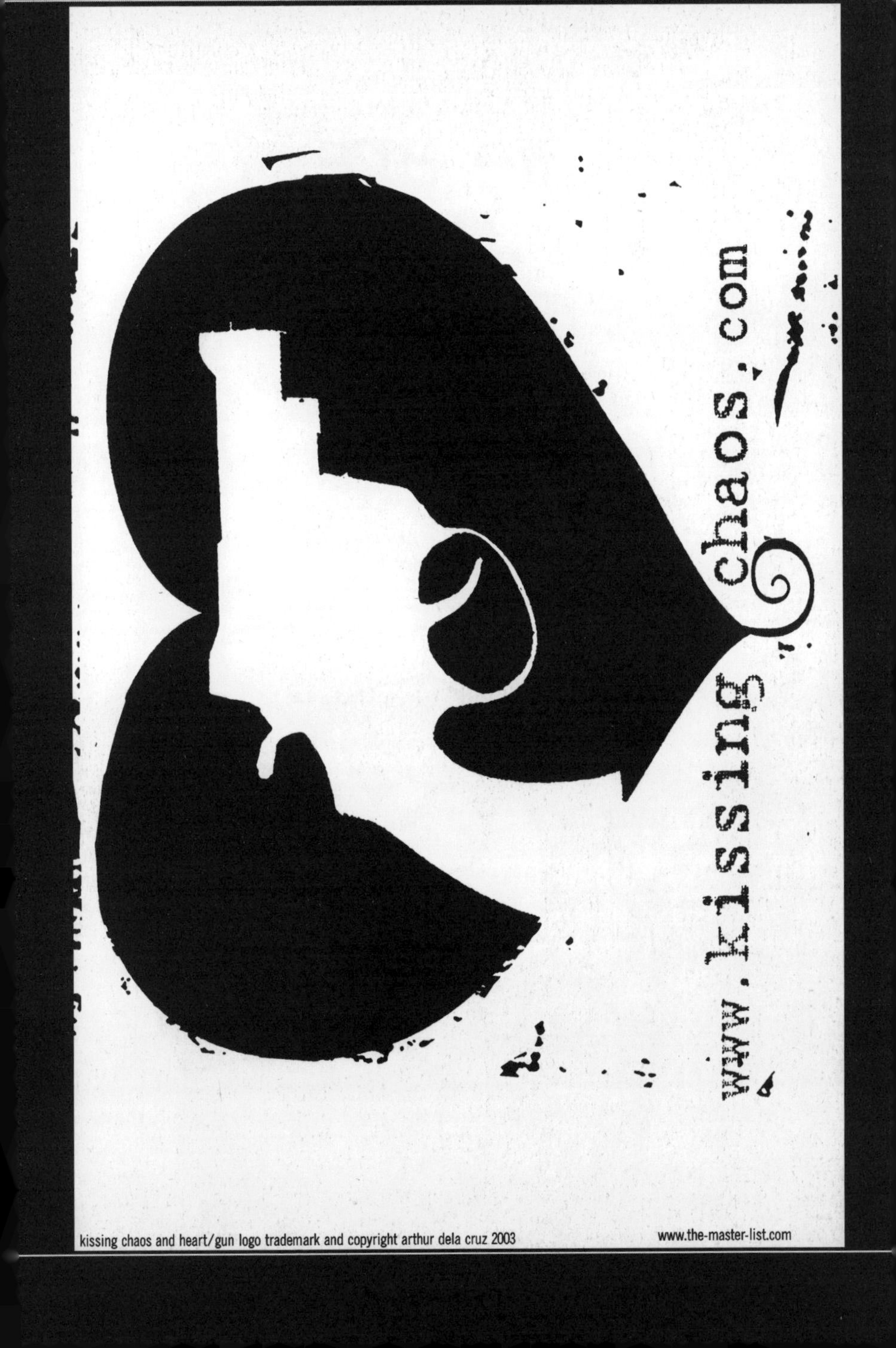
www.kissingchaos.com

we are the process..

kissingchaos.com
the-master-list.com

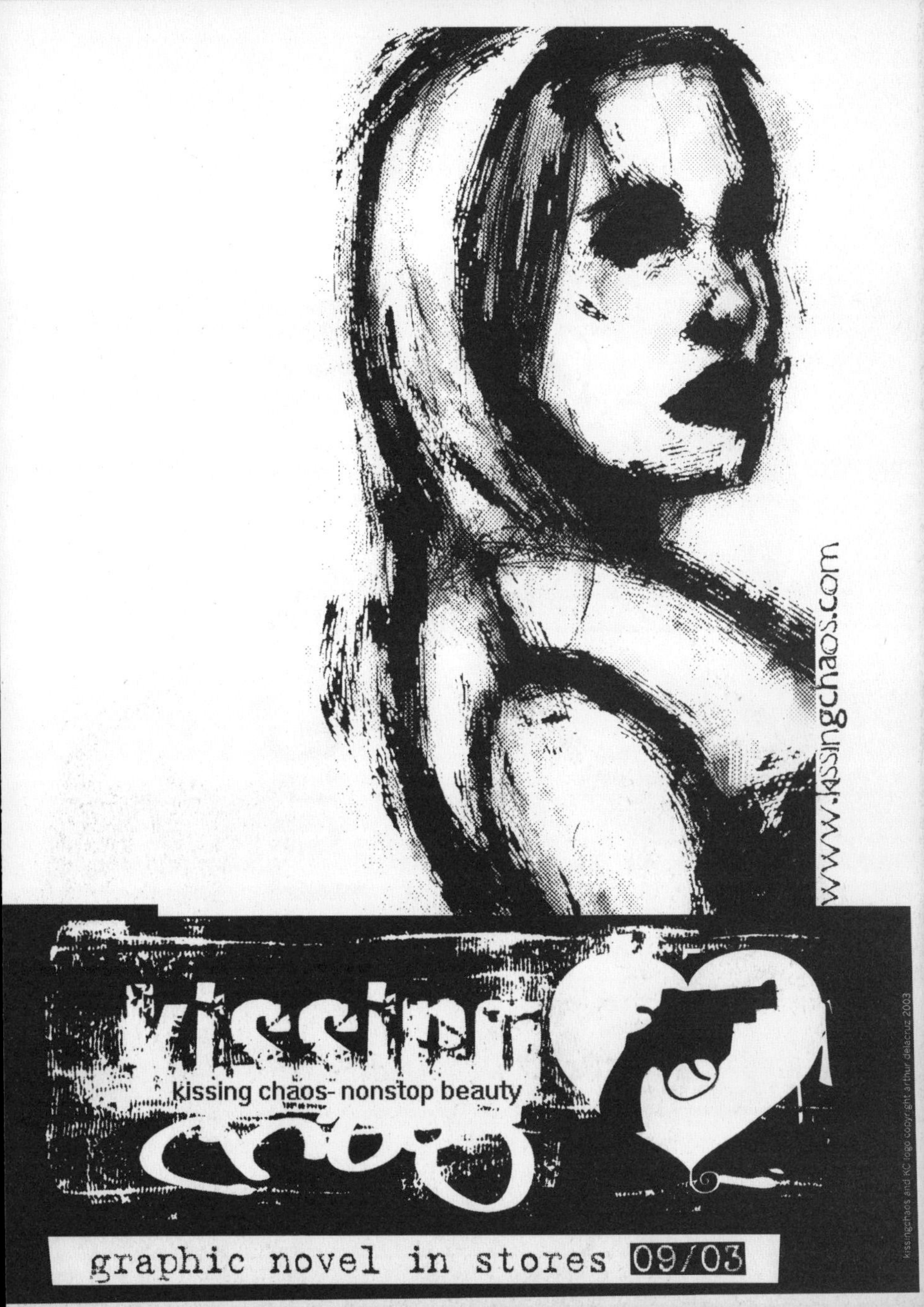
www.kissingchaos.com
kissing chaos
kissing chaos- nonstop beauty
graphic novel in stores 09/03
kissingchaos and KC logo copyright arthur delacruz 2003

Love, or death.

www.kissingchaos.com

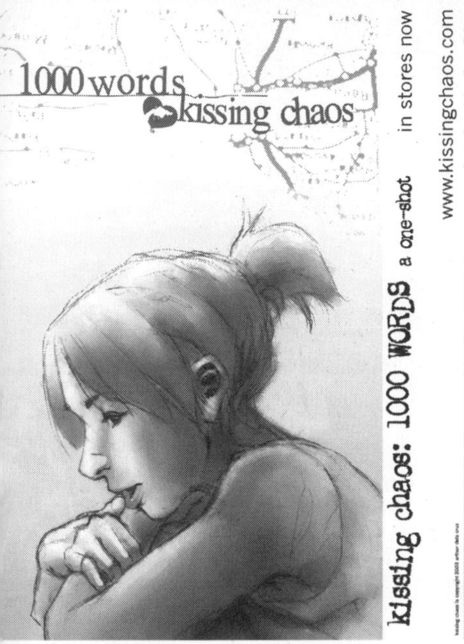
1000 words
kissing chaos
kissing chaos: 1000 WORDS a one-shot
in stores now
www.kissingchaos.com

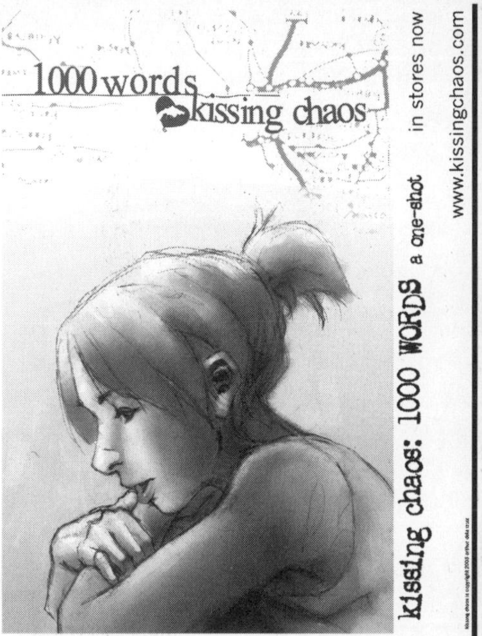
1000 words
kissing chaos
kissing chaos: 1000 WORDS a one-shot
in stores now
www.kissingchaos.com

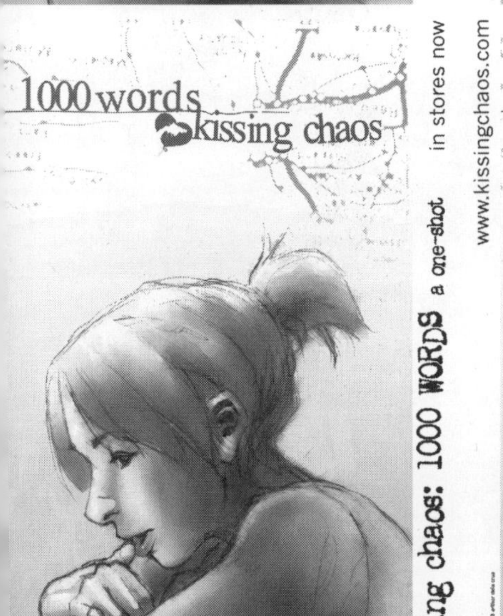
1000 words
kissing chaos
kissing chaos: 1000 WORDS a one-shot
in stores now
www.kissingchaos.com

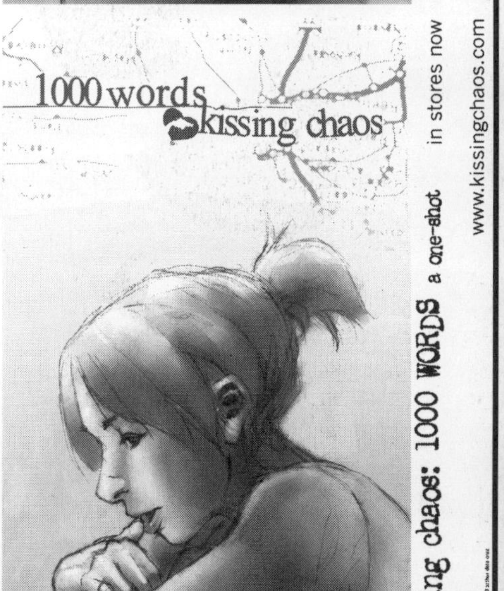
1000 words
kissing chaos
kissing chaos: 1000 WORDS a one-shot
in stores now
www.kissingchaos.com

this is a flyer specifically designed to be cut up and left at comics stores.

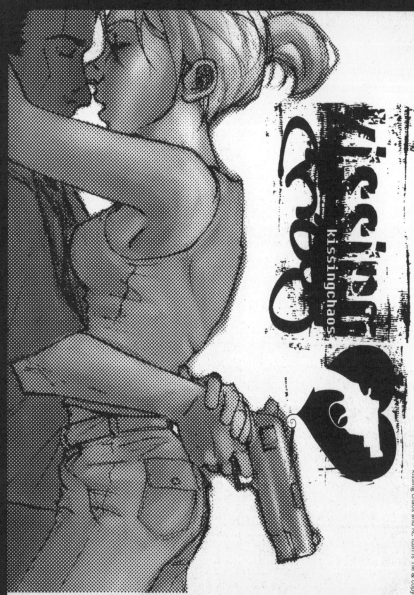

KISSING CHAOS tradepaperback
IN STORES NOW
KISSING CHAOS: nonstop beauty
4 issues starting 11/02

kissing chaos and KC icon is TM & copyrightArthur Dela Cruz 2002

another flyer made to be left at comics stores,
when the first series was collected as a TPB.

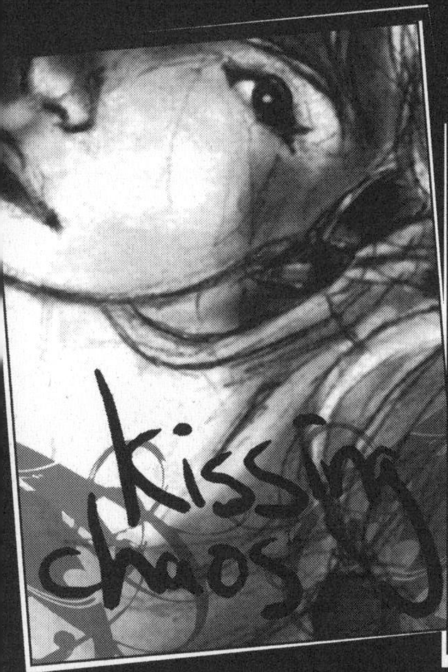
kissing chaos

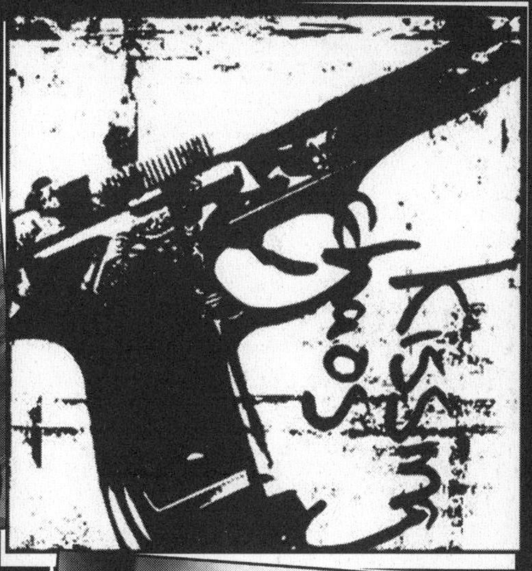

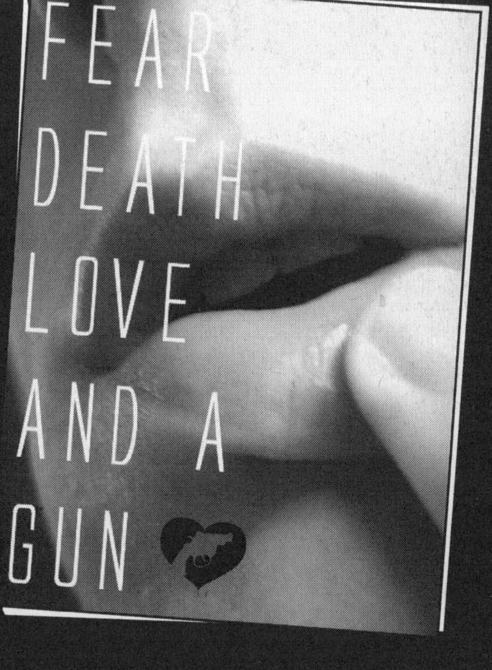
FEAR
DEATH
LOVE
AND A
GUN

Here are some flyer images submitted by street team member Tome Wilson.

He and a few others took part in the KC: Street Team contest, where I asked members to design their own flyers. The grand prize was having their designs published in this collection.

All those who participated made great flyers, and will recieve some sort of KC goods for their efforts.

A special thanks to all the members of the street team! You guys did a great job!

enemies**friends**beginnings**ends**love**hate**life**death**
all in one breath.

about the author.

hi, my name is arthur dela cruz. I like to make stories and pictures. That's about it.

The first volume of Kissing Chaos (which began in 2001) was my comics debut, and I was nominated for an Eisner award for that series. I plan to finally complete the Kissing Chaos saga in 2005, but you never know.

I'm currently developing several other projects so stay tuned for more of this nonsense.

other books from Arthur Dela Cruz & Oni Press

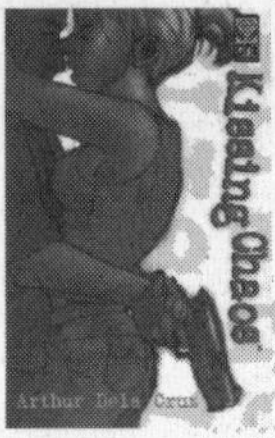
Kissing Chaos
Arthur Dela Cruz

KISSING CHAOS™
vol. 1
by Arthur Dela Cruz
196 pages, black-and-white interiors
$17.95 US
ISBN 1929998-32-5

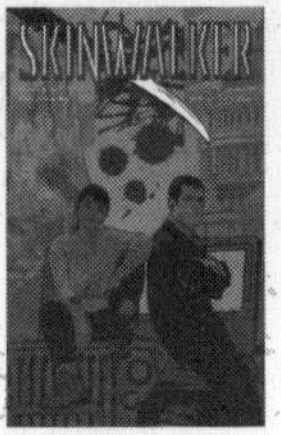
SKINWALKER

SKINWALKER ™
by Nunzio DeFilippis, Christina Weir, Brian Hurtt, & Arthur Dela Cruz
128 pages, black-and-white interiors
$11.95 US
ISBN 1929998-45-7

other Oni Press Graphic novels

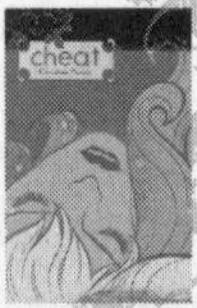
cheat

CHEAT ™
by Christine Norrie
72 pages, black-and-white interiors
$5.95 US
ISBN 1929998-47-3

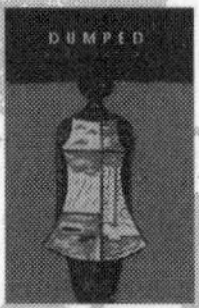
DUMPED

DUMPED ™
by Andi Watson
56 pages, black-and-white interiors
$5.95 US
ISBN 1929998-41-4

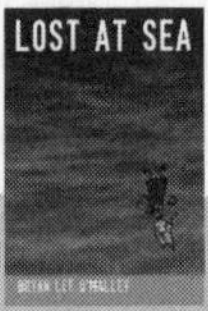
LOST AT SEA

LOST AT SEA ™
by Bryan Lee O'Malley
160 pages, black-and-white interiors
$11.95 US
ISBN 1929998-71-6
Available October 2003!

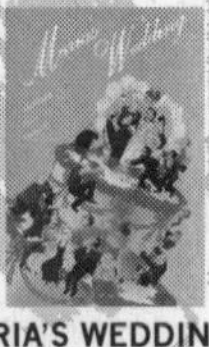

MARIA'S WEDDING ™
by Nunzio DeFilippis, Christina Weir, & Jose Garibaldi
88 pages, black-and-white interiors
$10.95 US
ISBN 1929998-57-0

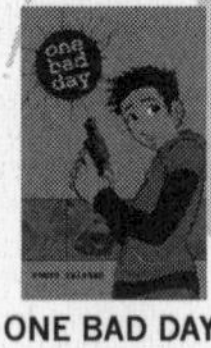
one bad day

ONE BAD DAY™
by Steve Rolston
120 pages, black-and-white interiors
$9.95 US
ISBN 1-929998-50-3

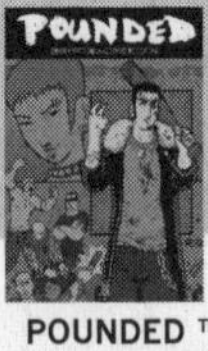
POUNDED

POUNDED ™
by Brian Wood & Steve Rolston
96 pages, black-and-white interiors
$8.95 US
ISBN 1929998-37-6

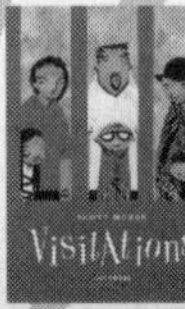
VisitAtions

VISITATIONS ™
by Scott Morse
88 pages, black-and-white interiors
$8.95 US, $12.95 CAN.
ISBN 1-929998-34-1

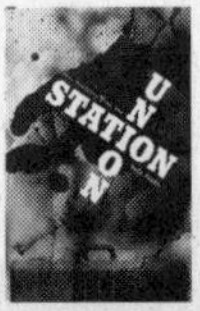
UNION STATION

UNION STATION ™
by Ande Parks & Eduardo Barretto
112 pages, black-and-white interiors
$11.95 US
ISBN 1929998-69-4
Available October 2003!

Available at finer comics shops everywhere. For a comics store near you, call 1-888-COMIC-BOOK or visit www.the-master-list.com.
For more Oni Press titles and information visit www.onipress.com.